MISSING LUCILE

Missing Lucile

Memories of the Grandmother
I Never Knew

A Shannon Ravenel Book

ALGONQUIN BOOKS OF CHAPEL HILL 2010

ℝ

A Shannon Ravenel Book

Published by
ALGONQUIN BOOKS OF CHAPEL HILL
Post Office Box 2225
Chapel Hill, North Carolina 27515-2225

a division of
WORKMAN PUBLISHING
225 Varick Street
New York, New York 10014

Sections of chapters 1 and 2, in different form,
have been previously published in *Harvard Review*.

The author gratefully acknowledges the following:
Excerpts from *The Kroger Story,* by George Laycock,
permission granted by the Kroger Company.

Excerpts from *Orlando* and from "A Sketch of the Past" in *Moments of
Being,* by Virginia Woolf, permission granted by Houghton Mifflin Harcourt
Publishing Company.

Excerpt from "Memory and Imagination" in *I Could Tell You Stories,*
by Patricia Hampl, permission granted by W. W. Norton & Company.

Permission to reprint photographs on pages 183, 218, 239, 240,
and 241 granted by the Wellesley College Archive.

Library of Congress Cataloging-in-Publication Data
Berne, Suzanne.
Missing Lucile : memories of the grandmother I never knew /
Suzanne Berne. — 1st ed.
p. cm.
"A Shannon Ravenel Book."
ISBN 978-1-56512-625-1
1. Berne, Lucile Kroger, 1889–1932. 2. Berne, Suzanne—
Family. I. Title.
CT275.B56537B47 2010
973.92092—dc22
[B]   2010019670

10 9 8 7 6 5 4 3 2 1
First Edition

For

Lucile's grandchildren and

her great-grandchildren

And might it not be . . . that we also have appointments
to keep in the past, in what has gone before and is for
the most part extinguished, and must go there in search of
places and people who have some connection with us
on the far side of time, so to speak?

—W. G. SEBALD, *Austerlitz*

FOREWORD

My father is eighty-two years old and lives alone in a small apartment off a busy road in Charlotte, North Carolina. He has had both lung and colon cancer in the last two years and suffers as well from high blood pressure. Last spring he fell and hit his head while walking inside his apartment and had to spend a week in the hospital. Afterward he had trouble remembering what day it was or with whom he had spoken five minutes earlier; his car had to be sold and someone found to come in to help him with cooking and bathing.

His children live far away and he wants to stay in Charlotte. Fortunately, he has many friends, among them poets and aspiring poets, members of his weekly poetry group, who visit and offer to take him shopping or to doctors' appointments. They appreciate his humor and his intelligence and his encouraging view of poetry, which is that any attempt is worthwhile as long as it's an honest attempt. Until recently, he himself wrote a poem every day, often about the park where he liked to walk in the morning, and then, when he could no longer take those walks, he wrote about the vine-draped oaks and tulip poplars outside his apartment windows, and about birds, clouds, the different light at different sunrises, spending hours scanning the near horizon, looking for what else life might hold for him, aside from more illness.

Though he has very little money and gets by mostly on Social Security, with help from a generous friend, oddly enough he's more contented now than he was during my childhood, when he owned big houses and cars and boats, flew first class on airplanes, hired caterers for dinner parties. Most of the anger that used to crackle around him is gone. He doesn't seem to mind the money much, except when he needs dental work and has trouble paying for it. Having to live so monastically suits him, comes even as a kind of relief. He has been married three times and divorced three times. After lengthy periods of estrangement, he is now on cordial terms, to different degrees, or at least on speaking terms, with his three ex-wives, his six children, and an ex-stepson.

He is a dignified, courtly looking gentleman with white hair, which has grown poetically long since he's stopped patronizing the barber shop, a neat white mustache, and a Vandyke beard; he dresses invariably in khaki trousers, collared shirts, and laced shoes. A throwback to when older gentlemen looked like gentlemen and would not think of appearing at the grocery store in Bermuda shorts and plastic sandals. Though he spent most of his adult life up north, he feels at home in Charlotte, the "Queen City of the South," his place of retirement dovetailing neatly with his birthplace, Cincinnati, Ohio, "the Queen City of the West." Queens, goddesses, earth mothers have long been his fascination. At Georgetown University in the 1970s, he taught courses on mythology that centered on the Great Goddess. He often writes of the Great Mother in his poems. Though he has difficulty with women in general, he loves the idea of them.

His deep voice has always had a southern lilt, the proximity of Kentucky to Cincinnati showing up in his softened consonants — "nothin'" instead of "nothing" — and in the way he says "Hah" instead of "Hi," when he greets an acquaintance. Formal in manner, and easily offended, he nevertheless loves to be self-deprecating. The technicians at the hospital where he underwent radiation treatments two years ago called him Colonel Sanders because of his white beard and mustache. On the day of his final treatment, he brought them a tub of fried chicken.

He takes special delight in absurdities: silly names, malapropisms, bad puns, which he'll repeat and then laugh out loud. My father has a deep, surprised-sounding laugh that often makes other people laugh when they hear it. Whenever he is not actually laughing, however, he looks painfully sad, partly owing to his long upper lip and pale blue, slightly watery eyes that are magnified by the lenses of his glasses. But he also looks sad because he often is sad. He has always been sad. Not depressed, which has a specific clinical definition, and which at different times has been the case with him as well. But *sad*. Melancholy. Inconsolable. A man who is missing something.

All my childhood I felt sorry for him and was impressed and frightened by his sadness, which seemed to threaten both his survival and mine. His unhappiness had an encompassing grandeur, almost Russian in its intemperance, but also a condemned quality. No matter what set off his frequent rages—burnt toast, no parking spaces, squabbling children—he seemed stricken by something far more serious.

Which I understood. He had lost his mother when he was a little boy. He'd hardly known her. An unthinkable disaster for me, who had a mother I loved passionately.

Logically enough I wished I could give his mother back to him. A wish I suppose I've held ever since I was old enough to wish for anything not directly involving myself, though of course self-interest was always involved. Loss for a parent is loss for his child, and parental sorrow is so atmospheric that its traces remain visible decades later, the way long-forgotten droughts can be detected in tree rings, and particles of volcanic ash linger for years in the sky.

MISSING LUCILE

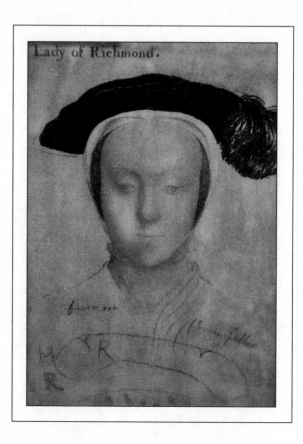

I

Lady of Richmond

DUKE: And what is her history?
VIOLA: A blank, my lord.

—SHAKESPEARE, *Twelfth Night*

Outside the bedroom windows the garden is full of snow. The lily pond is frozen, the dark branches of the apple tree, standing alone in its stone circle, are sharply defined against a winter sky. Snow caps the bronze statues at either end of the rectangular pool, each of a child offering water to birds. A thoughtful garden, with its matching statuary, its low hedges and flower beds flanking a sloping grassy avenue that leads outward to a wide lawn and a lily pond, the garden of someone more than casually interested in symmetry and perspective. In the spring the grass will turn a deep blue-green, just as the apple tree will be surrounded by a perfect circle of lily of the valley. But for now everything but the bare tree branches is white.

Upstairs in the master bedroom, a red-haired woman lies in a white-painted iron hospital bed facing the southeast window, which has a long view not of her garden, where she has spent so much time and to which she has given so much thought, but of the Little Miami River and the low hills of Ohio's Clermont County. Across from the foot of the bed is a fireplace, beside which is a chaise longue. A fire burns in the fireplace, firelight reflecting off the glass covering a very old, very simple pencil-and-ink drawing hanging near the bed. A sketchbook drawing of a woman in a plumed hat. Also red haired. The artist has shaded her hair, face, and lips with colored pencil. But only her hat and the black plumed feather are distinct, the woman's face is barely outlined, half smiling, the eyes mysterious, half closed, looking away from both the viewer and the artist. "Lady of Richmond" is carefully lettered in the top right-hand corner.

The woman in bed is my grandmother, Lucile Kroger Berne, the daughter of B. H. Kroger, the Cincinnati grocery-store magnate. Forty-three years old in December of 1932 and dying of abdominal cancer, though she, perhaps alone in her family, believes she is getting well.

This particular morning, a Thursday, December 1, she has enough energy to write to her old college friend, Ridie Guion. "Just a note," she apologizes, in a firm regular hand. "I am not allowed to do much in the way of correspondence." She is still in bed "with no immediate prospects of anything else," and with "no appetite," and not much strength. But, she insists, "I do feel that there is a slight but steady improvement."

MRS. ALBERT BERNE
BOX 456
MADEIRA, OHIO Thursday

Dearest Ride. —

Just a note as I am not allowed to do much in the way of correspondence. I am still in bed, with no immediate prospects of anything else. My strength does not come back very rapidly. and I have no appetite, but I do feel that there is very slight but steady improvement.

I spend my days doing picture puzzles and reading.

Of course this is not true. Her immediate prospects are as plain as the low hills of Clermont County beyond her window. She will die the Friday after next.

And yet according to this letter, she spends her days mildly, not in the extremity one would expect from someone with so little time left, not clutching at the coverlet or tossing restlessly from side to side on her pillow, not calling out for her children, so soon to be motherless, or weeping in her husband's arms. Instead she does picture puzzles in bed and reads. Every so often she looks at the old clock on her mantel, a clock set in a dark gothic wooden case above a glass panel painted with an idealized landscape in bright greens and blues. Then she glances away.

"I've gotten down to detective novels," she admits to Ridie, "as I can't take anything heavy."

She confides that she is being visited daily by her three sisters, Gertrude, Helen, and Gretchen, who all live nearby on Indian Hill; her father visits almost as often and sends her flowers. Her two little boys, Albert Jr. and Henry, like school and are doing well, though she has not yet seen their report cards. They are taking piano lessons. Of Albert Jr. she confides that he shows no "especial talent"; still, she does not doubt that "he'll be able to play acceptably," a prediction that unfortunately will not come true.

Christmas is upon her; she frets over being unprepared. "I have done nothing. I must start to make out lists and let Helen and Gretchen take care of things for me." She is still making plans, still determined to worry about Christmas presents and writing lists. Downstairs in the living room her husband is singing "Brahms and Schubert, etc.," accompanying himself on the grand piano. When they met at a reception at a friend's house he was a professional singer. A baritone modestly famous in Cincinnati, where he teaches at the conservatory. Every morning after breakfast he sings for an hour or more while upstairs his wife lies in bed looking toward the river and the woods and listening. "There are compensations for being sick," she writes.

Husband, children, sisters. Christmas, piano lessons, detective novels. Brahms and Schubert. Etcetera. These are the preoccupations of the woman who is about to vanish forever from her big cream-colored house on Indian Hill. She is concerned as well for her friend Ridie, apologizing again, this time for writing "a stupid note" and for having "no news," though she is fast approaching that strange dark frontier that lies beyond news, beyond even etcetera, a place that few of us can bring ourselves to contemplate for long or too closely. By the time her letter reaches its destination, she will have fewer days left to her than she could count on both hands.

Still, her final words in this letter are about Ridie, whom she cautions not to "work too hard and get yourself all tired out," understanding that Ridie, unmarried, with little money, an English teacher at Milton Academy outside of Boston, is delicate. Not someone who needs further worries. She has been sending Ridie checks for years; a week after her death, her husband, Albert, will send another, a Christmas one, "as Lucile would have done."

In that quiet bedroom she fits together pieces of a puzzle, turning the smooth colored cardboard pieces over in her pale fingers, hunting for the right shapes that will finish the picture. She follows clues in her detective novels, waits for a complicated story to come clear. She knows it will all end neatly enough—the last lobed piece will reveal a complete Taj Mahal, the detective will explain his final discovery and solve the crime—but she doesn't yet know exactly how.

FROM THE SLENDER evidence of this letter, my grandmother's death seems like it must have been a calm, dignified passage. One we could all aspire to—no railing against fate, no bleak hospital corridor. Visits from sisters, letters from friends. Downstairs her husband is singing "Ave Maria" as the children go cheerfully off to school on a Monday morning. By her last days the children will have been sent to a sister's house to stay, her husband will have stopped singing. In that elegant room full of wintry light, the only sounds are footsteps muffled by the hallway's thick plum-colored carpet, whispered conferences, and the distant crack of ice on the river.

And yet something remains out of place within this picture of my grandmother's quiet bedroom, where she lies in that iron bed with a crank, facing away from her garden. A piece does not quite fit. All that worrying about a friend while on her own deathbed, the stringent lack of self-pity, the serene contemplation of her children and their piano lessons. "It seems hardly possible," writes her sister Helen three weeks later, "that anyone could be so brave and meet death with so much courage."

It does seem hardly possible. And so one has to wonder if such bravery, like her careful account of the compensations of illness, isn't part of some final mutiny, a moment when she halts her subdued progress toward the frost-colored horizon beyond those low hills. A last-ditch defiance encoded in this "stupid note" that bears "no news," a small revolt that comes actually at the expense of her poor friend Ridie.

I am not so sick, that letter implies, that I forget myself: I am sick, not unfortunate. Here in my wide bedroom with a view of the river, where I lie in bed listening to my husband sing downstairs, anticipating my children's first report cards, awaiting another visit from my sisters and flowers from my father, I have no news. News is disasters and accidents, prizes, discoveries, events. Something unhappened that happened, something that was missing until now. But nothing is missing from my life. The pieces are all here, the clues all add up. I am not being brave, I am being practical. My sisters will take care of my lists.

I have no news, but I have everything else.

A last stand. An idealized landscape in bright greens and blues, overshadowed by a gothic clock. A pretense. Because of course she doesn't want to die in that iron bed. Of course she does not have what she wants most, which is more time, time for whatever she still wants to do, things she can't even imagine now, but knows that she wants to have done. Time to be part of whatever is going to happen, next year, and the year after that, as well as time to reflect on everything she has lived through, because that is who she is, a person to whom things have happened, but now who will know about it?

And her children, her two small boys with their unread report cards. What will happen to them?

She cannot think of that. And so she blazes up for an instant, like a log breaking on the fire under that ticking clock, fierce in her insistence that she has written "a stupid note," because there is no intelligence she can pass on about where she is going. Only that where she has been is worth envying.

("Of course we have known for some months how things were," writes her sister Helen, "but even so were not prepared.")

For a moment her red hair glints. Then the fire dies down again, the sparks subside. From her frame on the wall, the woman in the sketch looks down at the woman in the bed. The dark plume nods above her head, her eyes half closed, gazing past the artist who sketched her so many years ago, smiling faintly.

But this is not a real likeness, that smile seems to say. Only the barest suggestion.

That letter to Ridie Guion is the only letter of my grandmother's that survives, at least that I have been able to find. There were once many — my mother recalls visiting the attic of my grandfather's house on Indian Hill and seeing "stacks" of letters in my grandmother's handwriting, all now lost, thrown out, like the rest of the contents of that attic. Written during Lucile's last weeks, this one remaining letter has all the pathos of a final utterance, which must be why Ridie saved it and included the letter, along with one from my great aunt Helen and two from my grandfather, in a box of papers she willed to Wellesley College, where she and my grandmother had become friends. It is also the only remaining record of my grandmother's voice speaking to someone else. A stubborn voice, despite her apologies and graciousness. A willful voice. Not optimistic, but obdurate. The voice of a dying woman who wanted to sound as if she were doing well.

LUCILE KROGER BERNE died at home on December 16, 1932, attended by her husband, her doctor, and her faithful nurse, Chappie, and for a very long time her death was the most significant thing about her. She was a "lovely, lovely person," according to one of my father's cousins, who was nine when my grandmother died and despite her best efforts remembers her only as "very brave and uncomplaining." And so like many brave and uncomplaining women, who are admirable and forgettable in almost equal proportions, Lucile has slipped out of memory.

However he felt about her before she died, my father's enduring and unhappy impression of his mother was that he scarcely knew her during her brief parenthood, which lasted for him only until he was six. In his mind, she was always preoccupied by something other than himself. As she dressed for dinner in the evenings, she would often pause and stand for as long as half an hour with one elbow resting on the tall cherry wood dresser in her bedroom, smoking Chesterfields and doing crossword puzzles. He sometimes spied on her from the long gallery-like second-floor hallway, watching cigarette smoke curl into question marks above her head, enjoying a rare few moments of finding her alone but wondering with increasing impatience when she would turn to look at him. Later in life he would be addicted to crossword puzzles as well, his hand hovering above white and black boxes, just as hers had done, filling in the names of flowers and Greek heroes and the titles of Broadway musicals. Losing the trail of some clues, leaving some boxes blank. Perhaps without realizing it finding a few words she had found, following a few of the same hints, stumped by some of the same riddles. But for him the puzzle always remains unsolved; all the hints lead back to the same old question.

In his only other clear recollection of his mother my father was sitting on a stone bench in the garden behind the house one afternoon in early fall, watching her plant bulbs. He was eating little red cinnamon candies, Red Hearts, as they were called then, and still are, I believe. At some point she stood up and peeled off her gardening gloves, then asked him if she could have a few of the candies. He said no. She looked at him closely, then asked if he really couldn't give a Red Heart to his mother. He shook his head. She pulled on her gloves and went back to her bulbs.

By its survival, it's clear this memory long troubled my father and probably convinced him that his small act of selfishness was responsible for the tragedy that later befell him. Children are always claiming responsibility for tragedy based on a minor offense; their sense of cause and effect is not wrong—tragedy has often been the result of small offenses—just slightly out of true. In my father's childish reasoning, he had not given his mother a Red Heart and so she died. Without that small twisted "so" this sentence would be straight enough, sad but not ruinous.

I only wish he had been eating peppermints. But such is the tenacity of metaphor: this memory wouldn't persist, most likely, if my father hadn't been hoarding Red Hearts. As for my grandmother, the bulbs she was planting were surely narcissus.

THROUGHOUT MY CHILDHOOD Lucile was a perplexing, poignant figure, mostly unknown but never forgotten, remaining vivid for me because of her reputation for both reticence and restlessness. I understood, very early, that she was the cause of my father's own restlessness—to be with him was to feel, so often, that he would rather be somewhere else—and also his unpredictable temper, a nervous mix of irritation and impatience, always rumbling in the background which could flash out so suddenly that it was like living with summer lightning. Often, though, he was charming, funny, and sympathetic, the sort of father to whom a child could bring complaints about a dragonish third-grade teacher who berated students for failing to master the seven times table, and he would always side with the child and never the teacher. "Don't let the bastards grind you down!" he used to whisper to me, in ersatz Latin, his parting words whenever I returned glumly to boarding school after a weekend at home. Still, you never knew when you might get scorched.

In the few photographs I had seen of her Lucile looked disappointingly sedate, but she was the first person in her family to go to college, had marched (it was rumored) with the suffragettes in Washington in 1913, and been treasurer of her father's company during World War I. After the war, she sailed to France with an all-woman relief unit and spent a year rebuilding ruined villages. But this boldness of hers, so uncharacteristic of her sisters, was combined with a "remoteness," spoken of by my father with bitterness and longing. Soon after she died, he began to confuse his mother with a small marble statue of Athena that stood on a table in his father's bedroom.

"We were told she was gone," he told us, again and again, a hundred times, whenever he described how he and his older brother had learned of their mother's death. "No one ever said where."

Gone. As in hidden away. Kidnapped. Stolen. She was simply

waiting to be discovered, I always felt when I listened to this story, like a sarcophagus buried beneath the sands of Egypt. The missing mother, warm, vibrant, capable. The one who could put everything to rights.

We were told she was gone. No one ever said where.

Even as a child it struck me as manifestly unfair that someone's significance could be reduced to her absence.

OF COURSE PLENTY of people have endured far greater losses than my father and gone on to lead reasonable, even contented lives. But bereavement, like passion, has no proper notion of scale, and what form it takes depends mostly on the character of the mourner. His mother's death was the cause of all of my father's failings and mistakes, the reason why his many promising talents — including his singular ability to make another person feel promising and talented, when he chose, which alone should have guaranteed his good fortune — never quite added up to anything. That's what he believed, and because he did the rest of us did, too. Her absence became the Rosetta stone by which all subsequent family guilt and unhappiness could be decoded, especially a pervasive sense of deficiency. My father was different from his twelve cousins growing up with him on the sloping green lawns of Indian Hill: they had mothers, he did not.

Something for which he could never forgive them—at least, we never visited our numerous Kroger cousins in Cincinnati and only very rarely on Cape Cod, where they congregated in two enormous gray-shingled houses on the water in Harwich Port, just a few miles from my grandfather's house in Chatham. They were not like us. For one thing they were Republicans; for another, they did not sit inside and read all day long. The few times I did meet them, the cousins seemed like a sturdy, genial, attractive bunch, briskly sailing their catamarans into Nantucket Sound or organizing tennis games, later having drinks on the lawn, an American flag snapping smartly in the breeze, the men in khakis and boat shoes and seersucker shirts, the women in white sleeveless dresses, which showed off their tanned shoulders. But my father held a mysterious grudge against them, a grudge I could not fathom yet accepted anyway, as children generally accept the grudges held by their parents, because to do otherwise feels disloyal and somehow exposing.

Perhaps I figured that his cousins had been different from my father from the start. Their fathers played golf, for instance; his played the piano. And on Friday afternoons, while his brother and boy cousins stayed at school for football practice, from which my father was excused for being nearsighted and undersized, he went to the symphony with his father. As a teacher at the conservatory, my grandfather knew most of the orchestra musicians and was usually able to go backstage after a concert. He introduced my father to various luminaries, including Yehudi Menuhin, who would not shake my father's hand because he was afraid of having his fingers squeezed, and George Enescu, who shook hands vigorously. When Artur Rubenstein came to Cincinnati, my father met him as well; my grandfather and Rubenstein had studied piano with the same teacher in Berlin and were still on first-name basis. (Backstage, my grand-father asked Rubenstein how he handled stage fright. He leaned close and whispered, "Albert, I vomit.") One afternoon my father went to hear Rachmaninoff, to whom he was not introduced (the maestro declined), though later he was handed a signed program. He remembers watching the great pianist, tall and severe looking with an enormous bald head, stride across the stage of the Music Hall. The audience fell silent. Rachmaninoff sat down at the piano, and when he struck the first chord of his famous Concerto No. 2, collectively the audience shivered. Recalling the effect of that first chord, seven decades later, my father says hoarsely, "It was as if the world had changed."

And yet he felt disadvantaged. At dinner every evening, my grand-father lectured to his two young sons about German history, art, music. He talked for hours, filling the emptiness at the dinner table with stories of Beethoven's deafness, mad Ludwig's castle, Goethe's broken heart. My uncle dozed off, dreaming of football; my father listened. He loved history, art, music, but he suspected this was somehow out of order. It wasn't long before he began to feel smarter, odder, more artistic, less assured than his brother and his cousins, and gradually he developed a sense of separateness that was both su-perior and envious, and increasingly aggrieved, until finally it alien-ated him from his entire family.

SOMEONE ONCE TOLD me that irony is not a defense against feeling, as it's often understood; instead irony is the expression of in-tensely mixed feeling. Given that definition, my father is an ironic person. He has mixed feelings about almost everything, which is why he has left so many houses, jobs, wives, even his children. As I have lately been telling myself, it is not that he stopped caring for those places and people or didn't feel ashamed for letting go of them; it's more that he could not reconcile those attachments with his yearning for something else, another house, a different woman. Underscored by his perpetual feeling of being wrongfully denied what everyone else seemed to have, though he could not have named what it was. Perhaps this restlessness is also why, late in life, and after trying out various careers and professions (newspaperman, novelist, civil rights activist, academic, psychotherapist), he has chosen to become a poet. Ambivalence being the most resonant string on the poet's violin.

How much of my father's ironic nature has to do with being motherless, a deprived child of privilege, is anybody's guess, but quite early he began a romance with discontent, which I, at least, his most earnest listener, for many years found enthralling. Unhappiness can be as stirring a narrative, in its way, as war stories or surviving a storm at sea. But now that I am a middle-aged woman, with children and ironies of my own, I find myself growing restless, though in my case it's with that sense of deficiency. And so one day a few years ago, as I was listening to my father talk about his unhappy childhood, a subject that has obsessed him more and more in the last decade, I thought: My father has missed his mother all his life. Her absence has made him miserable.

So what if, at the end of his life, he got to have her?

"THE BIOGRAPHER IS, of course, the prisoner of his subject's facts," notes the biographer Geoffrey Wolff, who has specialized in writing about people of whom no one has ever heard including, memorably, his own father, who was a prodigious liar. The subject is, of course, also prisoner of the biographer's facts. In looking into my grandmother's life, however, I have an even more basic problem: there are so few facts about her with which to begin. Her letters and papers have been discarded, her house sold; her friends and family all gone, save for an elderly son who has spent most of the last seventy-five years furious at her disappearance and so did nothing to conserve what she left him. Including his inheritance and his family connections. Including his memories. While she has been the defining relationship of my father's life, until I sent him one several years ago he no longer owned a photograph of his mother.

And so I've decided to find out who she was, so that he might feel some kinship with the person he lost, but also for the simple reason that Lucile is a missing part of our family history, which is my link to general history, though it's taken me years to reach this conclusion. History becomes most transparent, and most believable, through one's relatives who lived through it. Without a grandmother I am missing a large piece of the past, and at least in my case, without believing in the past, it's hard to believe altogether in the present.

I'd also like to give her a little more time.

Not that Lucile ever did anything truly remarkable during the time she had, especially compared to the achievements one has come to expect from people who are the subjects of biographies. Nor did she do any of the outrageous destructive things we have come to expect when achievement is not the biographical point. She was an inconsequential figure—in the way that most of us are inconsequential, meaning that we matter only to a few people. Wealthy but not a Rockefeller, nice looking but not beautiful. Not even a rebel, though she was an intellectual, a feminist, and an aesthete in a conservative bourgeois family, whom she did not reject, as might be supposed, even hoped, but instead clung to with great determination. Conventional and restless in almost equal parts, she was strong-willed, practical, highly intelligent, a somewhat abrupt, rather shy woman who lived in a big staid house in Cincinnati. My guess is that she would have disliked the idea of anyone, perhaps especially a granddaughter (so often axe grinding, those granddaughters), presuming to reconstruct her life.

But then we don't really choose our subjects, do we, as much as we'd like to think the opposite. Any more than we choose our biographers, for the most part, should we be consequential enough to have them, or our relatives, or what in life and history is going to hold us prisoner.

II

The Box in the Attic

I dreamt the past was never
past redeeming.

—RICHARD WILBUR

The last time I visited Cincinnati was at Christmastime in 1973, a few days after my grandfather died. I was twelve years old. We had come from Washington DC for his funeral and then stayed on for a week while my parents got his house in order so that it could be sold. One afternoon when we children had been making too much noise and pestering sweet, palsied, gray-haired Anna, my grandfather's cook, for *kipfels* — wonderful sugared crescents made with ground almonds — my father became irritated and told us to go play outside. But it was December, and raining, so instead my mother, who was adroit at figuring out how to divert us and placate my father, led us up a set of narrow backstairs and turned us loose in the attic.

My grandfather had outlived his wife by more than forty years and in all that time he'd scarcely moved an armchair or shifted the placement of a vase. At least partly because he felt more like a tenant in that house than its owner (in fact, he *was* a tenant; his sons inherited everything, while he lived off dividends from a trust). But also because he was permanently staggered by his wife's death; he simply could not accept that he would now be in charge of the life they'd made together, a life that she had designed, for the most part, and paid for, and made sensible, while he sat by, grateful and admiring.

He was turning fifty when my father was born in 1926, already almost elderly. A man who had spent his entire life studying music, an only child who nearly died of typhoid fever when he was four and forever after thought of himself as frail, even when he was climbing in the Alps. Cared for first by an anxious mother, then by a wealthy wife. Even had he been so inclined, he was afraid to think about marrying again. Afraid of what the Kroger family, especially

Lucile's three sisters, his nearest neighbors, might think of a new bride installed down the road. Afraid even more of his spry, brusque, hard-nosed father-in-law, who had bankrolled everything. But how was he to manage the profound complexities of a big house, ten servants, and two frightened grieving little boys? By not altering anything and asking his mother to come live with him.

Maybe he also hoped, without admitting it to himself, that if he kept the house just as she left it, his wife would come back. And so nothing much changed after 1932. No new rugs or paintings, no new furniture. For forty years everything kept in the same places, as if some of Lucile's elemental geometry remained in the precise angles of end tables and chairs.

Except in the attic. High above that neatly furnished mausoleum on Indian Hill, the past had become a marvelous bewildering mind-numbing jumble. Ostrich feathers and opera glasses, half-torn receipts for lost purchases, invitations from forgotten acquaintances to forgotten events, unfocused photographs, newspapers gone yellow, cracked china, old books underlined and scribbled with old thoughts, knotted necklaces, stray buttons, collectibles that had lost their reason for being collected. Relic and rubbish and all the confusion that lies in between. Junk. Not heirlooms, which all have approved and edited stories attached. Things. As ephemeral as it may seem, the past is made up crassly of things, most of them unmemorable and therefore free for the taking, and such was the case with my grand-father's attic.

It was a long, low-ceilinged room with cork walls and a cork floor that smelled piercingly of cork, and it ran half the length of the house, filled almost to the ceiling with trunks, wooden wardrobes, souvenirs of travel, books, boxes of papers. And, it stands to reason, letters. Most likely diaries and journals as well. Lucile grew up at a time when wealthy, educated women typically kept diaries, if only to track whom they'd seen and where they'd been. The line-a-day type was very popular. "Dined with Mrs. Astor to meet Prince Louis of Battenburg," reads one entry from Edith Wharton's line-a-day diary in 1905. The next day's jottings might be restricted to traffic between Hyde Park and Lenox, Massachusetts. The mix of banality and occasion in those line-a-day diaries, noted mostly without editorial comment, comes closer than any biography to capturing the true texture of someone else's life, though Wharton could record more occasion and less banality than most of us.

Given that she was a great reader (and perhaps given that I was just thinking of Edith Wharton), it also occurs to me that Lucile might have tried to write a novel when she was young.

Novelists run in the family, along with nearsightedness and a certain self-absorption—which also tend to run in novelists. My father wrote a pair of novels when he was in his late twenties, though neither were published (one was a broad farce that was too broad, the other a hostile roman à clef that was too hostile). My older sister is writing one now. Lucile's sister Gertrude wrote a novel when she was middle aged but thought it was too risqué, so she threw it into the fire, creating, she claimed, "the hottest fire that fireplace ever saw!"

During her senior year at Wellesley Lucile took a yearlong course on American authors, taught by a reserved, correct male professor named Charles Lowell Young, who was passionate about American writers to the point of evangelism. He loved, in particular, Emerson and the Transcendentalists. On warm spring afternoons he paced back and forth in front of a classroom full of drowsy young women, lecturing in his stiff white celluloid collar, a hectic patch on either cheek, breathing heavily as the hour progressed and his theories became more intricate. His subject: Emerson's rational control of inspiration. What most of his students heard: heavy breathing. Correctness has its romantic aspects; so does literary fervor. The scarcity of men on the Wellesley campus in 1910 may have also increased Professor Young's attractions (he was related to the poetic Lowells of Massachusetts); it's not impossible that Lucile might have hoped to impress him with undergraduate efforts of her own.

She was a member, too, of the selective Shakespeare Society, Wellesley's version of a literary Skull and Bones. For her honeymoon, in July of 1923, when she and my grandfather could have gone anywhere, they stayed in Warm Springs, Virginia, at the home of Mary Johnston, the author of *To Have and to Hold,* a popular novel about the Civil War, and a well-known supporter of women's suffrage. For pecuniary reasons that affect even popular novelists, Mary Johnston had turned her house into the Three Hills Inn. Virginia in July is not an obvious destination; it is hot and muggy there that time of year, even up in the mountains, particularly if one is also floating in ninety-eight-degree bubbling hot springs, the inn's major attraction. Virginia Beach makes more sense, especially if you're traveling all the way from Cincinnati. But Lucile must have admired Miss Johnston's books (otherwise the visit might have been strained) as well as her politics and wanted to meet her to discuss them.

So it seems reasonable to wonder whether she ever tried to become an author herself.

Especially considering that for four years she was an intelligent, literate progressive young college graduate without a job, living in her father's house. She dabbled in courses in home economics at the University of Cincinnati and considered becoming a practical nurse.

She tried to study horticulture. Mostly she supervised the kitchen, making sure her father's meals were exactly as he wanted them and served precisely at six thirty every evening or he would explode in wrath. A fertile situation for a budding novelist: full of constraint and repression, plus three good meals a day.

Add a further ingredient: her father, B. H. Kroger, the perfect antagonist. Charismatic, tyrannical, humorous. Widowed and attractive to women (bound to provoke a daughter). A genius at making money, at marketing, at coaxing and bullying people into doing what he wanted when he wanted it. He shouted, he swore, he insulted with breathtaking dexterity. Like most competent people, he could also be extremely kind. Above all, he was oppressive. His pale, clever, bespectacled face peered out from billboards across Cincinnati. His name was emblazoned across storefronts, spelled out on the side of delivery trucks, capitalized in daily newspaper advertisements. KROGER.

Who wouldn't want to rebel against such an overweening parent? And what better way to rebel than to turn him into a fictional figure, comic if possible, and trap him between parallel lines on numbered eight-by-eleven-inch pieces of paper, with neat margins, where he must remain, unfinished, until you feel like coming back to him. Also, what better way than writing a novel to make a little room for yourself in a crowded house, where probably no one but you cares much about what you are thinking. Lucile paces the floor of her bedroom devising plots and reading novels—the Bröntes would have been just the ticket for this edgy period—brooding about her sisters' romantic endeavors (they are all engaged), acting as hostess at her father's dinner parties and contending with Aunt Ida, her father's unmarried sister, who as housekeeper holds the keys to everything and orders the household. Irksome when one is twenty-five or -six and believes it's time to hold the keys to everything oneself.

But then the war began and everything changed, briefly, startlingly.

Lucile was drafted by her father to be his private secretary and act as treasurer of his company, which was growing almost too fast for him to keep up with and by then comprised nearly five thousand stores. Overnight she became an executive, with her own office in the company's headquarters, her own typewriter, her own shelf of accounting ledgers, her own wooden swivel chair. She had the best head for business of all her father's children; she knew it and he knew it. Her two younger brothers, Henry and Chester, joined the army. Her sisters stayed home, knitting socks and getting married. Years later her father admitted he would never have sold his company if he could have left it to Lucile. Yet she sat in that office, day after day, with the understanding that she would surrender her chair and its 360-degree turns as soon as "the boys" came home.

So in between the office and the kitchen, perhaps on her new office typewriter, she writes (perhaps) a bildungsroman. The story of a smart, restive young woman living at home with her domineering father in a provincial midwestern city full of steep hills and middle-brow Germans. A young woman with red hair and a passionate nature, hidden behind a certain reserve. She leaves home for Europe, is briefly exhilaratingly free, dabbles with bohemian life, befriends actors and revolutionaries in cafes, and then falls in love with a dark dashing man she cannot marry. An officer in the French army. Married already? Poor? Suspected of being a fortune hunter? Anyway, they can't marry. She succumbs to despair. Survives. The last pages find her back in Cincinnati, dolefully deciding to marry a sensitive, palely handsome man who can't compare with the swashbuckling love she renounced.

Not much plot or suspense. Dishonest about the rage the heroine feels toward her father, too pious about the forsaken lover. Overwritten in some passages, sketchy in others, and the character of the plucky, independent young midwesterner owes a bit too much to Jane Eyre crossed with a Willa Cather heroine. Embarrassed by

the ungainly thing she has created but, like so many first-time novelists, unwilling to toss it out, Lucile carries the manuscript with her
through successive house moves and finally stuffs it into a box up in
the attic under the eaves.

Lost Opportunities, she calls it. Or *Love's Regrets.* Something that
makes her smile ruefully later when she happens upon it by accident,
and finger the pages, and be glad that she had put it away.

I did not find a yellowed manuscript of my grandmother's tucked under the eaves in my grandfather's attic in 1973. And if I had, I don't know that I would have bothered to look at it. Like most twelve-year-olds, my interest in the past was mostly ornamental. Of that afternoon in the attic, I recall only opening trunks and trying on wide-brimmed ladies' hats and an old steel army helmet, peering through a lorgnette, and finding an ancient baby carriage with a cracked bonnet, which my younger sisters and I wheeled squeaking back and forth. And the acrid, pensive smell of mothballs, mixed with cork. I'm almost positive I remember opening a wardrobe and finding a sash like the ones worn by suffragettes when they marched in Washington in 1913 and almost certain I recall a hatbox full of dance cards and music programs (one signed by Rachmaninoff?), but that "almost" is hazardous. These could simply be recollections of what I want to recollect.

Because while I had always been fascinated by my grandmother, whose early death struck me even then as the keynote of family history, I wasn't fascinated enough to look closely at all the evidence of her that lay in those boxes and trunks. Like squirrels my sisters and I ran wild among the trunks and tall oak wardrobes of our grandfather's attic, pillaging and pocketing whatever caught our attention. Usually, antique finery—black gloves and old fox pieces and long white silk scarves—in which we could become stars of our own version of history, which from our perspective was simply the present in old-fashioned clothing (a view shared, interestingly, by many writers of historical fiction). Whatever didn't concern us immediately, we ignored.

And my parents weren't in the attic to supervise. They were downstairs, creaking through shuttered high-ceilinged rooms putting color-coded stickers on etchings and lithographs and Chinese lamps and dividing up the books, the Persian carpets, the china and silver— solely responsible for this task because my tall, humorous uncle Albert, whose drooping mustache and big lower lip made him look like the drinker on the label of Moretti beer, had gone on a bender. Dazed and exhausted, they conferred only when they had to, my father trying to reassess his life now that he had no parent at all, my mother trying to understand why, when his parent had been almost a hundred years old, my father would need to reassess anything. The end of their marriage was beginning, though none of us, not even they, guessed it then.

Several times that week I searched out my mother as she drifted through those big shrouded rooms on the first floor (though none of the furniture was actually shrouded), her long dark hair loosening from the long clip that held it in a casual chignon, a checklist in her hand. Nominally, she was taking an inventory of the furniture, but I sensed she was taking an inventory of my father, noting whether he was standing too long by the windows facing the garden and its bare syringa hedges, gauging whether he was annoyed by our clamor as we tried to play with an ancient mah-jongg set in the front hall.

We were always looking for my mother; often so was my father. "Where's your mother?" he would demand, scowling suspiciously, as though we were hiding her under the bed. It was a never-ending tension between us, who would get her attention first, and who would keep it, though I think I always knew that she preferred to be with us children. A sunny, energetic person, she loved to be "out and about," as she would say, "doing something." Going to the beach, into town, for a drive. When it comes to "doing something" children are natural companions.

My father, on the other hand, loved to sit and talk, often critically of other people. He was hugely entertaining at fault finding, as are most gifted conversationalists, but my mother did not like criticizing other people; she got along with almost everyone, which left her without much to say in a family of critics. At cocktail hour at home she could always be found sitting with my father in the sunroom, sipping a very weak martini, listening to him inveigh against some hapless administrator or colleague at Georgetown. "Go on out," he would say gruffly to us. "Your mother and I are talking." And my mother would give us a slightly resigned smile and nod toward the door. Inevitably, his despondency wore at her good humor. She told me once how furious she was when he informed her that he could never be happy. "And I tried so hard!" she said, her eyes bright with outrage.

One evening in Cincinnati I recall coming upon the two of them in my grandfather's living room, which by then was filling up with color-coded stickers. My mother was bending over my father as he sat in a chair with his face in his hands, her arms around his shoulders, a worried expression on her lovely face, when she glanced up and saw me standing there and either beckoned to me with one hand or tried to warn me away. Or maybe this memory is of the two of them at home, in my father's study. The place is as uncertain as my mother's gesture. All that remains clear for me is the impression of my father weeping and my mother trying, unsuccessfully, to console him.

Whatever did not acquire a color-coded sticker that week vanished.

A GHASTLY WEEK for my father. First my grandfather's funeral, conducted in the cold rain at Spring Grove Cemetery under a tent; the coffin was invisible beneath a small mountain of roses, so that it looked as if roses were being buried instead of my grandfather, a gaudy gesture he would have disliked. Dominating the burial site was the Kroger monument, a bleak granite obelisk that looked even more uncongenial in the rain. Most of my grandfather's friends had been dead for decades and so no one outside of the family attended the funeral except the younger son of William Howard Taft, Charley Taft, for whom my father had once campaigned in his well-intentioned but hopeless run for governor of Ohio. Charley Taft was now an old man in a felt hat and a tweed coat who had driven to the funeral in a car with a canoe tied to the roof. Great-Aunt Gertrude, the would-be novelist, Lucile's one surviving sister, was in Palm Beach for the winter where she had sensibly decided to stay.

With the funeral over, my father had to turn his attention to selling that echoing house on top of Indian Hill, his childhood home. And to the remaining three old German servants who needed to retire, the beloved Paula, Anna, and Robert, as quaintly distant now as characters in the *Tales of Hoffmann*. And finally to the contents of the house's twenty-three rooms (or was it twenty-four?), to be divided among two sons and eight grandchildren. Trembling with impatience and grief, my father wanted only to get it all over with, and his habit was to throw away what he could not manage, which in this instance meant the attic, even though that was the one place in the world where he might have found his mother.

L ooking back, I am amazed at how casually my sisters and I regarded that house on Indian Hill, which, surprisingly, seems even larger in photographs than in my recollections. With the unconscious entitlement of children, we walked in and out of the front door without pausing to knock, not properly awed by the mahogany grandfather clock in the hall, the rattling elevator with its black metal accordion cage door, the Steinway concert grand piano in the living room, the Whistler and Dürer etchings on the walls. It was simply a house, there to receive us, as though we were small visiting monarchs come to view a far-flung duchy. Its history, and that of its former occupants, seemed similarly incidental.

One part of the house did impress me: the formal staircase, curving down to the entrance hall from the second floor. My grandmother had fallen down this staircase, nineteen stairs, all the way from the top step, when she was nearly eight months' pregnant; soon after, she miscarried what would have been her third child, a girl. She died two years later, and though that fall can't have caused her subsequent illness, I associated the staircase with her death, anyway. Each time I went down those stairs I would pause for a moment at the top, looking down the banister's nautilus curl; when I reached the bottom, I lightly tapped the carved newel post. Whether out of superstition or sympathy, I can't remember.

My father did not know about his mother's dreadful fall, I discovered during a phone call last year, to my amazement since that

accident has provided one of the few vivid facts in my version of family history, its awfulness ensuring its importance. He sounded shocked, though he'd once confided that as a child he'd had repeated dreams of falling down the staircase himself and could not figure out why this dream kept recurring or what it signified.

Should I have told him? I wondered afterward. I assumed he'd known, so I wasn't intentionally apprising him of anything. Yet what else was I doing but apprising him of a woman he had never tried to discover for himself? What else but stirring up lost opportunities and love's regrets.

THE DEATH OF my grandfather, whom I had actually known, and whose funeral we had just held, seemed comparatively benign. Born in 1877, he was ninety-six when he died, truly historic, so old that he predated electric lights, telephones, and automobiles. So old that his fine white hair was a nimbus above his head and we children were not allowed to touch his hands, on which he wore fingerless white cotton gloves, because he might bruise, like a peach.

We had seen him most often at his ancient shingled summer home in Chatham, on Cape Cod, where sea air blew in through the windows and on foggy days made the sofa cushions damp and lumpy, where the painted wood floors creaked and all the doors had iron latches instead of doorknobs and the mossy brick patio outside the kitchen was shaded by a hundred-year-old sweet gum tree with branches so low that I climbed it once like a ladder and stepped right onto the roof. It was my first-loved home, with all the space a child instinctively equates with beauty, and the smallness required for security, and so I have missed it ever since. Honeysuckle grew up the chimney outside, and an orchard of dwarf apple trees produced tiny parrot green apples. Nearby was a wooden wishing well with a lichen-covered roof, a murky goldfish pond, blueberry bushes, and a little fenced vegetable garden that produced baby carrots, cherry tomatoes, and lovely pale delicate lettuces.

Everything was on a smaller, more informal scale than at his house in Cincinnati, though even on the Cape my grandfather wore a coat and tie when we came for dinner, driving over most Sundays from our own summer house on the other side of town. And even on the Cape all of his meals—including breakfast—were served with ceremony by Robert, who doubled as butler and chauffeur, in a white shirt, black pants, and a black bow tie.

Like a dancer appearing onstage, Robert would emerge deftly from the swinging door that led to the pantry and the kitchen carrying a bowl of spaetzle or boiled red potatoes sprinkled with parsley, or a platter of broiled haddock, fragrant with the smell of browned butter. Gliding around the long trestle table, he leaned first toward my grandfather with the proffered dish, then insinuated himself gracefully beside each of us in turn. His bulging forehead gleamed in the candlelight. He reeked of an oily men's cologne. "Vould you like zome?" he would ask intimately, baring the gap between his great front teeth.

Lucile must have been so used to the presence of servants that she took it for granted that people other than relatives would live under the same roof and that those people would be dedicated to making life comfortable for the others. Even middle-class families had servants in those days, though not the staff that Lucile had required to run her big house, of which Anna, Paula, and Robert were the final representatives. My grandfather, who had grown up very differently (attended only by his mother and a pair of liverish great aunts, Mutti and Gotti), must have got used to the idea of servants as well. More than used to it: Though he never once shared a meal with them, by the last decade of his life Anna, Robert, and Paula were his closest friends in the world. He spoke only German to them when we were not around, his first language, though he had been born in Cincinnati. To him, it was the language of deepest intimacy.

Robert loved to appall us little girls by claiming that we had promised to marry him. When we protested that this was impossible, he would insist that we had forgotten. "Chust last veek I proposed!" Then he would produce a ring from a Cracker Jack box and try to press it upon us while we shrank back in horror. "Ach Robert, zee gurls," Paula would exclaim, shaking her head.

Robert and Paula were not married but quietly a couple. Paula was Catholic and Robert was divorced, so she could not marry him until his ex-wife died, which the ex-wife, back in Germany, was taking her time in doing. So Paula, a calm, smiling, kind-faced woman with soft brown hair even in her sixties and cats'-eye spectacles, waited. My mother says Paula was very pretty when she first entered my grandfather's employ, at seventeen; she spent almost her entire life in his house, much of it being paid the same wages as when she began as a teenage maidservant. Robert arrived a few years later, passed along by my father's aunt Gretchen, who may have objected to men's cologne. Robert and Paula had grown old together tending my grandfather and waiting for Robert's ex-wife to expire. As a child I assumed this wait must have been bleak—until one of my older sisters told me that once while visiting our grandfather in Cincinnati, she had been put in a room next to Paula's and woke in the middle of the night to a strange metallic sound; it was the rhythmic creaking of bedsprings in the neighboring room.

My grandfather knew nothing of this. To him, Robert was impeccably respectful if slightly patronizing, though in a protective way, as one might patronize a precocious but sheltered child. By then it was clear to me that my grandfather existed on another plane altogether from the rest of us, increasingly a foreigner in the world outside his own house. I understood that he was still in love with my grandmother and that he spent much time communing, somehow, with their past life together, though I don't recall wondering why he remained so devoted to a woman who had been dead four times as long as they had been married or whether the answer might lie more with him than with her. When at home on Indian Hill, he said good morning to his wife's portrait in the dining room every morning when he sat down to breakfast and he wished her good night every evening just before he went up to bed. It was simply how he did things, the way my father began every morning with a bowl of Special K and finished the day with a glass or two of Jack Daniel's.

From all reports, my grandfather was utterly unhinged when Lucile died. My father remembers him changing his shirt several times a day during those early weeks of mourning, sweating through one after another in anguished panic. He took sedatives for a year in order to sleep, and he wrote to Lucile's friend Ridie of "indescribable and heartbreaking days of despair when everything looks impossible and futile." One hopes he kept some of this despair from his wife in her last months. Regrettably, he did not keep it from his sons. My grandfather's histrionic misery must be one of the reasons my father did not try to remember his mother, except as a marble Athena, since any more familiar reference to her could send his father into a frenzy.

Robert was once driving my grandfather around Chatham in his black Buick station wagon (traded in for a new model every two years) when they were pulled over by a policeman for speeding. My grandfather, irate at having his afternoon drive interrupted, began fuming in German from the backseat. Robert gazed unperturbedly at the officer from under the shiny black brim of his chauffeur's cap. "Zee Ambassador from Loveland," he said, discreetly pointing a thumb toward my grandfather. Loveland is a suburb of Cincinnati. But the officer, taken aback at such an introduction, apologized for the inconvenience and waved them on their way.

AND SO MY grandfather contin-
ued on, decade after decade, the ambassador from Loveland, engrossed in his
biographies of important men whom most
people had forgotten (I recall him reading
The Diary of Calvin Fletcher), absorbed
by his memories of his wife and their too-
brief marriage, and by his painting. In his
late fifties, after Lucile died, he gave up
singing and the piano and became, unex-
pectedly, an abstract expressionist painter,
fond of stark whirling shapes in brilliant Fauvist colors. Every morning on Cape Cod he painted for two or three hours in his studio
across the driveway. Then he had lunch and took a nap. Then he had
dinner. He did not seem unhappy; he seemed poignantly preserved,
as if being a widower all these years were a kind of wistful brine.
Year after year we grew older while my grandfather remained the
same, awaiting us in his green chair in that cluttered living room,
surrounded by floral hooked rugs and his most recent jagged paintings. Always a glass plate of shrimp cocktail sat on the low wooden
table by the sofa. He would murmur greetings, hold up a white-
gloved hand. As I kissed his pale cheek, he smelled gently and deli-
ciously of beer.

Sometimes he would tell us stories of his days as music student in Berlin at the turn of the century, of visiting Napoleon's Tomb in Paris and climbing in the horned Alps with a bar of chocolate in his knapsack. My father ate shrimp and impatiently joggled his foot. Being with his father made him edgy. He was so old, so attached to his old stories. So anxious to show off his paintings, which my father thought amateurish, the same thing I was, one day, to think about my father's poetry. Critical parents produce critical children, I suppose, though my grandfather, at least, did not seem especially critical. At dinner he quizzed us on composers, making us spell Tchaikovsky and Rimsky-Korsakov, and then he would pretend to speak to us in Chinese, muttering meaningfully in gibberish with a mandarin look on his face.

Fifty years had passed since he and Lucile married on a hot July afternoon in Cincinnati, forsaking all others. The second time they met, she asked him to dance. According to my mother, who got the story from an aunt, Lucile kissed him on the dance floor. He was shocked. She kissed him again. What music were they dancing to? I hope it was a tango and not a waltz, and I hope after that second kiss my grandfather stopped being shocked. I hope he told her of visiting Napoleon's Tomb and of climbing in the Alps with a bar of chocolate and that she found these anecdotes stirring instead of tedious. I hope he whispered gibberish into her ear. She was almost thirty-three years old. She must have figured that if she wanted to kiss someone, she'd better go ahead. She was a pragmatist. A realist. She'd lived through a war. Forsaking all others wasn't going to cost her much of a pang.

One afternoon in the summer of 2005, while I was visiting my mother at her house on Cape Cod, she handed me a tin box embossed with Victorian-style cupids that had once held a fruitcake. "Here," she said. "I found this at the back of a shelf when I was going through boxes in the garage. I think it belongs to you."

She was wearing a bathing suit while cleaning out the garage, a blue-flowered affair; my mother is in her seventies and her confidence in bathing suits is still remarkable. I should mention that she was very beautiful when my father met her in the office of my uncle's advertising agency, where she was the secretary. So beautiful that during their honeymoon at the Breakers Hotel in Palm Beach, Marlon Brando, who was staying there, too, while he filmed *Mutiny on the Bounty,* saw her on the beach building a sand castle and offered to help. My father was reading in a beach chair. My mother and Marlon Brando built their sand castle and chatted for a bit; then he asked if she'd like to take a shower with him, at which point my father prudently put down his book and got out of his beach chair.

So I was complimenting my mother on her bathing suit that afternoon in the garage a few summers ago, and not really looking at what she was handing me, until I got back inside the house. It was a tin manufactured in western Germany, made to look old, but not old, and undoubtedly saved for the cupids. I'd had it in my room all through adolescence, though I rarely opened its hinged lid. Still, I recall considering that fruitcake tin one of my significant possessions. In it I had placed a few odds and ends I'd taken away with me from my grandfather's attic after he died in 1973, items that I'd left behind when I moved out of my mother's house a year after she and my father divorced. Until that afternoon when I lifted the lid and caught a whiff of cork, I had not thought of my grandfather's attic in over twenty years.

So much had transpired since then to make me forget it, including my father's remarriage, and my own wedding, which my father did not attend, and the weddings of my two younger sisters, which he didn't attend either, and the births of my children, whom he scarcely knew. It's a strange story, what happened to us, and I tell it here not in the spirit of recrimination, but of explanation: Soon after I left college my father disappeared. For eight years, I did not have an address for him or a telephone number. Various reasons contributed to his disappearance. After their divorce, he and my mother argued over money. He meanwhile had lost a lot of it, though not to her;

he was always incompetent with money, which he never seemed to understand except as a way to get out of things he did not want to do, a problematic attitude compounded by extravagance — he loved to give generous presents — and unwise investments, like buying a herd of Black Angus cattle that almost immediately contracted hoof-and-mouth disease. (My mother, on the other hand, who had grown up poor, had excellent business sense.) Worse, none of his children got on with his new wife. She thought we were selfish, and at the time, he agreed with her. Maybe we were. Though that's not how I remember it, more that we were rather too anxious to please. In any case, my father had a long history of blaming his troubles on who-ever, at the moment, seemed to be causing them, and for the moment it was all of us. So he vanished.

My brother maintained occasional contact with him and would periodically report that my father was in Richmond, or Ocean City, or Chapel Hill. What he was doing seemed as provisional as where he was living. Running a T-shirt shop; planning to start a bakery; learning massage techniques. Now I can see that he was a man marked by terrors and doubts which he was trying to erase, even at the risk of rubbing himself out. But of course I did not see that then, and even if I had it wouldn't have made much difference.

During those eight years I pretended not to miss my father, but I saw him in any tallish bespectacled gray-haired man who walked with his fists cocked backward and his shoulders rounded forward. At a rest stop in Utah, on a San Francisco street corner overlooking the bay, in a dingy Cambridge laundry with a gray linoleum floor. One brilliant afternoon I saw him in Monte Carlo, where I had stopped for a day with my husband a few years before we were married, on a trip from Italy to Spain. My father was reading the paper at a little green metal table in an outdoor cafe. Beside the table sat a lemon tree in an orange clay pot. People in sunglasses walked back and forth on the sidewalk, on their way to the beach or the casinos. I can still see him so clearly: his large shapely hand holding up the newspaper, sunlight shining hotly on the green metal tabletop and along the glossy dark leaves of the lemon tree. I am still stunned when the paper lowers and the face behind it belongs to a stranger.

More time passed. Slowly my father reappeared, coming gradually into focus after his murky absence like a figure in a Polaroid photograph. I was living outside of Boston by then. He called a few times. He made a few brief visits. Very awkward visits, which demanded courage on his part. His marriage ended; the calls and visits increased. Yet despite sincere efforts on his part to make amends, which I appreciated but found hard to accept, there wasn't much left between us. We no longer had friends or acquaintances in common — most of them had fallen away after his second divorce — and family was a subject to be avoided, since he was barely speaking to most of my sisters, or they to him, and he certainly wasn't speaking to my mother, whom he blamed for their divorce, though he had left her for another woman. I couldn't refer to him as "my father" without feeling slightly false. It wasn't a term that quite applied to him, something he seemed to feel even more strongly than I did.

Seeing me with my children, for instance, did not prompt memories of being a parent for him, only memories of himself as a child and the parenting he hadn't received. When I spoke to him on the phone, our conversations inevitably reverted to his sad childhood, perhaps because he sensed it was the one part of his life that continued to exert an almost tidal pull on me. The bad nanny, the weak father, the careless aunts and uncles. But most of all the missing mother who had never really loved him. As if the entire middle period of his life, the years between being a child and an elderly man, had never existed.

Though he was clearly lonely and wanted to talk, I dreaded those calls. I avoided them whenever possible, letting the answering machine pick up for me, and when I did pick up the phone myself it would often be at a time when I knew I'd have to leave soon to fetch the children from school or a playdate. The back of my throat would start to ache. When I hung up, I felt guilty and sad, ashamed of my unwillingness to give him what he was calling for, which was reassurance that he was not alone in the world, but also deeply furious. Why should I feel sorry for him? He was the one who had vanished.

So MUCH HAD transpired, so much had been lost. And yet as I stood there staring at the jumbled contents of that fruitcake tin, it was as if no time had passed at all. There was my grandfather's attic, in all its manifold confusion, still waiting for someone to sort it out.

A complete list of the tin's contents, in no particular order:

1. A small navy blue leatherbound gilt-edged book stamped TAGEBUCH, or diary, which contains fourteen pages of a journal Lucile Kroger kept at Wellesley at the beginning of 1911, the last semester of her senior year. Within this journal are also twelve loose notebook pages, half of them written in French, all that survives of a record she kept of the year she spent in France between 1919 and 1920 as a relief worker with the Wellesley College Reconstruction Unit.

The rest of the *Tagebuch*'s pages are blank, save for the very back of the book which contains several long lists of expenditures, mostly for groceries, dated the month of January, year unknown. She may have been fond of lists. The sign either of an organized person or of a person who desperately wants to feel organized.

Lists are revealing of other things as well. On January 8 Lucile spent thirty cents on marshmallows and ten cents on carfare. But what is revealed? That she liked marshmallows? That in those days carfare was relatively cheap while marshmallows were expensive? Or only that when presented with a list that also includes stamps, pork chops, and shelf paper, I will focus on marshmallows?

2. Two booklets of postcards she brought back from France, depicting the devastation after the Great War. One of the booklets, *"Ruines de Lens,"* shows before and after scenes on alternating postcards. A terrible magic trick. On the postcard to the left: a prosperous French boulevard with a vegetable market, a school, and rows of tidy brick storefronts. Now the postcard to the right: the same view — except it's a twisted metal gate opening onto piles of dirt and rubble. The other booklet gives postcard views of the stark lunar aftermath of the Battle of the Somme.

3. An olive-drab cardboard packet, a Kodak *Album Classeur* of undeveloped negatives of pictures taken in France, each one neatly identified in my grandmother's handwriting on several pages labeled SUJET at the back of the packet. When I first held these negatives up to the light, I saw that several of them were of a handsome man in uniform. He was identified only as "Brigadier." The other repeated *sujet* was a big shepherd dog named Wolf.

4. A crumbling black leather scrapbook of snapshots she had taken of friends and family in Cincinnati with her No. 2 Brownie box camera and also on a holiday in Michigan, between 1904 and 1905.

5. Her engraved metal bookplate stamp, which reads EX LIBRIS and has her name, Lucile I. Kroger, in gothic script, underneath. It depicts a cozy library scene with a bench and an enormous stone fireplace and a mantel with framed pictures resting on it, surrounded by leafy trees instead of walls. The Three Bears' reading room. Did she choose this scene as representative of herself as a reader? Did she find reading a warm, reassuring experience? Did she choose cozy books? Probably not, especially if one considers that she named her Indian Hill house Thornefield, which she must have known was the

name of Mr. Rochester's house in *Jane Eyre,* though spelled without the first *e.* My father named his first daughter Catherine after the heroine of *Wuthering Heights.* A few years ago I visited the Brönte home in Haworth and was so transfixed by the parlor sofa on which Emily is said to have expired that finally I had to be elbowed out of the way by another visitor. What lies behind this family affinity for the Bröntes? Is it only that we are somewhat morose?

6. A small bronze French medal with ALSACE engraved in the upper left-hand corner. Below is the embossed profile of a beautiful, stern-faced young woman in an elaborate medieval-looking headdress. On the reverse side, a pair of storks nest on a steep rooftop. A commemorative medal. But what does it commemorate?

7. A battered, annotated copy of Washington Irving's *Life of Oliver Goldsmith,* which Lucile read as a teenager when she attended the Collegiate School for Girls in Washington DC. A book that she underlined here and there, occasionally adding penciled comments. This stanza of a poem by the impecunious Goldsmith, written after a gift of some game from his patron, Lord Clare, received her particular attention:

> But hang it — to poets, who seldom can eat,
> Your very good mutton's a very good treat;
> Such dainties to them, their health it might hurt;
> *It's like sending them ruffles, when wanting a shirt.*

"Condition of poets in age of changing standards," noted Lucile dutifully in the margin. Alas, she was wrong, the condition of poets, who are always needing shirts but getting ruffles, never changes much, age to age, which is why Goldsmith italicized that last line. Neither does the condition of collegiate girls, who will always read more dutifully than thoughtfully.

8. A green paper-covered exercise book in which she copied out poems to practice her penmanship, probably in grammar school. It's a collection of remarkable variety, rendered without editorial comment, from "Pitty Pat's Prayer" ("We've a dear little damsel we call / Pitty Pat / She's got a wee kitten she calls / Kitty Cat") all the way to Byron's "The Field of Waterloo" ("Stop! For thy tread is on an empire's dust! An earthquake's spoil is sepulchered below!")

9. A few gold hatpins and four or five brooches, including her Shakespeare Society pin from Wellesley—a bronze tragicomic mask with a silver quill pen stuck through one eye—and some little bar pins for holding one's bra straps in place.

10. And finally a silver charm bracelet that has, among its other charms, a tiny matchbook stamped HOT TIP, a miniscule pack of Chesterfield cigarettes, and a marriage license that opens to reveal the words *State of Bliss.*

THIS IS WHAT I HAVE: Snips of historical DNA. Some photographs. A letter. A fruitcake tin embossed with cupids which holds a minute helix of allusions to a long-dead woman who contributed one-quarter of my genetic makeup, along with possible freaks of temperament. Though I wonder if I had more whether I would make less of it.

Actually, it's a sizable archive in its way, an archive of oddments, things that mattered to Lucile, if only briefly, and that from the beginning suggested that I might discover something meaningful about her if I could only arrange them in the right order. Or perhaps it's more like a crossword puzzle, with hints and riddles as well as blank squares that I would never fill in. Which is as it should be. Every life has its blank squares.

But riddles often have obvious answers that obscure a truer complexity; hints can hint at more than one thing. The real puzzle, it seems to me, lies in finding the right question, not a right answer. And when I first began to sift through Lucile's past, that question remained disappointingly crude, a note written in crayon and torn from a child's old exercise book: what did I hope to find, by finding my father's mother?

The Kroger children on the stairs of their house in Cincinnati.
Lucile is seated far left, top row

III

The Grocer's Daughter

Man is a stream whose
source is hidden.

—EMERSON

Whenever people ask me where I am from, I answer "Virginia" or "Washington DC." Those are both places where I lived as a child, first on a horse farm in Fauquier County, later in different neighborhoods off MacArthur Boulevard in DC. But always I feel that I am not telling the truth. I am not "from" that horse farm (we didn't even ride horses) or those Washington neighborhoods; I happened to live there for a while with my parents, who never seemed to feel committed to one residence over another. Over the last fifty years, for instance, my father has lived in more than twenty houses or apartments, and he was not in the real estate business. Where I secretly feel I am "from" is Cincinnati, a place I visited only a few times as a girl, and know hardly at all, and yet like "the old country" for an exile's children, it absorbs the past for me. Cincinnati may not seem as romantic as St. Petersburg before the revolution, but it is where my father's family has lived for a century and a half, and where his grandfather transformed grocery stores into supermarkets, and himself into a brand name. To find Lucile, I decided, it would make sense to find the place where she was born, the family she was born into, and maybe stake a small claim to both of them myself.

BERNARD HENRY KROGER was a small, wiry, bony-faced man with a large Bavarian nose. He had big ears and, for someone so slight, big wrists that stuck out from the cuffs of even expensively tailored coats. Not a handsome man, but in the photographs I've seen there's something sensual about his wide, full-lipped mouth, something generous and humorous that is complicated, though not quite contradicted, by his alert, shrewd dark eyes. He looks avid.

Born on January 24, 1860, a year before the start of the Civil War and the same year the Prince of Wales visited Cincinnati, or "Porkopolis" as it was known (during his visit the prince noted the astonishing number of hogs running wild in the streets), Bernard was the fifth of ten children, all of whom lived in a small, dark apartment above their father's dry-goods store. They grew up breathing the anxious air of retail. I have difficulty believing this story is not apocryphal, but apparently little Bernard's first toy was a cigar box which he fashioned into a tiny grocery. He began commercial life in earnest at thirteen, a skinny yellow-skinned peddler shaking with malaria as he hawked tea and coffee on the pig-infested streets of Cincinnati. His last name is now known to millions of Americans because they buy their bacon and ice cream and hamburger buns at one of his supermarkets.

I shouldn't say "his supermarkets"; the Kroger Company is now a megacorporation, with annual sales of around seventy-six billion dollars, with 2,486 supermarkets and 750 "fuel centers" spread over thirty-three states. As recently as a decade ago, one in every ten American dollars was spent at a store owned by the Kroger Company. Unfortunately, no one in my branch of the family, at least, owns more than a few shares of stock in it anymore. But my great-grandfather started the company in 1883 and his name is still on it. Whatever understanding his children had of the American dream would have been formed almost entirely by him and they in turn passed that understanding on to their children, who passed it on again. Though, like the American dream itself, that understanding has acquired more ambivalence, and lost economic underpinning, with each generation.

I have never stepped inside a Kroger store (we don't have Kroger in New England) so I've never had a chance to get used to it as an entity, and all my life I have been startled whenever I see the Kroger brand name in print. The first time was when I was in seventh grade and writing a paper on Andy Warhol. In the course of my brief research in the school library, I discovered that one of Warhol's early artistic epiphanies came in the aisles of a Kroger supermarket. I remember staring in amazement at the book I was reading—not amazement that Warhol, a famous and influential American artist, should have begun his artistic life in a supermarket but amazement that I was connected to something large enough that people I would never know could refer to it, even have their own histories with it. I might belong to the Krogers, but Kroger had nothing to do with me. My introduction to the endlessly beguiling question of how much history has to "do" with the people it produces.

BERNARD HENRY'S FATHER, John Henry Kroger, was in his own way as classic a type as his rags-to-riches son: a child immigrant, who traveled alone and penniless from Europe to America. My father is not certain, but he thinks the Krogers lived in Landau, Germany, close to Alsace, territory that was itself uncertain, sometimes German, sometimes French. It seems reasonable to guess that the Krogers were shopkeepers ruined by the political turmoil and financial panic that swept Germany between 1845 and 1848.

It's not hard to imagine those early Krogers, small people with big wrists and large ears, minding a little grocery in the *Marktplatz* tucked beneath steep forested hills and medieval stone castles, vineyards stretching out below. Just to the south lies the ancient Schwarzwald, the Black Forest. Even the name carries a kind of music-box enchantment: Tall pine trees. Drifts of snow. Hunting lodges with gingerbread trim, haunted by the ghosts of Bavarian kings who rode out after stags and then, after a lunch of Rhenish wine and blueberries, fell asleep in the woods and woke up on convent tapestries. A strange place, the Black Forest, full of brooding bedtime stories; even the layer cakes it has inspired are unusually heavy. A place that casts a genetic shadow.

In the turbulent mid-nineteenth century, Landau is a green, bosky fortified city, full of handsome stone buildings and old parade grounds and pink-cheeked students who attend the university and dream of revolutions. The students always have a bit of pocket money for beer and a loaf of rye bread and the occasional dill pickle when everyone else is down to his last mark. But finally even the students run out of money and have to go home to plot their revolutions. The Krogers live on behind their shop, amid ropes of garlic and onions and barrels of unsold pickles; in the evenings the mother sits tiredly at her spinning wheel with a hank of tallowy grayish wool while the father puts on his green felt hat with the little red feather and trudges over to the *Rathaus* to hear the latest bad news. The children cry. There are too many of them to feed, so one day the mother hands the oldest boy a change of underwear and says it's time to go fend for himself.

Or maybe his parents died or maybe John Henry Kroger was wayward and ran away from home. He paid for his passage across the Atlantic by working as a deckhand on a small sloop headed for Baltimore. Finding nothing to keep him in Baltimore after he landed, he then walked over the Allegheny Mountains to Pittsburgh.

I'm sure none of this experience was as phlegmatic as I'm making it sound, especially given that John Henry was the age of a fifth-grader and should have been spending his time learning geography rather than navigating great tracts of it by himself. Also, he didn't speak any English. He may have been preyed upon; probably he missed his mother. He must have often felt lost and cold and hungry. One of my daughters is around his age now, and the thought of her spending even five minutes on her own in a foreign place is unendurable to me. But children belong to the times they live in, like everyone else, and children a century and a half ago were quite different from children now. Perhaps they were more resilient. Or they simply had other things to be resilient about.

Whatever he felt about his life at this point, with no recorded difficulty John Henry got hired to work on a flatboat in Pittsburgh and floated down the Ohio River, landing in Covington, Kentucky, with a capital of six cents, where he found a job in a cracker factory. Not a bad beginning. At least he was guaranteed something to eat and a cracker factory had to have been reasonably warm and dry. This I know not from family lore but from a book called *The Kroger Story,* written by a man named George Laycock. I bought it off Amazon.com for twelve dollars. Surprisingly, or perhaps not, given his family feeling, my father did not own a copy. This remarkable book was commissioned by the Kroger Company in 1973 and is a handsomely produced coffee-table book with a glossy cover that traces the fortunes of the Kroger Company from my great-grandfather's humble beginnings to the year Nixon faced impeachment.

The Kroger Story does not specify what year John Henry appeared in Kentucky, though by figuring backward from his son Bernard's birthdate, January 24, 1860, and surmising that John Henry had to have been at least in his early twenties by then to have fathered five children by the same wife, I can assume he arrived between 1846 and 1848. Which, again figuring backward, allows me to guess that when he stepped off that flatboat, jingling his six cents, he was roughly the same age as Samuel Langhorne Clemens, about to go out on his own as well, four hundred miles to the west in Hannibal, Missouri.

It is one of the tasks as well as one of the pleasures of biography to finger the loose weave of history this way, to consider the distant significance of a little German boy in an old serge jacket and dusty wool pants. To envision him stepping across rocky outcroppings of the Alleghenies, bending down to pull up a blade of grass, chewing it as he walks along squinting in the cool sunshine. A particular boy, a real boy, fully alive within his own flesh as he walks those real miles, kicking a rock. No one has thought much about that particular boy for over a century; he survives now only as a name. But the idea of him has become legendary because another boy about his same age went on to create a character named Huckleberry Finn who has defined forever what it was to be a boy living on his own in nineteenth-century America. We all fit into someone else's story somehow; the trick is to figure out which one.

SAM CLEMENS FIRST heard the term *mark twain,* which means "two fathoms," as he floated away from Cincinnati on the *Paul Jones,* in 1855. He went on to be a genius; John Henry Kroger went on to run an unsuccessful dry-goods store. Eventually the latter married the formidable Gertrude Schlebbe, another German immigrant and something of a religious fanatic (she attended Mass three times on Sundays), who was as relentlessly industrious as her husband was lazy and affable. That they maintained a store at all was mostly due to her efforts. She put her ten children to work almost as soon as they could walk; she beat them if she thought they were wasting time. It's tempting to disparage such an uncompromising mother, but Gertrude deserves, if not affection, then a certain deference. All ten of her children survived; more astonishingly, so did she. If she was worried about wasting time perhaps it was because she understood how little time was usually allotted to people like her.

(All the same, perhaps it is the lingering influence of Gertrude Schlebbe, dealing a hereditary swat to her descendants, that has made me all my life so terrified of being late. My father hates to be late as well. We arrive at airports hours earlier than necessary, hurry into doctors' waiting rooms long before the doctor can see us, appear at parties when the hosts are still getting dressed. We actually waste time in our anxiety about being late—one of those evolutionary twists that signal imminent obsolescence, like a fish with fur. Was Lucile also nervously punctual? Her father became Vesuvian if he wasn't served dinner at exactly six thirty every evening. Isn't it likelier than not?)

Bernard, who rechristened himself Barney as soon as possible, left school at age thirteen when his father's store failed during the business panic of 1873. I have heard both that his father died the same year and that his father became a hopeless drunk; whatever happened to him, it was always his mother Barney wanted to impress. He worked first as a delivery boy at Rheum's Drug Store in Cincinnati, seven days a week, until Gertrude got mad at him for working on the Sabbath and made him quit. The only other job he could find was as a field hand on a farm in Warren County, thirty miles away on the outskirts of Pleasant Plain, which might have seemed like a hard-luck position to anyone but somebody whose father had hiked from Baltimore to work in a cracker factory.

It was March when Barney presented himself at the farm, a bleak stretch of fields and a huddle of ramshackle outbuildings, near Pleasant Plain in name only. He was shown his quarters, an unheated loft over a shed where he had to sleep wrapped in a smelly sheepskin rug. In the winter he lay awake shivering. In the summer he was bitten all night by mosquitoes. Then he had to get up at four thirty in the morning for chores, followed by a long day of plowing in the fields. By lantern light, he milked the cows every evening, fed the hogs, pitched hay to the horses. All for six dollars a month.

"He met the mornings with dread and the evenings with reluctance," notes George Laycock in *The Kroger Story.* Somehow Barney must have also found time during his busy day to eat a bowl of gruel, though it was thin gruel. By the next winter he weighed one hundred pounds and had malaria, thanks to those mosquitoes.

On a cold December day, physically exhausted, Kroger finally quit his job, stuck his corduroy pants legs into the tops of his muddy farm boots, pulled up the frayed collar of his brown overcoat and set off, on foot, for Cincinnati, walking the entire distance to save train fare.

It is peculiarly gratifying to have a description like this written about one of your ancestors by someone who is no relation but who nevertheless cares about intimate details like your great-grandfather's corduroy pants legs and the frayed collar of his brown overcoat. A bit like finding a respectful inventory of your pantry shelves published in the local newspaper. *The Kroger Story* is a fascinating book, one I recommend to grocery-store aficionados (unfortunately, it's out of print). Filled with early advertisements and photographs of the first Kroger stores as well as later supermarkets, it also contains a time line that tracks the progress of the Kroger grocery chain alongside U.S. history, often insisting on parity between the two.

> 1883 is the year for great beginnings. Buffalo Bill Cody launches his first Wild West Show. The world's longest bridge opens in New York linking Brooklyn and Manhattan. And on a crowded street near the Ohio River waterfront in Cincinnati, Ohio, Barney Kroger opens his first store with $722 in cash and big dreams.

And a little later on:

> A new century brings new kinds of transportation, new kinds of ideas, and a new hope for a better life. Automobiles, airplanes, telephone, telegraph, motion pictures, recorded music and radio promise a better life. In Kroger stores there are fresh fruits and vegetables, a variety of

canned and packaged foods and new kinds of foods such
as breakfast cereals, desserts and baking products.

Buffalo Bill, the Brooklyn Bridge, and Barney Kroger—all in the
same paragraph! Heady stuff for a descendant. Not to mention the
revelation that "hope for a better life" once
came in cans and packages, purveyed by
that same ancestor. No wonder everyone
in my family has remained intimidated
by Barney—everyone falling short of his
mark, some of us falling so far that we appear to have made no mark at all. Barney
went on to hobnob with congressmen and
senators and at least two U.S. presidents,
to belong to the most exclusive clubs in the
country (including the Pelee Club on an island in Lake Erie, limited to fifty members
at a time, where Barney smoked cigars and
went fishing with Robert Todd Lincoln and
Marshall Field), to have his own private Pullman car, and a Palm
Beach villa and a "cottage" next door to Joe Kennedy's place on Cape
Cod, and to live the rest of the time in a Cincinnati hillside estate
which he called, waggishly, Slant-Acres. He not only survived the
Great Depression, but he also somehow saw it coming and sold the
Kroger Company to Lehman Brothers for almost thirty million dollars six months before the stock market crashed. A year or so later he
quietly bought back a lot of those shares for a song, gave them to his
children, then decided to start his own bank.

If Barney made money fast, he gave it away at nearly the same
pace: He donated five Bengal tigers to the Cincinnati Zoo. He donated a public golf course to Palm Beach. He donated two summer
camps for tubercular children, and a cow to a midwife working in

the backwoods of Kentucky. Most of the other things he donated no one ever heard about; by then he was rich enough not to care anymore who knew how rich he was. Certainly Lucile must have found him an exciting if daunting parent; he was forever hurrying off somewhere in his frock coat and striped trousers, like the cartoonish banker on the Monopoly board, his thin white hair neatly parted down the middle, spectacles glinting as he turned to bark an order about dinner, or make a joke, always nimble, nervy, exacting, and slightly hallucinatory, since he moved so fast he sometimes seemed to be in two places at once. He was a midwestern icon before she left college, a man referred to in newspaper profiles as a "Horatio Alger character."

Then again, aren't most of us overshadowed by our ancestry? Scratch deep enough in the dust of anyone's background and you'll find the seed of a looming archetype. This is especially true of Americans, who belong to a nation that sprang from variety and contradiction. (My mother's father was an Irish policeman, for example; one of her grandfathers gambled.) This may be why Americans are so devoted to tracing their family backgrounds: we're all convinced we come from some kind of notoriety, it doesn't really matter what kind.

GEORGE LAYCOCK IS an assured writer (he was nominated for a National Book Award, though not for *The Kroger Story,* alas, but for a book on bald eagles). He does a nice job of describing Barney's rise from a "skinny, yellow, long-haired" yokel tramping around Cincinnati with a basket of coffee samples to a savvy, dapper, door-to-door salesman working first for the magisterially named Great Northern and Pacific Tea Company, a small grocery near the riverfront, then for the equally small but more modestly designated Wm. White and Company.

During these stints of employment, Barney carefully noted failures. In the first case, the store owner was selling below-market goods for above-market prices (e.g., mealy apples for too much money); in the second, the manager was too sluggish to get up from his stool at the back of the store and attend to his customers. Both businesses went under.

Barney went off to drive a delivery wagon for the Imperial Tea Company, "cracking up the goods" as he was said to describe it. But soon the Imperial Tea Company began to fail as well. More laziness, greed, and incompetence. Saved only when the despairing partners hired "the hustling young Kroger" to take over their ailing store. He said yes on the condition they granted him total authority; then he fired everyone but a delivery boy. When, after twelve months and a one-thousand-dollar profit margin, the owners of the Imperial Tea Company refused to make him a full partner, Barney quit and started his own store, and pretty soon took away all their business. (What happened to the delivery boy, I have no idea. I hope he got a raise.)

Many years later the Kroger Company was a focus of trust-busting efforts for having tried to monopolize the grocery business in the Midwest. My husband remembers reading about the case in law school. One could say it all started with the Imperial Tea Company, which hired a starveling free marketeer and then, by refusing to reward his successes, turned him into a true imperialist.

It seems inevitable to me now, knowing the trajectory of this kind of narrative, that Barney and his grocery business would prosper, but at the time Barney himself must have been less sanguine. As Laycock reports him saying years later, "In the early days, I have many times started from my store with my room key in my hand, so dead tired that I climbed the steps, unlocked the door and tumbled into bed without being able to remember what I had done. Many a time I have dropped down on my bed with my clothes on and slept until morning without getting under the covers. I would get up at four o'clock, crawl out, get something to eat at the market house and go at it again."

Within that slender, rumpled figure of the young man facedown on his bed, "many a time" still with his shoes on, sleeps both the person and the story of that person. Fraternal twins, one of whom will eventually, inevitably murder the other. The hero of the story is the eager, hustling lad who hurries forever from the market house at daybreak, striding across shadowed streets with a roll in his hand, rushing toward his empire in the sun. "You can't fool people on food!" he shouts. Every thing he says becomes an instant slogan.

But the other brother, the one with his rundown shoe heels pointed toward the ceiling in some dive near Sausage Row, dreaming his exhausted dreams—what happened to him? He was once alive as well, more alive, in fact, than his famous twin, because he was completely preoccupied with the precariousness of ordinary living.

Day after day he woke dry mouthed on his lumpy cot, shirt collar chafing his neck, to confront the bare floor and torn blind of his ugly cheap little room. "Many a time" he wanted to stay in bed, but always he remembered something he was afraid of forgetting—a mouse behind the cracker barrels, a bag of shelled walnuts to check for hulls—and sat up, heart thumping, already fumbling with his crumpled tie. What precise mixture of excitement and terror woke him up every morning without an alarm clock? What chased him as he ran down those rickety stairs?

According to Laycock, in a moment of psychological daring that may not have been commissioned by the Kroger Company, it was his mother. Gertrude Kroger, she of the hard swat, handed Barney his favorite word—*particular*—the way John Henry Kroger had been handed a change of underwear and told to make his own way. Be particular, she told him, and you will succeed. Gertrude herself had been very particular about the quilts she made and the ones she commissioned for her husband's dry-goods store. If she didn't like a quilt enough to have it "on her own bed," she wouldn't sell it. For the rest of his working life, Barney Kroger dedicated himself to being particular. Great artists dedicate themselves to the same principle, with the same single-mindedness, but Barney's medium was groceries: "I meant to sell things," he said simply, "that I would want to have myself."

The flip side of all this particularity, of course, as my father was to discover, was shame instead of a shrug when something was not quite good enough. Another kind of Black Forest, with its own genetic shadow.

IN 1883, HAVING left the Imperial Tea Company, Barney opens his own store at 66 East Pearl Street in downtown Cincinnati using $372 of savings and borrowing $350 from the bank. He takes a partner, Barney Branagan, who shares his first name but none of

his business acumen. From the first, Barney Kroger displays a virtuosity for marketing. Cunningly, he paints the outside of the store "fire-engine red" and chooses an appropriately grandiose name: the Great Western Tea Company. "I don't see what's so great about it," a passerby remarked as Kroger was painting the store name on the front window. "You will!" he cried with characteristic brio.

Kroger realizes that they need a delivery wagon and buys "the finest-looking horse he could afford—a big, smart-stepping sorrel named Dan." For Dan, he purchases "a brightly gilded harness" and buys a wagon, which he also paints red with the store's name spelled out in gold letters. Such a hopeful image: high-stepping Dan in his shiny harness, standing proudly against the backdrop of dusty, dirty East Pearl Street in 1883. Signs for saloons hang everywhere: JOE'S PLACE. LAGER BEER. A WIENERWURST FREE WITH EACH DRINK. (One of these saloons a few blocks away on Vine Street is owned by Rudolph John Berne, father of a frail musical little boy who will grow up to be my grandfather.) Dogs bark, pigs run past the wagon wheels nosing in the mud for fallen cabbage leaves and potatoes, odorous mounds of droppings steam in the cold morning sunlight as people pick their way along, pausing to admire proud glossy Dan and his gleaming red wagon. Cincinnati is a rough, busy, stinking place, and one must savor moments of beauty where one finds them.

Steamboats whistle from the river; a streetcar rushes past. The air is cindery, rank, damp with the tannic scent of river water. Up and down the street, mixed in with the saloons, are German bakeries, brick churches with tidy white spires, barber shops, harness shops, dry-goods stores and other small newly swept groceries, opening their doors for the housewives lined up with baskets on their arms. And there, taking it all in among his canisters of Moon Chop tea, his cakes of pine tar soap, his tins of tobacco, his barrels of flour and sugar, his bins of ginger snaps, his crates of apples, picked through so there isn't a single rotten one and the apples on top polished with a shirtsleeve to make them shine appetizingly, is Barney Kroger.

Twenty-three years old and almost insane with ambition.

He works "longer hours than ever, laboring over his records, cleaning the store, packaging and delivering groceries and taking orders." He schemes, he calculates, he chats up housewives to find out what they like to buy. He gets up even earlier to get the farmers' business, peddling them groceries as they come around on their wagons to peddle vegetables. What Barney Branagan was doing meanwhile we aren't told, though according to family hearsay he was drinking at one of those nearby saloons—a suspicion borne out by what happens two weeks after the Great Western Tea Company opens its fire-engine red doors:

> Branagan, who was delivering groceries with Dan and the new red wagon, approached a grade level railroad crossing one day. He could plainly see a train engine chugging toward the crossing, its stack puffing black coal smoke. But Branagan decided he had ample time to beat the train, so he spoke to Dan and set the horse into a brisk

trot. All but the rear half of the wagon cleared the tracks. As the cowcatcher splintered the red delivery wagon, parts flew in every direction. So did groceries. Dan was dead in his harness. Branagan, who was thrown clear of the wreck, had narrowly escaped injury.

Until he limped back to the store, that is, and reported the day's events to Kroger. Despite his mother's religious instruction, Kroger did not prize forgiveness and "profanity, not German, was his second tongue." Whatever he said to Branagan that day was certainly not commissioned by the Kroger Company.

They replace Dan with an ancient nag. Kroger tells Branagan not to make the nag try to pull their new delivery wagon up a certain steep hill; Branagan ignores him. The nag drops dead on the hillside. One February morning a few weeks later the Ohio River floods, cresting at over seventy feet. Muddy water cascades down East Pearl Street. Kroger swims into his store to save the cash register, but everything else is flotsam.

Incredibly the Great Western Tea Company survives and by the end of its first year even turns a profit. Gertrude is partly responsible. Another Kroger Company history, this one published on the company website, recounts a Friday in early winter when Barney bought a cartload of cabbages from a local farmer. Belatedly realizing that he had too many cabbages to sell, and no room to store them, he drove the whole cartload across the river to his mother in Covington, Kentucky, and asked her to make sauerkraut over the weekend (rather like the miller in *Rumpelstiltskin,* presenting his daughter with a wagonload of hay to spin overnight into gold, as Gertrude had only Friday evening and Saturday to turn that cartload of cabbages into sauerkraut since, famously, she went to Mass all day on Sunday).

Never one to shirk a challenge, she dispatches those cabbages with the same gusto she employs when spanking her ten children.

Using an old family recipe that is heavy on sugar, she produces several barrels of sauerkraut. The following Monday Barney rolls the barrels into his store, opens the lids, and hangs up a sign: KROGER SAUERKRAUT, 3 CENTS A POUND. The sauerkraut is a hit with German housewives, who are delighted not to have to go home and chop up their own cabbages. Gertrude follows this success with her own pickles, and store-brand products are born.

BY THE END of his first year in business Kroger has learned to buy in bulk so that he can cut prices (he is Wal-Mart before Wal-Mart), to make use of what he can't immediately sell, to buy directly from farmers and to seize the opportunity to sell them their groceries at the same time, thereby repocketing whatever he's just paid out. Branagan has learned nothing except that he doesn't want to work as hard as Kroger. "Branagan enjoyed visiting with the customers more than he enjoyed working," notes Laycock diplomatically. It was John Henry Kroger all over again, affable and indolent, with Barney Kroger in the role of Gertrude. A marriage that needed repeating only so that it could finally be escaped.

Kroger buys out Branagan, who ambles out of history, at least this history, and it's not long before Kroger opens another store, then another. Soon he has four Great Western Tea Company stores, one of which is managed by his mother.

Be particular, don't charge too much, advertise cleverly, drive yourself like a donkey, and you will prosper. Barney never mistrusted the basic fairness of commercial success. Life rewarded those who deserved to be rewarded.

"In the early days," he said, "it never occurred to me that I could be wrong."

No one in my family recalls a single detail about Barney's wife, Mary Emily Jansen Kroger, except that she succumbed to an overdose of ether during an appendectomy, leaving her husband with seven young children. According to burial records at Spring Grove Cemetery, she was born May 11, 1867, and died on April 22, 1899. My father has a vague impression that she was "sort of a nobody." One of those unmemorable women who "did" nothing but marry and have children; she was probably very brave and uncomplaining. But as Diane Johnson points out in *Lesser Lives,* her biography of the deliberately forgotten first Mrs. George Meredith, "a lesser life does not seem lesser to the person who leads one. His life is very real to him; he is not a minor figure in it."

Given her present obscurity among even her grandchildren it's hard to believe that Mary Emily once seemed major to anyone, herself included. She lived, she died. The end. It's unfortunate, but the uncelebrated also seem undeserving. At least Mrs. George Meredith was married to a famous poet and dramatist, and also the daughter of Thomas Love Peacock and a friend to famous men and women, plus a writer herself who had a scandalous affair with the artist responsible for the famous painting of John Keats on his deathbed.

But who is Mary Emily Jansen Kroger that we should bother to remember her? Nobody. To invest this woman with a mind, with moods, to picture her as someone capable of bad dreams, who sometimes woke up thirsty, who tugged at her eyebrows when she was distracted, who enjoyed a mild spring breeze and two teaspoons of sugar in her coffee, is more than an act of will—it's an act, almost, of subversion. Because this is the danger in looking backward at people who don't "matter": there are so many of them. And as soon as one begins to consider those billions of forgotten nobodies, like any rabble they threaten to overwhelm all social order, not to mention one's own self-importance. "Hold your breath," my children cry whenever we pass a graveyard, a game of theirs based on an old superstition that graveyards are places of contagion, based on the old fact that they sometimes were. Best to give those lesser dead a sympathetic nod, then hold your breath and keep your eyes on the road. Though every so often someone like Mary Emily sticks up a pale hand from the depths of irrelevance and asks to be counted anyway.

THE JANSENS LIVED in Newport, Kentucky, just across the river from Cincinnati, and Barney met Mary Emily on his delivery route. According to Laycock, Barney continued to deliver the Jansens' weekly order himself even after he had hired men to drive his wagons. What Mary Emily's father did for a living I haven't been able to discover, but he must have been somewhat prosperous, enough so that he "speculated aloud that his daughter could do better than marry the man who delivered the groceries."

Though he was short and unprepossessing, with his big nose and big ears, and by now also spectacles, Barney was never more persuasive than when he was selling himself. He wanted Mary Emily—who must not have been altogether unmemorable if she inspired desire in such a notoriously particular man—and so he said and did whatever was necessary to get her. Determination can be its own aphrodisiac. They were married in 1886 when Mary Emily was nineteen years old. Marrying the delivery boy for love soon turned out to have been a smart idea, as business began to improve rapidly for the Great Western Tea Company. Barney was still working from dawn to midnight seven days a week and can't have been the most attentive of husbands, and yet they were an amorous couple; she was either pregnant or nursing a baby for the next twelve years.

Two photographs survive of Mary Emily. The first I found in a small canvas bag, along with two more of Lucile's photo albums and

some miscellaneous letters, none by her. The contents of this bag belong to my older brother, Henry, who made his own token appearance in the attic after my grandfather's funeral, collected a few things to carry away, and quietly kept them in his own attic all these years. Last fall he sent me this canvas bag in care of one of our sisters. A generous gesture, possibly a leap of faith. My brother is a loyal, good-hearted person, but he has been burdened with five younger sisters. We are, he feels, unserious. Gossipy. Meddlesome. He is right. I am perhaps the most meddlesome of all. Look at what I am doing to the lives of relatives we have never even met. Still, he delivers his canvas bag. History demands a historian, even if only a gossipy, unserious one.

The photograph of Mary Emily is a studio portrait printed on a stiff cardboard panel taken around 1887 by J. P. Weckman, a Cincinnati photographer on Fifth Street. She is a mild-looking young woman with a round chin, sweetly bowed lips that conceal a slight overbite, and large tranquil wide-spaced blue eyes. Her brown hair is not especially luxuriant, but it's nicely curled over her broad forehead. In three-quarter profile, hers is not a striking face. Compliant, reasonable, modestly expectant. A face with more than a suggestion of German milkmaid. But she does have a taste for adornment. She wears ear-rings and a paisley shawl, fastened with a little jeweled filigree pin. Ribbon threads through her back plait of hair. One can imagine her wearing neat, pretty leather boots that show off nicely turned ankles, a welcome antidote to dour, pickle-scented Gertrude.

There isn't much else to say about her. Mary Emily Jansen Kroger sinks back down into the past, floating through darker and darker green depths with her filigree pin and paisley shawl, her ringlets and plaited hair. Though the present glimmers there as well. Her eyes have resurfaced in one of my sisters, and also something of the shape of her brow. She is recognizably One of Us. And yet we will never make her out; at most we can make a few educated guesses based on a few details about who she was and what mattered to her. Which is perhaps only an exaggerated version of our relationship to anyone, including the people we believe we know best.

THE SECOND PHOTOGRAPH is a group portrait that I've had hanging by my desk for twenty-five years, carrying it with me from apartment to apartment, then later from house to house, one of the first things I hang up when I arrange my desk and books in a new home. For twenty-five years I have assumed this portrait is of Mary Emily sitting with her seven children — the seven children are easily identified.

They are all posed on the front steps of the big crenellated stone house B. H. Kroger (no longer Barney, he has rechristened himself again) has built for his family in prosperous Avondale, a neighborhood full of newly elevated families, recently incorporated into the seven hills of Cincinnati. It's summertime. No one is wearing a jacket and the little girls are dressed in white. Two hieratic-looking women are in-cluded in the photograph as well, one older, one young, acting as book-ends, each standing and leaning an elbow against opposite stone posts. They appear to be members of the household staff, cook and nanny, though the younger woman could be a Kroger or Jansen cousin. The older woman looks like the stern-faced woman wearing a large white apron in a photograph preserved in Lucile's 1905 album, the one I found in the attic; that photograph is respectfully labeled "Miss McGrath."

Neither woman is smiling. Why are these cheerless women included in a formal family portrait? A question that, for a long time, I asked myself without bothering to try to answer.

The third woman is sitting on the top step with the three youngest children grouped around her. One of them, little Chester, a future war hero, leans against her knees, an arm placed confidingly across her lap. Baby Gretchen, who as baby should by rights have been in her lap, is instead sitting alone off to the side. Behind her, the four older children are ranged along a bench: Lucile, on the far left wearing a sailor dress, gazes gravely into the camera; unruly hair frizzes over her forehead, though you can just make out the neat plait down her back. The oldest, Raymond, is twelve.

This woman looks grimly exhausted. She has a thin, strained, diminished face. Her hair is pulled severely back and she wears a starkly plain, high-necked white blouse. Not long ago as I was peering at this woman in the group portrait and comparing her to the photograph by J. P. Weckman, confidently labeled "Mrs. B. H. Kroger," with a positive cursive flourish, I began, reluctantly, to realize that these were not pictures of the same woman.

AT FIRST I simply assumed that twelve years of childbearing had reduced the soft-faced Mary Emily, with her pretty trinkets, to this whittled-looking person on the steps. But the features are too different, down to the shape of her mouth and the curve of her chin. And the children look reduced as well. Not just solemn, which one expects from old photographs, but miserable — except for little Chester, who, befitting a future war hero, is bravely trying to smile. (And why is no one holding the baby?) That the children should share such similar expressions does not make sense given how many of them there are, even allowing for the length of time a person used to have to sit still for his picture to be taken and how odious sitting still is for children. Again, it's summer. No school. A time for holiday jaunts and picnics. All of the women and children, save the two babies, have shadows under their eyes. Perhaps everyone looked happier half an hour earlier, but from their set faces it looks as if they have not been happy in months.

So who is this woman, if she's not Mary Emily?

After going through Lucile's photograph albums again, this time with a magnifying glass, I recognized that I was looking at Aunt Ida, Barney's sister, who moved in with her brother after his wife died in April 1899 to become his housekeeper. Only then did I understand that this was not a portrait of Mary Emily with her seven children but rather a portrait that must have been taken very soon after her death. That I know for certain because Raymond, the oldest, sitting on the bench with Lucile, died within eight months of his mother, of diphtheria.

For twenty-five years I had been looking at the reverse of the picture I thought I was seeing: these are the children *without* their mother. It's a portrait of a newly configured household, a document of family loss and not, as I had assumed, a proud display of family expansion. The ever-scrupulous B. H. Kroger, who recorded all his transactions carefully, whether with tradesmen or with fate, must have been the one to arrange and pay for this portrait — it is a professionally produced eight-by-ten-inch enlargement, not a snapshot. A terrible bit of bookkeeping that he nevertheless figured had to be done.

Susan Sontag, who has thought more carefully about old family pictures than just about anyone, defines a photograph as a "tiny element of another world: the image world that bids to outlast us all." But the image world is never as plainly before us as we might like to think. "Photographs, which cannot themselves explain anything," says Sontag, "are inexhaustible invitations to deduction, speculation and fantasy."

We shouldn't count on photographs too heavily, in other words, when we are trying to understand the past. Unless we have nothing else to count on. Unless deduction, speculation, and fantasy are all that's left in the attic. As Sontag also observes, photographs are "not so much an instrument of memory as an invention of it or a replacement."

So what can this photograph tell me that is not invented, not a replacement for what was really going on at the time?

There were once seven Kroger children who lost their mother, lost her so suddenly they never had a chance to say good-bye. ("We were told she was gone," one can imagine them saying, an inverted echo of my father years later. "No one ever said where.") Afterward they had to make do with a maiden aunt and a succession of servant women hired to take care of them. Lucile was not yet ten when her mother died. I don't know that my father has ever examined just how closely his experience of losing his mother compares with her own experience. Perhaps if he did he might realize that he knew her better than he thought.

Lucile Ida Kroger arrived in the world on Monday, October 28, in 1889, the 301st day of the year. A Scorpio. She would be 119 if she were alive today—an impossible age, and yet only two years ago a woman named Maria Capovilla from Ecuador died at 117, the last remaining person on earth to have been born in the 1880s. It is always astonishing how impossibilities turn into possibilities. Lucile was born the same year the world's tallest building, the Eiffel Tower, was completed. Another impossibility: most people thought the Eiffel Tower was ugly and wanted it torn down. Yet there it still is; I took a picture of it myself, just last summer. La Tour Eiffel. A monument either to solipsism or the human desire for transcendence, depending on your point of view, something that could be said of biography as well. Especially biographies of relatives.

She was born in Newport, Kentucky, where her parents had bought a house on Monroe Street soon after they were married. George Laycock notes that neighbors recalled seeing Barney Kroger "playing on the lawn with his children" during this period "and acting out the drum major's role as lines of boys and girls followed him through the yard and up and down the stairs." Barney was twenty-nine years old when Lucile was born; even after a long day of managing his quickly multiplying stores, he had energy left over for cavorting in the front yard. As the third child, Lucile wouldn't have held the novelty for him of her older brother and sister. But her arrival must have been greeted with satisfaction. Three children is a convincing family, the beginning of a tribe. And Barney, at least, was always thinking big.

A charming sight, those impromptu parades in the warm pink dusk of Newport, with half a dozen merry little Krogers trying to keep in line to the beat of their father's invisible drum, as they will do for the rest of their lives, staggering after him on fat legs, tumbling up and down the porch steps, careening off the brick walkway and onto the Kentucky blue grass. Up and down they marched, the girls in white petticoats and brown laced boots, the boys, too—in those days little children were dressed alike until they were about four, an early egalitarianism that was as easily discarded as those petticoats. In the twilight of the nineteenth century the children of a rising young midwestern businessman would have been nicely attired on summer evenings when Papa came home to play with them.

And yet Barney's success felt tentative. Money was still tight. The

earliest photograph of Lucile that I've been able to find has her posing with her first school, Park Avenue Primary, an institution that, despite its glamorous-sounding name, has a workhouse ambience. Around the turn of the century, nearly half of all children born in this country died before they reached the age of five, an unhappy statistic that broods over Park Avenue Primary. Some of  the boys have the rough uneasy swagger of children who know they will not be in school long; some of the girls look vacant. A few of them appear malnourished and no one is very clean. Except Lucile. Amid thirty or forty pasty, squinting, consumptive-looking children in clownish adultlike clothing, Lucile stands on a bench at the extreme right of the second row in a neat black dress, black stockings, and black shoes. She must be about six years old. Most children are slouching or leaning against one another, but she stands a little apart and very straight, her expression attentively frightened.

She looks like an exclamation point.

LUCILE DOES NOT languish at Park Avenue Primary for long. By the fall of 1898 the Krogers have moved across the river to a big stone house on Reading Road in the new suburb of Avondale, perched on the side of one of Cincinnati's seven green hills. Business is looking sunny for Barney. He is planning to install bakeries in his seventeen grocery stores — now called B. H. Kroger's Tea and Grocery Stores — so he can sell Kroger bread for two and a half cents a loaf, half of what you'd pay for bread at a bakery. His ads run in all the Cincinnati papers, hawking groceries "of the finest quality." Chili sauce, corn meal, Smyrna figs, coffee, cigars, toilet soaps. He is buying goods by the trainload now, as he explains cannily in his ads, so that consumers can reap the benefits of his "remarkably low prices."

Far from content with seventeen stores and a platoon of red-painted Kroger delivery wagons rumbling out to all the suburbs of Cincinnati, Barney is also planning to open fifteen new stores in Dayton, Ohio—just as two local Dayton boys, Orville and Wilbur Wright, are tightening screws on their flying machine and dreaming of hauling it out to Kitty Hawk. Along with Orville and Wilbur, Barney has trouble thinking about anything except where he's going and how he's going to get there. The sky's the limit. His heart is a kite. He has fresh ideas every ten minutes. He will give his customers everything they could ever want at a fantastic bargain! He will sell them hope for a better world in cans and packages! He is a winged capitalist, flying ecstatically into the empyrean of Big Business.

By the following spring Mary Emily is dead. Outside, daffodils bloom in a profusion of yellow. Saplings unfurl leaves of the tenderest green. The sky above Avondale is forget-me-not blue. Inside the new house on Reading Road everything has turned gray. People keep shutting the windows and pulling the curtains, closing the doors. The air loses its springlike scent, becomes laden with something else, a smell like old candle wax.

"I want a photograph of the children," Barney tells his sister Ida.

IF I COULD contact anyone in that Kroger family portrait on the front steps of the Reading Road house it would not be Lucile, who is only nine, and not a reliable source for reporting on the unreliable world of adults—despite her mother's death and all the evidence before her, she would have still considered adults trustworthy—but Aunt Ida. Of everyone posing on the front steps that day Aunt Ida could tell me the most about that household, being a relative and an insider as well as a newcomer. Which child was having tantrums, which one cried herself to sleep, which one wet the bed. Who was being eerily "good," who had tried to run away. Whether any of the servants were stealing, or had been stealing and now had to stop, and who was threatening to quit now that "Missus," who had always been so kind, was gone. As for B. H. himself . . .

Poor Aunt Ida. Suddenly responsible for seven bereaved children and for managing the household of a brother who dealt with his own grief by becoming more "particular" than ever.

Aunt Ida was said to be very strict. "From what I heard," my father says, "she was just as tough as B. H." In a story my grandfather used to tell, Aunt Ida came to visit my father soon after he was born; the moment she entered the nursery my infant father began to wail and

Back row (left to right): Helen, Gertrude, and Lucile; front row (left to right): Aunt Ida, Grandmother Gertrude, and Gretchen

would not stop until she left. My father's uneasy relationship with women may have begun, in fact, at that moment. Aunt Ida was an old crone by then, withered by years of being strict with someone else's children—which she would have thought of as simply doing her duty by them—probably with little thanks, and even less remuneration. She did her best. Undoubtedly she was kinder and more lenient than her own mother. But those children knew what they had lost, as children always do, and the older ones, at least, would not have taken easily to substitutes, no matter how well intentioned.

My baleful impression of Aunt Ida was furthered by yet another incorrectly identified photograph in which I had her confused with Grandmother Gertrude, who is tiny and shriveled and dressed in black and looks like a bad fairy from a Bavarian folktale. Aunt Ida is, in fact, included in that photograph as well, which also features the four Kroger girls as teenagers (Lucile glaring beneath a hat shaped like a salad bowl and trimmed with a black ribbon the size of a bunch of spinach). Sitting next to her forbidding parent, Aunt Ida looks quite pleasant.

But in the photograph taken with her nieces and nephews on the steps of the house on Reading Road, Aunt Ida looks neither pleas-

ant nor unpleasant. She radiates relinquishment. She is not yet old, in her high-collared plain white blouse, no more than thirty-five or so. But she is old enough that she would have seemed almost elderly to the children who could not themselves imagine life beyond twenty-two. I have just noticed that she is wearing earrings. Perhaps not long before she sat for this portrait she'd dreamed of having her own children, her own house. Perhaps there was even a suitor, who gave her those earrings (she does not strike one as a woman who would buy jewelry for herself). But unmarried sisters did not have the choices in 1899 that they do now, and people also felt quite differently then about family duty. Had there been a hesitant suitor, who finally came to the door one afternoon, bowler hat in hand, a carnation in his buttonhole, Ida may well have told him tartly to save his breath, that it was his bad luck he'd waited too long. Now she was spoken for.

AT MARY EMILY Kroger's funeral, the local priest took the opportunity to chastise her family for not attending Mass more frequently, including her band of motherless children lined up in the church's first pew, none of their feet quite reaching the floor. Barney sat stony-faced through the rest of the service, tossed a spadeful of earth onto his wife's coffin, then took his children home and declared that none of them would ever step inside a Catholic church again.

My father always told this anecdote to illustrate Barney Kroger's intolerance of sanctimony (an intolerance shared by my father), but I wonder if instead it illustrates the first time Barney lost faith in himself. He had never before believed in bad luck. He had persisted through hunger, calamity, and floods, overcoming every setback simply by working harder than before, but his wife's death was something entirely new. This was a loss that could not be recouped, and it made no sense. His golden rule was "the rule of giving full value for money received," one of the bedrock beliefs of free enterprise, which he must have thought God believed in, too. People who worked hard and were fruitful were supposed to be happy. He knew he had a bad temper, but he didn't smoke or drink or chase women. He gave to charity. Amid all the famed excesses of the Gilded Age he wasn't very gilded, still getting up at dawn every morning and cracking up the goods. And he had loved his wife.

THERE IS, ACTUALLY, one more photograph of Mary Emily Kroger — or, to be exact, there's a picture of her picture. In 1918 B. H. Kroger was photographed by the *American Magazine* sitting

at his desk in his company headquarters. It's a huge handsome mahogany roll-top desk, with papers neatly tucked into wooden slots,
ledgers perched here and there, along with a small brass reading
light and two framed photographs of young men in uniform, Bernard
Henry Jr. and Chester Kroger, who have both enlisted in the army.
Just across the hall sits Lucile, in her swivel chair, going over receipts.
Kroger himself sits in an upholstered leather chair wearing striped
trousers and a black frock coat, his stiff white wing collar pressing
under his chin, holding the speaker of an early model telephone.

It's the desk of a busy important successful man, phone in hand,
who clearly has no time for a photographer fussing with flashpans
and tripods—he's a man with sons in the war and a company to
run, not to mention local government to reform (like many other
self-created millionaires, he's gotten involved in politics, unable to
resist sharing his bootstraps wisdom). But there, right in the center
of his desk behind that early telephone, that gadget that allows you
to communicate with unseen people as if they were right in the next
room, is a photograph of Mary Emily.

Or at least it's a photograph of a young dark-haired woman, and I
can't imagine that B. H., a stickler for propriety, would have allowed
himself to be immortalized by the *American Magazine* with a photograph of a young woman on his desk who wasn't his wife. As he had
four daughters, all living nearby and one working across the hall, it
also seems unlikely he would have chosen one of them to be honored
so centrally. Having made such grave mistakes with photographs, I
am trying to be careful.

My father says that in 1918 B. H. was conducting a long-standing
affair with a working-class woman out in Western Hills to whom
his oldest daughter, Gertrude, was once introduced. A woman he
must have cared about as well and respected enough that he wasn't
ashamed to have one of his children to meet her. Ten years later,
when he finally got remarried (to a socialite), he gave a million

dollars to each of his children and a million dollars to his mistress—
a gift that his children, though probably not his new wife, most
certainly knew about. Still, a mistress was a mistress. Maybe having a photograph of Mary Emily on his desk was his way of being
careful, too.

And yet despite his frock coat and starchy wing collar, B. H.
doesn't seem to me as emotionally straitlaced or as "tough" as my
father describes him. There is that sensual mouth. That slightly wistful avidity. When she died, Barney and Mary Emily had been days
away from embarking on a trip to Europe, their "honeymoon trip,"
since they had never had the freedom, or the money, to go anywhere
together before. They had booked an early May sailing for Europe,
when the sea was calm and the weather most likely to be fine.

And that was when God chose to smite him. Or that's how it must
have felt.

When his eldest son, Raymond, died the winter after his wife,
what had seemed to Barney like divine punishment for his success
became divine persecution. Always short tempered, he now became
a much darker presence, driven to work harder than ever, but also
increasingly irascible and demanding. Nothing pleased him. One of
his employees remarked, "He snapped out commands and he seemed
unable to praise a man for a job well done or a good idea."

He might apologize later for chewing someone out, but as Laycock
notes with a trifle too much satisfaction, "the explosion was always
there just below the surface." If that's how Barney treated his employees, who could quit if they had to, imagine how he treated his
children.

An irrational fear of punishment has traveled down
through the family. If something good happens, it will be followed by
bad luck. Never think of yourself as fortunate or you will be doomed.
If someone praises you, deflect the compliment. Knock on wood.

"Don't toot your own horn," my father used to warn us, the implication being that if you did someone would run you over.

Did this anxious pessimism spring from my great-grandmother's death just before she and Barney were to leave on their belated European honeymoon? Did Barney Kroger's rejection of Catholicism after his wife's funeral signal the beginning of a deep familial skepticism?

Who knows, but at least it's a story that makes sense, and the function of family history is to explain what is essentially inexplicable — how we came to be ourselves. With time that explanation becomes something coherent and useful, if egregiously incomplete, and also hopeful: every family narrative makes a bid to be handed down for generations.

The memoirist Patricia Hampl sees it even more urgently:

> The self-absorption that seems to me the impetus and embarrassment of autobiography turns into (or perhaps always was) a hunger for the world. Actually, it began as hunger for a world, one gone or lost, effaced by time or a more sudden brutality. But in the act of remembering, the personal environment expands, resonates beyond itself, beyond its "subject," into the endless and tragic recollection that is history.

Of course, how you choose to narrate your family history, what you emphasize and what you ignore, makes all the difference. As Hampl also points out, "We carry our wounds and perhaps even worse, our capacity to wound, forward with us."

From the patterns of our past we cut the fabric of our future. That my great-grandmother Mary Emily, survivor of seven nineteenth-century childbirths, died during minor surgery from too much ether, the very thing that was supposed to spare her pain, is one of those mournful ironies that fits my family all too well.

In other words, if you don't own your family history, it will likely own you.

One of my daughters has started knocking on wood.

IV

Child of a New Century

A biography is considered complete if it merely
accounts for six or seven selves, whereas a
person may well have as many thousand.

—VIRGINIA WOOLF, *Orlando*

Whenever my father has visited me over the past ten years, inevitably during his stay one of my children has thrown a fit about losing a game or feeling insulted, has shouted various denunciations, and then required soothing. Then off she's skimmed, fully recovered, at which point my father has always observed (unhelpfully), "If I had done that, I would have been murdered." He himself did not tolerate much childish drama as a parent; our shrieks were often met with savage disapproval. Apparently a learned response, at least to some degree. "She was always severe," my father said not long ago, when I asked what happened when he ran to his mother with injuries. "She didn't have time for that kind of thing."

Instead of sympathizing with my father, as he was probably hoping, I found myself wondering whether Lucile's perceived severity wasn't instead a well-worn stoicism. People who have learned early to be brave and uncomplaining often have trouble attending to the complaints of others. And children have so many complaints and are so desperately attached to them. Which doesn't mean they shouldn't have complaints, only that different mothers will hear those complaints differently; the main thing for a child is to have someone to hear them at all.

Just yesterday I was waiting outside my younger daughter's school when I discovered a little boy of about five, wearing bright red rain boots and a fireman's raincoat, sobbing in the dirt behind a holly bush. Sobbing with that wild, heaving, shuddering abandon to which only children can surrender, a mixture of rage and despair that is truly existential, directed at the unfairness of *everything*. Still, one never knows, so I bent down and asked the child if he needed me to find someone for him.

Instantly he sobered up, stuck his fists in his eyes, and muttered in a mortified tone that his mother was "over there." I walked away regretting that I had intruded, but it impressed me, yet again, to see how quickly a person can recover from misery, if he believes he has someone "over there."

As a little girl Lucile assumed that everyone's father owned grocery stores, that every grandmother was German, that the seven hills of Cincinnati were mountains, and that Lake Michigan was as big as an ocean. No one explained these things to her, still she knew them. We believe what we see, not necessarily what we're told. So she must have also assumed, at ten, that dying was commonplace, and hard to avoid, since two members of her own family died within months of each other, and also that there was no saying who might be next.

She would have been correct in this assumption. In 1899 most large families could expect to lose several family members along the way and frequently one of the first to be lost was the mother. Often she died from childbirth complications, puerperal fever, or childbed sickness, being prevalent, particularly among women who gave birth in the hospital. One of my grandfather's heroes was Ignaz Semmelweis, the Hungarian physician who figured out that germs killed human beings and that bleach and water killed germs. In 1847 he insisted that doctors and medical students working in the maternity ward of his Viennese hospital wash their hands between treating patients. Immediately maternal mortality dropped by 20 percent. A discovery that should have netted Semmelweis at least a comfortable retirement, but he was ridiculed for years by other physicians, who thought he was a superstitious quack, until finally he had a nervous breakdown and spent his last years raving in a sanatorium. (My grandfather particularly loved stories of great men whose lives ended sadly.) Of course, mothers also died of all the usual ailments that were untreatable back then, and given those large families, and few labor-saving devices, some of them simply died from exhaustion. It being the timeless fate of mothers to do everything no one else gets done.

And yet there's no reason to think that losing one's mother in 1899 was any easier to bear than it is nowadays. It was only less exceptional.

VIRGINIA WOOLF WAS only a few years older than Lucile when she lost her own mother in the spring of 1895. Woolf's mother, Julia Stephen, had also borne seven children and, like Mary Emily Kroger, was more a general mother than a particular one, having had to belong to so many people at once. ("Can I remember ever being alone with her for more than a few minutes?" muses Woolf. "Someone was always interrupting.") Julia Stephen had occupied "the very centre of that great Cathedral space which was childhood," as do most mothers, except the deranged and truly infirm, and often even them. And, again like Mary Emily, Julia Stephen had married a difficult man, who was hard on the children after she was gone. The children themselves were devastated. In "A Sketch of the Past," written forty-four years after her mother died, Woolf attempts to describe the weird boredom and self-consciousness that for children accompanies mourning, the persistent sense of unreality, and the frank bewilderment.

> I see us now, all dressed in unbroken black, George and
> Gerald in black trousers, Stella with real crape deep on
> her dress, Nessa and myself with slightly modified crape,

my father black from head to foot—even the notepaper was so black bordered that only a little space for writing remained—I see us emerging from Hyde Park Gate on a fine summer afternoon and walking in procession hand in hand, for we were always taking hands—I see us walking—I rather proud of the solemn blackness and the impression it must make—into Kensington Gardens. . . . And then we sat silent under the trees. The silence was stifling. A finger was laid on our lips. One had always to think whether what one was about to say was the right thing to say. It ought to be a help. But how could one help?

And this was an intellectual British family who read poetry and Greek drama and drank tea with Henry James. Imagine the Krogers, who despite that fancy new house were still just two steps out of the cracker factory, and who not only didn't know what to say about what had happened to them but wouldn't have thought it was a good idea to try. Plus they had just left the Catholic Church.

A mother's death is such a profound shock for a child that it does not register for long on the surface of daily life, since everything changes because of it. Like relocating to another country. Aunt Ida moves in. Papa becomes a furious stranger. Adults come and go, talking of God's will and of Mother being in "a better place." No one says anything comprehensible.

Gone are the small vital irreplaceable things that for Lucile previously meant home: Her mother's footstep, rapid, definite. Her voice at the breakfast table, patiently firm about drinking milk. Her hand smoothing the hair back from Lucile's forehead. It takes a while to understand that no one will ever smooth her hair like that again.

When Lucile's older brother, Raymond, died it was different. In a smaller and more immediate way, it was worse. He died of diphtheria, a disease that could have killed any of the children—that should have killed more of them, given its virulence—but mysteriously didn't. He died eight months after their mother, falling sick without anyone noticing. He was simply tired one morning in January, with a bit of a sore throat.

JANUARY. A SLOW, cold, muted month in Cincinnati. Skies the color of an old pie tin. Frigid afternoons where the light begins to fade by four thirty, and as it fades even the snow looks bereft. Inside the house on Reading Road the curtains are drawn against the cold, leaving each room shrouded in chilly gloom. Already the children have acquired the listless, lank-haired look of the uncherished. Barney leaves for work every morning while it's still dark. One morning he storms out of the house, enraged that his boots weren't polished the night before. "I won't have it!" he bellows from the front hall. What he won't have does not need to be specified.

To recover from her brother's departure, Aunt Ida scolds all the children for not sitting up straight at breakfast and gives them an extra dose of cod liver oil. Then noticing that one is missing, she sends Lucile upstairs to see what is keeping Raymond.

Lucile dawdles on the stairs, pressing the toes of her black boots against each riser. She has no appetite for oatmeal and stewed prunes. She has also been having trouble feeling things lately, even sharp things, like pins, and so it is with some relief that she feels her toes hitting the wooden risers through the thin leather of her boots.

Raymond is lying in bed in the little corner room he shares with Henry. A skinny arm flung over his eyes, elbow sharply bent, sheet pulled to his chin. Icy sunlight pools on a corner of his white pillowcase. "Get *up*," she repeats, for the second time, from the doorway. The room is airless and smells of wool carpet. There is also another smell. She can't define it. Something like old apple cores.

"Are you sick?"

She takes a step backward. Raymond is always leaping out at her from closets and grabbing her ankles from under the sofa. Putting frogs in her bed. Spiders in her dresser drawer. It's Lucile he targets. Gertrude does not scare. Gertrude is taller and heavier than Raymond, though a year younger, and can knock him down whenever she feels like it. But Lucile shrieks satisfyingly.

"Get up," she says once more, from out in the hall. He stirs and lifts his arm. Murmurs something she doesn't stay to hear.

"You'll catch it!" she cries, as she runs down the stairs.

Lucile dislikes Raymond. He is a boy. The oldest. Their mother's favorite. Probably their father's, as well. A prime target for both reverence and hatred. He teases, is lordly. Pulls hair ribbons, spoils drawings, delivers stray insults. Though often she adores him, too, with that innate attraction younger sisters feel for older brothers. She would like to marry him. He has swank and glamour. He comes home from school with stories of boys being caned so hard they can't sit down for a week, of boys who can throw a baseball across the Ohio River, of boys who are "good fellows" and intend to join the circus and become lion tamers or at least "hop a train" for the West and hire themselves out as cowboys. If Raymond and his friends read anything, they read girl-free books like Walter Scott's *Ivanhoe* (except for boring Lady Rowena) and Robert Louis Stevenson's *Treasure Island*. Then they discuss how to behead people with broadswords or how to find buried treasure and cut people's throats with daggers. The thrilling, brutal, exaggerated world of boys.

Or perhaps not.

Perhaps she feels sorry for Raymond. Perhaps Raymond is sickly and small for his age, with a tracery of blue veins that show through the skin at his temples and spatulate fingertips that are always damp. Perhaps he is a disappointment to his father because he won't play street hockey, and when it snows he wants to stay inside and help in the kitchen, rolling out dough for strudel. Reads even more omnivorously than Lucile herself, is didactic and fussy and slightly perverse. Collects, for instance, moths. Likes to press a square of velvet against his cheek. Wept once when he found a dead blue jay under a laurel bush. A mama's boy, an oddball.

Perhaps.

Somehow Raymond must be fished out of *per-haps*, that immeasurable pocket of a word, only two syllables but holding everything that is possible but not certain. He's in there all right, among cough-drop wrappers and bits of lint, but where? Was he a redhead like Lucile? Did he also have blue eyes? There's a lot I'd like to know about Raymond but never will, and yet I'm determined to write about

him anyway, even to make extravagant claims for him, because I feel sorry for him, swept away at twelve, leaving nothing behind but a few question marks, and because I need him. My family history, if it's to be interesting to anyone besides me, requires pathos, a commodity supplied in abundance by childhoods tragically cut short.

All of which leads me to wonder if *perhaps* isn't fatally compromised by what we wish we knew. It's supposed to indicate what's possible, but those possibilities have been tainted by preference. There are certain things I want out of Raymond—boyish valor, red hair—and so that's what I look for, discarding myriad other possibilities. And I lean on *perhaps* because it sounds so dispassionate. *Perhaps* has a scholarly mien, more authoritative and less coy than *maybe*. A word that wears spectacles. We rely on it all the time. I've used *perhaps* twenty-six times before reaching this page. We rely on it especially when we are trying to write about truth and history, both of which change every time the light shifts or the phone rings.

But perhaps we should be more cautious and remember that what we don't know can be more revealing than what we do. And that what goes unsaid is often unsayable. As with his mother, Mary

Emily, Raymond was rarely mentioned during my father's childhood. No tales of boyhood adventures passed along. No namesake, even in a family fond of recycling names (Henry, Chester, Ida, Gertrude). Not even a photograph, except for the one in that family portrait in which he is fair skinned and freckled and sadly truculent, sporting a pair of Barney's big ears. Sandwiched between Henry and Gertrude, Raymond leans as far back from the camera as he can get — the camera that can capture but not hold him. His expression is mutinous. Hands laced across his stomach, sandy eyebrows pulled down, a tweed newsboy cap pushed back on his head. *I am not here.* Yet one-sixtieth of a second of his life has been documented, at least, as having existed.

Did he deliver newspapers? Did someone order him to take his cap off for the photograph — none of the other children are wearing hats — and he refused? Is that why he looks so forlornly defiant? Trying desperately to keep his lid on.

He was born in 1887, the same year as Rupert Brooke, "Shoeless" Joe Jackson, and Prince Felix Yusupov, any of whose vocations — poet, baseball hero, Rasputin's assassin — might have fit Raymond's own youthful ambitions. He died of diphtheria, which killed scores of children in Cincinnati in 1900, a bacterial disease that, like typhus, probably came from polluted drinking water siphoned from the Ohio River. A disease that terrified parents, who could only watch helplessly while their children's necks swelled and they slowly suffocated. The first diphtheria antitoxin wasn't available until 1905.

He wore a cap, at least once. He had his father's ears. On the spectrum of boyhood he existed somewhere between Tom Sawyer and a young Truman Capote. That is as much as I can say for certain about Raymond and even here I've supposed far too much.

As they grew older, the four Kroger girls grew increasingly different, though they were all, my father says, "tough." Decided,

irreverent, demanding, proud — and with enough money to do whatever they wanted, including marry whomever they wanted. Within
reason (and with Barney's permission). A daunting quartet.

Gertrude, or Tutu, was the outrageous one. A smart flibbertigibbet. She married a New Englander with an engineering degree from
Brown University; but when he wanted to leave Cincinnati for a fine
job in Cleveland, she blithely dismissed the idea. Arguing with a
flibbertigibbet is like boxing with a hummingbird,
so at last, despite the advantages of the job, and
of living in a city not occupied by his father-in-
law, the New Englander gave in. They had five
children and Tutu treated them with autocratic
benevolence. Unlike Lucile, she avoided the
kitchen — so assiduously, in fact, that when her
cook took a yearly vacation, Tutu and her husband
went on vacation, too, and didn't return until the
cook was safely back at the stove. My father's word for her was *in-
souciant,* a rare quality, which only a lifetime of avoiding the stove
can afford. On her ninetieth birthday, he called to wish her many
happy returns and asked how she was feeling. "I *couldn't* be better!"
she exclaimed, though she was in the hospital re-
covering from her third heart attack.

Helen became the sportswoman, a golf champion at the Camargo Club. The prettiest of the
Kroger girls, she married a man with a glamorous
side part in his brilliantined hair and who liked
martinis and polo ponies. While she cultivated a
reputation for hardy brainlessness — Helen was
called "Fuzz" by her own children — she was ac-
tually quite intelligent and also, when it mattered, self-sacrificing.
During World War II, when there was a nursing shortage, she volunteered for three years as a scrub nurse in the operating room at a

local hospital and, according to the doctors she assisted, should have considered medical school herself.

As for Gretchen, the baby forever sitting by herself on the front steps, she married three different men, the first for less than forty-eight hours; the last one had claims on being a German count, or  related to one. My father believes he had been a Luftwaffe pilot in World War I. He once took a gaggle of nieces and nephews on a daylong hike up a steep ridge called Devil's Backbone. He pronounced Worth Avenue in Palm Beach "Worse Avenue," possibly on purpose. After he and Aunt Gretchen divorced he married an oil widow in Dallas who lived in a house where the dining room was on an island in the middle of the indoor swimming pool. Aunt Gretchen carried on, madcap and friendly. My father remembers her getting down on her hands and knees in an evening gown to roll dice in a crap's game in the men's bar of the Camargo Club. She was not much better at craps than at husbands, but she enjoyed the former a good deal.

They were all so different and yet all four sisters built their big houses within earshot of each other on Indian Hill, along with their brother Chester, who built himself a farm across the road from my grandparents. Henry Kroger, whom my father remembers only as "a pleasant-faced man with red hair," died before he had a chance to get married, or I'm sure he would have built a house on Indian Hill, too.

Henry, another forgotten son. Briefly CEO of the Kroger Company, later demoted by Barney. While his siblings were building houses and planting gardens, Henry rented a room in the Queen City Club at Fourth and Broadway. Rumors of a thwarted romance: Henry had been in love with a nurse, whom he wanted to marry, but Barney (forgetting his farmhand days) thought she was too low class for his son. Henry gave up his nurse. At the time he was still living in his father's house — a bigger, fancier house now, on Crescent Road. Then in 1928, the same year Barney sold his company and did not put Henry in charge of it, Barney himself got married, to a fashionable club woman from Palm Beach whom he directed his children to call "Aunt Alice." Only after Henry saw that he and "Aunt Alice" were the same age did he move out.

Why didn't Henry marry his nurse once he was on his own? Say nuts to old Barney and blow a kiss to Aunt Alice? In that photograph in front of the house on Reading Road, Henry is a little boy of seven or eight with a curlicue of dark hair on his forehead and a look of doglike dread in his eyes. Life, he already seemed know, was mostly about submission. So instead of lighting out for the territories, Henry stayed in Cincinnati and drank too much. One wintry night in 1933, a year after Lucile's death, he smashed up his car on a  dark road coming home from a party. Somehow he staggered a mile through the snow to the Queen City Club, telling no one what had happened. Three days later he died alone in his room.

Barney, according to my father, "was pretty cut up."

Those Krogers, they clung like burrs, no matter how spiky things got among them. Though there was really no question of letting go — they were all bound forever by what they had lost, and kept on losing.

NONE OF HIS aunts or uncles ever spoke to my father about the loss of their mother and brother when his own mother died. They should have, of course. He might have gained some comfort from knowing that people do continue on after such unhappiness; at least he might have felt slightly understood. But the Krogers weren't known to be especially expressive people and whatever they might have said to him they kept to themselves. They went on with their parties, even stepped up the pace and became more riotous. From his drafty hiding place at the top of the attic stairs, my father hugged his knees and gazed out the window at the bare trees across the road, waiting for someone to come talk to him. Later he blamed all his adult relatives for their silence, believed them to be shallow and uncaring.

"No one said anything to me," he repeats bitterly even now.

But maybe when Lucile died it all came back to them, those aunts and uncles. The closed doors and pulled curtains, the terrible smell of wax. In the midst of such dark déjà vu, what could they really say to comfort a little boy who'd just lost his mother? What could they do but pour each other another drink?

Neither my father nor his brother was allowed to go to their mother's funeral; they weren't even told about it until after it was over. I can't imagine such a thing now, and yet the feeling in 1932 must have been that children should be shielded from death, even the deaths of their own mothers. Children would not feel loss if it was not pointed out to them—that must have been the idea, the way pediatricians used to believe that infants did not experience pain. Just before their mother died, the boys were taken to stay for two weeks at Aunt Tutu's house.

Of this visit my father recalls very little, only that Aunt Tutu had a red cut-glass sugar shaker, which sat on a sideboard in the dining room table. He'd never seen anything like it. Every so often during those two weeks at her house he would slip into the dining room to shake sugar onto his palm. For years afterward he looked for a glass sugar shaker just like it, but he never found one.

The century ends. The world does not, despite the terrible things that have recently happened. It is 1900.

In a gilt-framed oval photograph Lucile appears in a Victorian white dress, a confection of lace, ruffles, and puffed sleeves. She is ten and a half, posed with one elbow on the back of a chair in a photographer's studio — in the background hangs a draped cloth. Her long red hair is tied back with a white ribbon and arranged loosely over one shoulder. Her hand is at her cheek, fingers bent artificially. But her smile seems genuine, if a bit theoretical. The other hand rests on the chair just below her elbow, creating an L with her arms, most likely coincidental. A sweet-faced, bright-looking little girl who seems to be making an effort to cooperate with the photographer.

B. H. Kroger has portraits made of all six of his remaining children, insurance against the unaccountability of time. He is a good businessman. He is a prudent father. A photograph lasts even when its subject does not. Sentimentality has nothing to do with it.

THE WORLD IS still lit by gas lamps. In the streets horses haul carriages, cabs, wagons, milk carts, all of which creak and rumble, and the horses leave immense droppings in the middle of the streets. Drivers yell at the horses and at each other. Streetcars rattle past. Newsboys shout and wave papers. Cincinnati is no longer the largest city in the West, but it's busy and big enough. High-rise buildings are springing up across the basin, like the Traction Building at

Fifth and Walnut, designed by Daniel Burnham, chief architect of the Chicago World's Fair. Vast department stores like Pogue's and Shillito's sell everything from handkerchiefs to mink coats. Factories loom above the river. Barges choke the wharves. Commerce fills the air with smoke and mirrors. Playing cards are manufactured in Cincinnati, and soap, and Baldwin pianos. All essentials in the twentieth century, era of musical innovation, improved hygiene, and gigantic gambles.

Late March. Evening is coming on. The light is turning blue. A girl in a frothy white dress steps out of a doorway, pulling on a coat. She has just been posing for her portrait in a third-floor photographer's studio, which smelled dizzily of developing fluid and unwashed hair. *Don't move!* the photographer kept begging, fingering his wilting collar. *Stay just as you are!* Grateful to be out in the cool air at last, she pauses with her brothers and sisters on a street corner and looks with interest about herself. A black dog trots past, pink tongue lolling. A woman with a fox stole bumps into her and says *excuse me* sharply just as a farm cart trundles by with a load of potatoes. Lights come on in a shop window across the street at the same time as a train whistle sounds in the distance. It's a high plaintive exhilarating sound, and as the girl pauses to listen she suddenly realizes, as everyone eventually realizes, that there is no such thing as staying just as you are and also that the world is rushing away as fast as it is rushing toward her.

IN 1900 HER mother and older brother are buried next to each other in Spring Grove Cemetery. Her father is fast becoming one of the richest men in Cincinnati. He is irritable and particular and tremendously important. Her grandmother, a frequent visitor, is terrifying. Her black silk dress smells of naphtha. She pokes into every room of the house, looking for dust and irreligious thoughts. Fortunately, she is ancient and does not see or hear very well.

What else is happening around Lucile in 1900? Julius Fleisch-mann, of yeast and margarine renown, is mayor of Cincinnati. McKinley, not yet assassinated, is president of the United States; in April he orders a commission headed by Cincinnati's own William Howard Taft to report on the Philippines. *The Cincinnati Post* and the *Commercial Tribune* are full of Taft. Enormously fat Taft, the size of a Clydesdale horse (his teenage nickname was "Big Lub"), who breaks people's dining room chairs when he sits on them but is invited to dinner anyway. Taft, future president and future B. H. crony, currently Teddy Roosevelt's friend.

Alice Roosevelt, Teddy's young daughter, is adored by American girls, who follow her exploits and her outfits with equal fascination. Alice's mother is dead as well. Perhaps Lucile feels a special connec-tion. Alice is also blonde and seraphically beautiful and not afraid of saying cheeky things to her father, so perhaps not.

Alice will go on to marry Congressman Nicholas Longworth, an-other Cincinnatian. In 1912 Longworth will abandon his father-in-law during Roosevelt's Bull Moose campaign for a second term as president and support Taft, a longtime friend, instead. Such are the ties that bind people from Cincinnati.

Besides Taft, the Cincinnati newspapers are full of the Panama Canal, which North America wants to dig and own, shutting France out of the deal. This subject interests B. H., who will profit by a more expedient and American-controlled route for imports. "Point to Panama!" B. H. orders a passing child after dinner, taking up a globe from the polished bookcase in his study. The child, most likely bookish Lucile, successfully points out Panama. "Good," snaps B. H., in the same tone he might have used had she been incorrect.

Nietzsche is dead. Kaiser Wilhelm rules Germany. The Dreyfus affair still rules France. In England, Queen Victoria is eighty-one years old. Newspaper photos show a dumpling-shaped old lady in black, who does not look like a proper queen, in the Kroger children's opinion, but like the cross old Austrian woman who runs the stationery shop near Eighth and Broadway.

More interesting to them is a total eclipse of the sun that occurs in May and lasts for two minutes and ten seconds. During the eclipse the children stand outside the house with pails of water, ordered by Aunt Ida not to look into the sky because they could go blind without even realizing, burn their eyes right out of their sockets. So they must view the eclipse reflected in the pails of water. The day darkens. Picture all the Kroger children looking down at pails of water. Picture pleasant little red-haired Henry looking up. Picture him being swatted and sent into the house. Eclipsed from the eclipse.

CINCINNATI IS FULL of music. Singing societies, choirs, orchestras, military bands. The New Vienna! An open-air opera house will be built, curiously, inside the Zoo, where arias from *Lohengrin* will mingle with the moaning of lions and the howling of monkeys. But as yet there is only the Music Hall. Also a music conservatory and a college of music (arch rivals), though truly talented young Cincinnatians are sent off to study in Europe, to Berlin and Italy. Usually, they come back. Famous musicians and singers like Jenny Lind and Enrico Caruso make a point of stopping in Cincinnati on tour. Also famous songs have been written here, including "O Susanna," composed by a shy young man named Steven Foster, and first sung in the Over the Rhine neighborhood in Cincinnati as

> *Ich kam von Alabama,*
> *Mein Banjo auf dem Knie—*

Lucile and her siblings are taken to the Orpheus Club's *Somnernachtfest,* to listen to local tenors and baritones sing lieder. On warm afternoons they go to band concerts in Burnet Woods and sit under a pavilion. In spring there is the May Festival, held downtown. Four evenings plus a matinee of oratorios and choral music, not to mention a few masses. Outside the Music Hall, Fountain Square is decorated with Chinese lanterns, lovely and exotic at night. Transformed as well is the celebrated fountain, adorned with bronze figures illustrating the various uses and blessings of water. A landmark revered by Cincinnatians, whose water is so often befouled, their version of the Arc de Triomphe or Trafalgar Square but dismissed by the gimlet-eyed journalist Lafcadio Hearn as "that old bronze candlestick." For the May Festival, the fountain becomes a magnificent rainbow, the water lit gorgeously by colored calcium lights.

THE KROGERS HAVE a medium-size household, given the times. Six children plus Aunt Ida, plus Papa. Plus whatever cousins have come to visit. The maids and the cook have attic rooms; the nanny sleeps next to the nursery. The house is ugly, imposing, comfortable, more or less Victorian, with gables, a wraparound porch, cool spacious downstairs rooms, a wood-paneled library and, upstairs, a warren of narrow bedrooms. It requires endless attention. In the summers, Aunt Ida directs the installation of striped awnings over

all the windows to the keep the house cool, and still the air is thick with insects and humidity and the legs of the piano have to be wiped down weekly or they turn green. In the fall, the awnings are taken down and heavy storm windows put up to keep the house warm during the bitter midwestern winter. Then the fireplaces smoke and soot must be washed off the walls. Endless.

Twelve to fourteen people live in that crenellated stone house on Reading Road. Because it is a modern house, quite recently built, there is indoor plumbing and an indoor bathroom, but only one, for twelve to fourteen people. Most of the servants use the privy out back. Not so bad in May and June but unpleasant in the winter. Try to think of music then.

CATHARINE BEECHER's *American Woman's Home* is the bible for housekeepers like Aunt Ida. Especially housekeepers who suddenly have sole charge of a large stone house, six children, and assorted domestics. Catharine Beecher, sister of Harriet Beecher Stowe, had been a resident of Cincinnati in the 1830s and '40s (an unpopular resident, being a noisy and persistent abolitionist who also tried to take over the literary society, the Semi-Colon, but her reputation improved with time); Miss Beecher could be trusted to know what households in Cincinnati were like.

> There is one great mistake, not infrequently made, in the management of both domestics and of children, and that is, in supposing that the way to cure defects is by finding fault as each failing occurs. . . . There are some minds very sensitive, easily discouraged, and infirm of purpose. Such persons, when they have formed habits of negligence, haste, and awkwardness, often need expressions of sympathy and encouragement rather than reproof.

They have usually been found fault with so much that
they have become either hardened or desponding. . . .

Poor Aunt Ida. Stuck with six negligent, hasty, sensitive, easily
discouraged children who, no matter how often she scolds them, remain infirm of purpose. Still, one doesn't want them to be desponding. Thank goodness for such a sensible guide
as *American Woman's Home.* Even the chapter
headings are instructive. One glance tells you all
the things you are most likely neglecting: Home
Decoration ("Exemplification of economical and
tasteful furniture"); Healthful Food ("Evils of
over-eating—Structure and operations of the
stomach"); Cleanliness ("Scientific treatment of
the skin, the most complicated organ of the body"); Domestic Man-
ners ("Serious defects in manners of the Americans").

If only the children would read *American Woman's Home.* Perhaps
Lucile, who reads all the time, could be given a copy.

AUGUST. ONCE AGAIN no trip to Lake Charlevoix in Michigan, where the Krogers have often gone in the summer. No rowing
on the bright cold choppy water. No scrambling on the rocks and
tossing pine cones at each other and getting sap on one's hands, so
hard to wash off, so fragrant of woods. Instead the children are taken
to Spring Grove to visit their mother's grave. They visit Spring Grove
every Sunday afternoon. Thirty-two years later, Lucile's sons will do
exactly the same thing.

Spring Grove is one of the most beautiful cemeteries in the world,
more beautiful even than cemeteries in Europe, which by now are
getting overcrowded. Spring Grove's landscape architect, Adolph
Strauch, believed a rural cemetery "should have the character of

untrammeled Nature." Perhaps to remind visitors that death has the most untrammeled nature of all. Lush vines cover the trees of Spring Grove. Weeping willows, enormous oaks. In 1788, a group of settlers landed at Yeatman's Cove, took a hatchet to their boats, and used the wood to build a few houses in what they decided to call Losantiville. Twelve years later they changed it to Cincinnati. Much better name. Does not have that French influence. Does not sound like an insane asylum either.

IN AUGUST SPRING Grove is hushed and verdant. The lake is filled with water lilies. In the middle of the lake sits a small island covered with dark green shrubs. The children pause to gaze at the island, imagining what it would be like to live there. Untrammeled, like Robinson Crusoe. Eating berries, twigs, the occasional tadpole.

Henry and Chester have to be prevented by Aunt Ida from skipping stones and looking for frogs under lily pads. Henry accidentally steps into a marshy spot he thought was dry ground and soaks his pant leg. *Heinie,* the other children have taken to calling him. *Heinie Kroger.* But that's just Henry in German, they say, poker faced, whenever Aunt Ida reprimands them. Everyone yawns from the heat. Little Gretchen trips over a curb, tears the knee of her stocking. Is lifted to her feet and dusted off.

"Hush," says Aunt Ida. Gretchen keeps crying. Despondently.

The Kroger monument, that impressive thrusting gray obelisk, has yet to be erected; the Kroger plot is still quite humble and still sparsely tenanted. Lucile stands for a moment in front of her mother's small flat headstone before placing a bunch of wilted violets at its base. It has been over a year since her mother died and seven months since Raymond's death. His headstone, even smaller, lies beside their mother's. Lucile lays a bunch of violets there as well. Then she steps back and looks at both graves. She is having trouble recalling what either her mother or Raymond looked like, though she can, if she makes an effort, recall her mother's voice, the way her mother said "Lucile," stretching her name into three syllables, and how she said "Why hello!" in a surprised tone whenever they passed anyone they knew in town.

Gertrude says she is the only one who remembers their mother and so she misses her the most. She will name her first child Mary Emily, so maybe this is true.

Cicadas buzz in the trees, a drowsy green rattle. Lucile wonders how all the people buried here feel about being dead. ETERNAL REST, reads a nearby headstone. Not far away is a tomb topped with a Sphinx. Her stockings itch. The sun is hot on top of her head. A dragonfly lights on the sleeve of her sailor dress. The air is dense and heavy with the smell of mud and grass and stagnant water from the lake.

At last they turn to leave, the children walking single file. Someone's stomach growls. They have been promised lemonade this afternoon, if they are good. Chester and Helen push each other. Gretchen is still crying. Green leaves blur and shift. Somewhere in the distance a deep baritone voice begins singing a gospel hymn. A gravedigger, a gardener. As Lucile passes under the dappled shade of a maple tree, a robin startles from a branch in a flash of wings and flutters into the sky. Her heart lifts with a sudden flight of grief.

"*Stop that,*" orders Aunt Ida. Heinie is throwing violets into the lake.

IN 1900 KODAK was just introducing the Brownie box camera, which Lucile would put to such good use a few years later when she started her photo albums. The men she saw on the streets wore bowler hats and homburgs; girls like her, and women as well, frequently wore straw boaters (Aunt Ida continues to wear a straw boater long after they go out of fashion). The Gibson girl look was everywhere, women sweeping their hair into high bouffants almost impossible to maintain and cinching their waists as small as possible. They all ate cabbage. Every woman Lucile knew wore a white blouse and a tight-waisted long dark skirt; they suffered from gas and shed hairpins.

ALONG WITH ALL the singing societies in Cincinnati were the saloons. They swarmed in the basin, particularly on Vine Street, among the brewery wagons and the sweetish-loamy smell of malt. The best beer, according to many people, was brewed by old John Hauck, whose granddaughter would someday marry Lucile's older son. Workmen crowded saloons at lunchtime, ordering a schooner of John Hauck's beer for a nickel and eating, for free, from plates of dried herring, pigs feet, liverwurst, blutwurst, boiled eggs. Less openhanded at lunchtime were saloons in the West End, frequented by bookies and gamblers and low-life con men. During their 1874 crusade, members of the Women's Christian Temperance Union, well-bred ladies in bustles and black silk hats the size of turkey platters, marched into saloons all over Cincinnati and knelt on sawdust floors, praying ferociously. The hats alone inspired sobriety. Saloon keepers began nailing NO CRUSADERS ALLOWED signs on their doors, as if they were in medieval France.

It was said that people in Cincinnati drank more beer than water. Men sprawled in the gutters after a night in the saloons; dogs ran past them unnoticing. Prostitutes thronged the sidewalks at night on Longworth Street at the corner of Central Avenue. The Kroger children were never taken on outings to Longworth Street, though sometimes they went to Mecklenburg's beer garden to sit under the grape arbor and watch their elders quaff steins of cold beer and listen to men in lederhosen sing and play the zither. And to see the *Kasperle theater*, the Punch-and-Judy show, and eat delicious potato pancakes and hasenpfeffer, rye bread and wiener schnitzel.

LATE OCTOBER. THE Kroger children are on an outing to the Zoological Gardens in honor of Lucile's birthday. Later that day there will be a chocolate layer cake and candles. Because it is her birthday, Lucile is wearing a new fawn-colored wool coat, which Aunt Ida ordered a size too large from Shillito's. The sleeves are so stiff Lucile cannot bend her elbows. She walks with wooden importance ahead of the other children with Aunt Ida, trying to pretend that she loves her new coat, that it doesn't feel like she is wearing fawn-colored chain mail.

They pass the Lookout House and the refreshment stand, pausing to gaze stolidly at the monkeys, the giraffe, and the lioness. The monkeys smell atrocious. They scratch at their private parts and bare their teeth mockingly. Aunt Ida hurries the children along. Let's go see the ostrich! She buys them a bag of peanuts and they throw some to the elephant.

Finally they arrive at the Japanese pagoda that houses the cage of Martha, the last remaining American passenger pigeon. Her feathers are bluish and pink. Otherwise Martha looks like an ordinary pigeon. Lucile stares at her gravely. She wonders what it is like to be the only creature of one's own kind on earth. She wonders if Martha is sad. What is it like to vanish forever? It occurs to Lucile that her own birthday marks the vanishing of another year. Martha's head moves robotically back and forth. She fixes Lucile with a round yellow eye.

FRANK LLOYD WRIGHT was busy designing his low-slung prairie houses, which would morph into the ubiquitous 1950s ranch, but for the moment many upper-middle-class houses, like the houses in Avondale, were still built along Victorian lines, which meant they were tall and drafty, with parlors much bigger than they needed to be, especially since they were so often unused, and kitchens much smaller and darker and less ventilated than they should have been. In those kitchens toiled women like Miss McGrath, in her stern apron. She was occupied all day with baking brown bread, roasting chickens, chopping cabbage, boiling carrots, rolling out dough, beating eggs, making gravy from gizzards and stock. And, of course, baking cakes.

Though Miss McGrath baked Lucile's birthday cake, Aunt Ida will have the honor of carrying it in to the dining room, all eleven candles lit, plus one to grow on, where she will place it shyly in front of Lucile. Aunt Ida is discomfited by celebrations (too indulgent, too much money, too sad when they are over), though she loves them as much as the children. Her brother is not present for this celebration—businessmen do not come home in the afternoon for children's birthday parties in 1900—so she can allow herself to linger for a moment over the scene at the table as she sets down the cake. The little mound of gifts, wrapped prettily, on the wooden sideboard; the silver dish of butterscotch candies; the string of paper dolls cut out by Helen and Gertrude. Ranged on either side of the table are the children, hands and faces scrubbed, gazing with reverent lust at the cake. Late afternoon light slants in through the windows. Slightly overcome, Aunt Ida steps back and claps her hands briskly together, as if dusting off a bit of flour.

THE KITCHEN IS easily the most interesting room in the house on Reading Road and yet it is not often visited by the Kroger children, who would love to be there among the marvelous smells and fascinating sights (headless chickens, monstrous blobs of rising dough). But in the kitchen they are In the Way. They are also in the way in the dining room, unless actually seated; and in their father's study; in the laundry room; in the sewing room; in the maids' rooms. They are in the way in every room of the house, in fact, but their own rooms. What they are obstructing is unclear, but being in the way is a permanent condition until one is about seventeen.

To get out of the way, Lucile lies on her bed and reads. Like most bookish young girls, her feelings about life at any given moment are determined by what she is reading. So what is she reading? *The Wizard of Oz* has just been published and *The Tale of Peter Rabbit.* Also *Little Black Sambo.* But more likely at eleven she is immersed in Louisa May Alcott. She has three sisters, just like Jo March in *Little Women,* and she, like Jo, is the second daughter. Her sisters annoy her, though thank goodness there isn't a sickly one like Beth March. Like Jo, Lucile loves to run and is faster than most of the boys in the neighborhood (she will one day be head of the Wellesley running team). She feels restless, obstreperous, at odds with everyone in her family, but she also cannot imagine living without them. She adores the theater and sometimes organizes her brothers and sisters to put on plays. She has a secret hideout in the attic. She dreams (maybe) of writing a novel. But she does not have a mother like Marmee. (No one has a mother like Marmee, but she would not have known that at eleven.) Instead she must settle for sharp-elbowed Aunt Ida.

She plays jacks. She rides a bicycle. She ice-skates. She has a doll, which she ignores. Dolls are large and unwieldy, with glass eyes and porcelain heads and real human hair. Girls must play with them carefully. Boys must not touch them. Damaged dolls can be a gruesome sight.

She battles with her sisters, especially Gertrude who is only eighteen months older. Gertrude is wild. Wilder than anyone, even the boys. A hedonist, a provocateur. Perfect foil for Lucile, who wants to be serious instead. It is Gertrude, or Tutu as she is known, who later in life enjoyed walking naked through her house, "airing the body," as she called it. One afternoon Tutu would encounter a nine-year-old nephew, Lucile's younger son, in an upstairs hallway. He would stare up at her bare breasts in alarmed fascination; she would calmly inform him that she had ordered a badminton set for the back lawn.

Lucile is good at school, better than her brothers, much better than her sisters, who soon acquire, perhaps by unfair comparison, a reputation for being dim. Not her. She reads. She does sums. She studies geography. (Panama!) She practices her penmanship by copying poems neatly into a green-papered, lined notebook. "The Death of Napoleon," "The Grave of the Indian Chief," "Mark Antony on the Death of Ceasar." Death is a popular theme in poems considered suitable for the study and contemplation of children in 1900:

> Friend after friend departs
> Who hath not lost a friend?
> There is no union here of hearts
> That finds not here an end!
> Were this frail world our final rest,
> Living or dying none were blest.
> Beyond the flight of time,
> Beyond the reign of death,
> There surely is some blessed clime,
> Where life is not a breath.
> —James Montgomery

December.

A whole year has passed and at last it is Christmas. Lucile loves Christmas. Last year her family barely celebrated Christmas. But this year the house is decorated with candles, red ribbons, holly branches, sprays of bittersweet.

Miss McGrath and her kitchen girls are busy till late every night, serving up chickens, turkeys, hams, sweetbreads, quivering aspics, fried oysters, cakes, cookies. Outside the windows snow flurries whirl. A fire leaps in the dining room fireplace. Huge tureens of hot punch and eggnog sit on the sideboard in the evening when Papa invites guests. During the day, ladies and gentlemen come to call, leave their cards in a silver salver on the front hall table. Thursday is calling day for Avondale. Bowls of nuts are set out for callers, candies, pyramids of oranges.

The tree is a handsome blue spruce, decorated with tinsel and glass balls. On Christmas morning there are packages for everyone, wrapped in bright silver paper. Lucile is given a white rabbit fur muff.

She loves dogs. She loves chocolate. She wears enormous hair ribbons.

She is now her father's favorite. ("My little redhead," he called her.)

This is Lucile's world in 1900.

Perhaps.

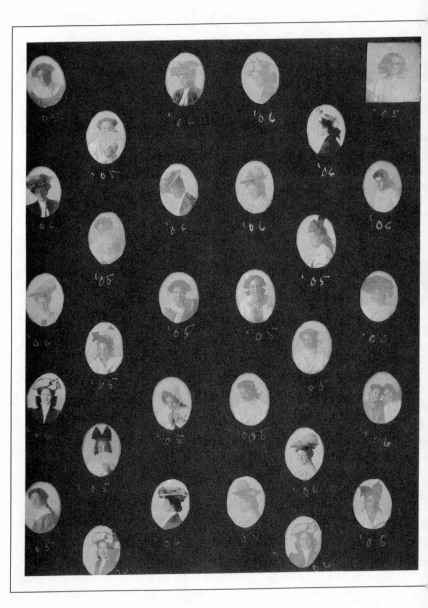

V

Camera Lucida

: an instrument that by means of a prism of a peculiar form or an arrangement of mirrors and often a microscope causes a virtual image of an external object to appear as if projected onto a plane surface (as of paper or canvas) so that an outline may be traced.

—*Webster's Third New International Dictionary*

When she was thirteen or fourteen years old someone, probably Barney, gave Lucile a No. 2 Brownie box camera. What I know or can infer about her adolescence is based almost entirely on snapshots she glued into two photo albums, one begun "Christmas 1904," according to the flyleaf (though she's stuck in some snapshots from 1903), and "Finished August 9, 1905," just before she left for boarding school. The second, which came to me from my brother's invaluable canvas bag, that mail pouch from the past, was started immediately afterward.

The first album is made up almost entirely of pictures of Lucile's sisters and brothers, friends and neighborhood children, babies, dogs, all against various backdrops. "A family's photograph album is generally about the extended family," notes Susan Sontag, adding, "and, often, is all that remains of it." She calls snapshots like these "souvenirs of daily life," and Lucile's first photo album—the size of a paperback turned sideways, bound in rusty black leather with black pages—certainly looks like a turn-of-the-century memento of a pleasant upper-middle-class midwestern world. Skating parties at Worken's Pond, a holiday visit to Lake Charlevoix, boating at Grande Pointe (the girls in long dresses with huge floppy bows in their hair). Trips to Eden Park, which had a scenic reservoir with a valve house and a water tower that looked like something that belonged to a German *Schloss*, also a fountain and a beautiful stone bridge, an aquaduct, arching above the entrance. Drives into the countryside. Rides in the carriage and in a wobbly-looking black runabout. Steamboat excursions on the Ohio River to visit Coney Island. On the Island Queen's top deck Lucile and her siblings lean against the railings, a breeze in their faces, and listen to the calliope. Tree branches hang down to the water and houses slide dreamily by on the opposite bank, while the children breathe in the river's muddy ferrous smell and wonder idly where they are really going, which is what children always wonder onboard ships, just as surely as they always climb to the topmost deck, and turn their faces to the breeze.

Whole pages are labeled simply "At home." Avondale is an attractive, though stark-looking neighborhood—the trees are spindly and the big houses have that gaunt, aggressive look that attends new houses of every era. The usual accoutrements of a comfortable childhood are featured: bicycles, swings, a tall dollhouse set up in the shade of a cherry tree. Despite his severe reputation, B. H. was indulgent enough to allow his children a plethora of pets: a pony named Boyd, a dachshund named Hans, a Saint Bernard named Doc, a collie named Kelpie.

The photographs are all carefully labeled in white ink: "Henry at home, 1904." "Gertrude and Corinne, Grande Pointe, 1903." (Corinne was Corinne Ashbrook, repeatedly featured, a blonde snippet in a sailor dress and black tights, a plaid cap tilted gaily on her head. Who was she aside from these details? A small hand rising from the deep.)

Dogs figure prominently. Lucile lies in the grass with her head pillowed on Doc the Saint Bernard. Kelpie scratches fleas. Henry makes Hans the dachshund ride on Boyd the pony. Tutu and a smirking, heavyset boy try to get Hans to ice skate. Hans again in a family picture, with Chester firmly holding his collar; everyone stares at the camera except Hans, who gazes thoughtfully into a middle distance. A resigned-looking animal is Hans, though perhaps that is simply the look of dachshunds, whose center of gravity is so unusually low.

CHERISHED PETS, MERRY skating parties, steamship excursions, outings to Eden Park. Is this what Lucile's childhood looked like? Or what, at thirteen or fourteen—a notorious age for self-invention—she wanted it to look like? What do we know of anybody's childhood? Mostly that it exists within a different cosmos than adult life, operating by a wholly different set of elementary principles.

My younger sister Evie recently told me that when she was in kindergarten she assumed that all the seventh- and eighth-graders at our school were married to each other. This was reasonable empiricism: height equaled adulthood; adult-hood equaled marriage. Lucile must have likewise arrived at her own un-derstanding of the world based on the conclusions she drew from what went on around her, an understanding that is not reflected in this album except in its heavy emphasis on children. The adults who are pictured are often stand-ing alone and those photographs have a slightly obligatory look, as if she had felt required to take them, the way one feels required to photograph historic sites.

"Papa, 1904": Barney stands in the bright sun on his front steps, legs apart, hatless, coatless, gripping a rolled news-paper as if it were a rifle stock. He might have just returned from shooting one of the Bengal tigers he would instead some day donate to the Cincinnati Zoo. His big ears and big nose stand out even more prominently than in most of his photographs. He looks small and surprisingly young. He looks a lot like my father. He also looks superimposed on those steps, standing in that conquering attitude, as if he were somewhere else at the time

the picture was taken. Islamabad, Nepal, the Gobi Desert. He has the pure and relentless gaze of an adventurer.

In a photo from 1905, "Papa and Myself," he and Lucile stand together on the front steps. The only photograph I have found featuring the two of them. It must be early spring, around Easter, cool enough for coats but warm enough in the sun to go without gloves: both are dressed formally for the middle of the day, wearing handsome light-colored wool coats over dark clothing. B. H. has donned a bowler hat and a suit and tie, his shoes freshly shined—he is definitely B. H. in this outfit, not Barney—so they must be heading out to an occasion of some importance. Lucile sports a flying saucer of a black hat. A windless day, otherwise she would be clutching that hat to her head. B. H. stands one step above her (to make sure he was taller?), an arm around her shoulders; his other hand grips a cane too thin to be anything but an affectation. He frowns superciliously, his nose in the air, quite clearly pretending to be a snob. Lucile smiles at the camera and looks as if a moment before she was laughing. Her father's success is still recent enough to be the subject of some amusement in the family—when Papa is in the proper mood, and if you are a favored child.

Lucile's photo album was composed when she was well into adolescence. A less jaded state of being in 1904 than it is now but still cagey and observant. The Judgmental Age. Other people are suddenly to blame for everything for which you had previously blamed yourself. Bad grades, bad skin ("the most complicated organ of the body"). Bad humor. Aunt Ida comes into focus now as the ogre of family fables. Ordering children to keep their elbows off the table, refusing to buy new kid gloves (what's wrong with your old ones?), insisting that everyone swallow a tablespoon of cod liver oil after breakfast, banishing dogs from the house. In one snapshot of her, she ascends the steps of the house, all in black, looking critical. Yet in others she is smiling, kindly and approachable, and like her brother, surprisingly young.

It is startling to realize that the people who were once in charge of one's life were often most in charge when they were young. The mercurial father, the distant mother, the scolding aunt. People in their twenties and early thirties. Yet they had seemed so imposing. So absolute in their authority. The child stares up at them hopelessly. How have they come by their knowledge of money? Of railway timetables? Of how long to bake a ham? How could anyone ever know so much? They command the world, these venerable young adults. Until the world spins the wrong way on its axis, that is, and then what they do not know could fit neatly between the North and South Pole.

BY THE TIME she took these snapshots and assembled her first album, Lucile had learned to put some distance between who she was and what she saw. And to arrange and select how she herself wanted to be seen. Very little gloom in Lucile's photo album between 1904 and 1905. Smiling children, laughing babies, adults who appear serene and tolerant. Piggyback rides, tennis games, girls on swings carefully keeping their legs tucked so their petticoats will not show. Quite a few snapshots of grinning boys who were not Lucile's brothers. Romance, or at least flirtation, seemed suddenly a tremulous possibility, pushing up here and there on those pages like purple crocuses in the grass.

But quietly mixed in with the capering holiday snapshots, the dogs, the girls in hair bows and sailor dresses, are also two very different pictures.

One was taken in 1904 from a steamboat on the Pine River. A bleak farmhouse, wooden fences trailing crazily down the steep bank to the water; inside the fences roam skinny-looking pigs. The other was snapped in August 1905 from the deck of the Island Queen, on a day that must have been sweltering. Factory smokestacks— perhaps it is a foundry—spew black smoke. The factory itself is black and infernal, a Dickensian pile.

Disconcerting. What do a dilapidated farmhouse and noisome smokestacks have to do with Avondale? The world, Lucile was just beginning to discover, is made of eggshell, which could crack open at any moment to reveal the mysterious yolk of everything. But her Wellesley course on American authors, with its special emphasis on Emerson and the Over-Soul, remained in her future, along with those postcard scenes of the Somme battlefields and pulverized French villages. For the moment Lucile had only floating glimpses of skinny pigs and dirty smokestacks while she drifted down the river on a pleasure boat, and perhaps *Oliver Twist,* and the dire mutterings of Grandmother Gertrude, to help her understand that not everyone lived in Avondale.

THE ONE OTHER dark hint in this album is Lucile herself, caught here and there in a sullen attitude by someone to whom she handed her Brownie camera. Pouting by a shrub in one picture, wearing a fussy cloth jacket and a dress with a ludicrously wide collar, her hair pulled upward in an uncomfortable topknot. Frowning as she balances on "Helen's wheel" (did she not have a bicycle of her own?). Though elsewhere she is smiling.

The final snapshot is captioned simply "Lucile." No date. It has her lying on her stomach in the grass, her chin propped on her hand, scowling fiercely. Behind her is the house, the dollhouse, the bicycles; it's a sunny day. She is in a rage. The world is as black as her own black heart.

Most teenage girls would leave out such an unflattering picture of themselves, but she chose to include it and even made it the album's grace note. Either she was being honest about how she often felt at the time — regardless of the bicycles and the sunny day — or she thought the photo was funny. Self-deprecation also runs in my family, along with novelists and nearsightedness.

How much of the girl in this album became my father's mother?

Katherine Mansfield, who was a year older than Lucile, considered exactly this question in 1920, in a curiously contemporary-sounding entry in her journal: "Is it not possible that the rage for confession, autobiography, especially for memories of earliest childhood, is explained by our persistent yet mysterious belief in a self which is continuous and permanent"?

With my magnifying glass, I hang over those yellowed black-and-white photographs from 1904 and 1905, trying to see through them into what Lucile saw and what she cared about (at least enough to photograph), and therefore believed in (home, family, dogs), because I think I will then know something about who she was. I will discover something "continuous and permanent" about her. But is this even slightly possible? Who was I at fourteen and fifteen? No one very recognizable to me now. Perhaps I can understand Lucile best by accepting that these photographs are indeed souvenirs of daily life, and nothing like the trip itself.

The only one in that Kroger family with any brains," Senator Robert Taft's wife once remarked of Lucile — a comment my father has always enjoyed repeating. Mrs. Taft had sought my father out at a party at the Camargo Club in Cincinnati specifically to voice this opinion, though she never said how she had come by it or what had prompted her to deliver it. In those days my father was a skinny, ginger-haired young man with horn-rimmed glasses who wanted to be a writer like John O'Hara; he always had a cigarette in one hand, a glass of bourbon in the other, and a skeptical look on his face. It was valiant of Mrs. Taft to ignore that skeptical look — literary young men are rarely receptive to the opinions of middle-aged ladies — so she must have believed that what she had to say was worth hearing.

As a teenager, Lucile attended two different boarding schools in Washington DC: the Collegiate School for Girls and Mount Vernon Seminary. She recorded the names of these institutions and their street addresses, in firmly rounded schoolgirl handwriting, inside her *Life of Oliver Goldsmith,* along with the years of her attendance, 1904 to 1907. Both the Collegiate School for Girls and Mount Vernon Seminary had fine academic reputations in their day, and Lucile had to have been pretty brainy to be admitted and pretty serious minded to have persuaded her father, who had already lost a wife and a son, to let her travel fifteen hundred miles to be educated in Washington DC.

Except that I can find no independent record of Lucile having been a student at either the Collegiate School for Girls or Mount Vernon Seminary. I have called and e-mailed the registrars and alumnae offices of both schools, in their current incarnations, and called and e-mailed all the people they suggested that I call and e-mail, and no one can find a trace of Lucile Ida Kroger. It's possible that in the days before alumni fund drives, schools kept skimpy records. On the other hand, Lucile's Wellesley College transcript states she prepared for Wellesley at neither of the aforementioned institutions but instead "at the College Preparatory School for Girls in Cincinnati," a maddeningly generic name for a school; not surprisingly, I can't discover whether such a place ever actually existed.

Another testament to her intellectual powers. Many people would like to forget their high school years, but few can claim to have erased them altogether.

So let's just say she went to high school in Washington. I myself went to high school in Washington and I don't remember it very well either. Stateless, sleepy, scheming Washington, always shifting one way or another, depending on who's in office, built on a swamp, girdled by the Potomac River, and the C&O Canal. A city of cherry blossoms and black slums and, even more noticeably, of white marble monuments. The Lincoln Memorial, the Jefferson Memorial. So white and monumental they seem to be floating in the mists of Valhalla. A skeptical place, a city of frauds and heroes. Where the frauds behave like heroes and the heroes, not surprisingly, often behave like frauds. But most of all a city of mind-altering humidity. Stepping outside on a July day can feel like walking into a sponge. In such a distracting miragelike city, it's quite possible that one could believe one is attending high school and yet be doing something else entirely.

By the fall of 1905, the wildly appealing and strenuously naughty

Alice Roosevelt had been First Daughter for four years at 1600 Pennsylvania Avenue. Alice was nineteen and preparing to marry Ohio representative Nicholas Longworth, from Cincinnati. Longworth was thirty-three. A famous roué who played the violin, swilled whiskey, ran after women, and could charm even the most bumptious crowd of voters. He was also handsome, though bald, and rich. To fifteen-year-old Lucile, raised in the shadow of the aristocratic Longworth family, perched in their Tudor mansion, Rookwood, atop Walnut Hills, he must have been a matinee idol.

That fall a flurry of parties, teas, bridal showers precedes the Roosevelt–Longworth wedding. Let's say Lucile is invited to a reception for Ohioans, hosted by Alice Roosevelt as a gesture to her fiancé's constituents, an invitation secured for Lucile through the Tafts. On a damp November afternoon she is escorted by the math teacher of the Collegiate School for Girls, a tall thin woman from Cleveland with dark Spanish-looking eyes and a high forehead, who belongs, distantly, to the family of President Benjamin Harrison. The math teacher has noticed Lucile's head for numbers. In the carriage, they discuss quadratic equations. Lucile is in a white shirtwaist, a black wool skirt, and a black wool Eton coat that when damp smells like Hans the dachshund. On her head she wears a flat little black felt hat trimmed with an ostrich feather. The hat is insecurely pinned and keeps slipping over one eye during the ride to Pennsylvania Avenue, while the ostrich feather tickles her nose.

The White House, impressive from the lawn, inside looks bare and utilitarian. Despite numerous brass chandeliers, the light is poor; the mauve carpets are threadbare in places, and spotty, and the windows, Lucile notes, need to be washed. Well-padded Ohioans crowd the overheated reception rooms, where spindly wooden chairs have been pushed against the walls. Not enough teacups. Not enough crabmeat paste sandwiches. Too much damp wool that smells like Hans the dachshund.

But it is all splendid, splendid, anyway. It is the White House! On the walls hang dark oil portraits in heavy gilt frames, former presidents, august in their high collars and waistcoats, somber with accomplishment and tints of burnt sienna. Lucile lurks in a doorway, hoping to see something a little livelier than these portraits—a few of President Roosevelt's five young children, for instance, who are said to race about the White House wearing stilts. Instead, men in black suits stride back and forth cradling sheaves of papers. Maids in white caps and aprons hover with mostly empty silver trays. The math teacher sighs and touches her high forehead with excitement.

Because there, at last, is Alice Roosevelt! Beautiful and impatient looking, superbly dressed in cream-colored French lace from Rheims. She stands by the French windows leading out to the Rose Garden with its rows of box hedges, brown and drab this time of year, and holds out her hand to a shuffling line of round-shouldered, brown-suited Ohioans, who resemble box hedges. Lucile and the math teacher join the reception line. By the time she reaches Alice, Lucile is blushing to her hairline and perspiring. Taking Alice's proffered hand, so pale and slim, so dry, Lucile stammers out something, then sneezes. (Drat that ostrich feather!) Alice lifts her blue eyes briefly, curls her lips into a vague half smile.

Extraordinary red hair, she thinks as Lucile backs away. But what did the girl say her name was? Croaker?

The Roosevelt–Longworth wedding took place at the White House on February 17, 1906. Undoubtedly several girls at Lucile's school, daughters of Washington politicians, were invited to the wedding with their families. Various prominent Cincinnati families—the Tafts, for one—were invited as well. Not invited herself, Lucile nevertheless enjoys close proximity to this legendary event, hears firsthand accounts of the dress, the flowers, the dignitaries who drank too much champagne and fell into potted palms, the passionate looks exchanged between teenage bride and bald groom. (Though newspaper photographs show the wedded couple standing rigid and unsmiling.) At night Lucile huddles cross-legged on her bed in her dormitory with a scratchy wool blanket around her shoulders, drinking tepid cocoa and listening to whispered ecstasies about the snake Alice totes along to parties, how Alice likes to play poker, and chew gum, and smoke *in public*. Alice is already, at nineteen, a celebrated smoker. Lucile's deep, abiding romance with cigarettes begins with Alice.

As a role model for teenage girls, Alice Roosevelt wasn't so bad. The other young woman in the news at the time was luscious Evelyn Nesbit, leading lady in the famous murder trial of her psychotic and depraved millionaire husband, Harry K. Thaw, who shot her former lover, the architect Stanford White, on a rooftop in Madison Square Garden. If she was wild, at least Alice was sensible. She chose a good-natured midwestern husband who may have liked whiskey too much, but appreciated her intelligence and thorny sense of humor. He went on to have a series of lovers but so did she, including one who fathered her only child, Paulina, whom Longworth adored and treated as his own. (Alice herself wasn't much of a mother.) And Alice's politics remained unshakably decent: she refused, for instance, to allow Senator Joe McCarthy to call her "Alice," although she said it was fine if the garbageman did so.

If that half-imagined glimpse of a suffragette's sash in the attic is any indication, Lucile's political sympathies fell in line with Alice's, from whom she may have also garnered a shade of self-importance. Like Alice, she deliberately chose a Cincinnati husband who admired her intelligence and independence, though in no other way did my grandfather resemble the winsome, brilliant, dissipated Nicholas Longworth. (He did, however, have a full head of hair.) Aside from her father, Lucile was the only one in her family to be interested in politics, a trait she passed down to her younger son. And it seems reasonable to guess

that her interest in politics began to take shape in Washington (if she was actually there), which from 1905 to 1907 was tightly wrapped up in Roosevelt's Square Deal.

Because while she was at the Collegiate School for Girls and/or Mount Vernon Seminary, studying Latin and French, and reading about Oliver Goldsmith, and memorizing the table of elements, and learning how to waltz, and stand still for dress fittings, and smoke cigarettes, Lucile must have also been listening to talk about the need for a living wage and for regulating railroads. The Meat Inspection Act and the Pure Food and Drug Act were passed in Washington in 1906, at the same time that Barney Kroger was installing meat counters in his grocery stores and waging a terrible battle with butchers.

It was to be one of Barney's defining ideas, hiring butchers to work in his yet again renamed B. H. Kroger Baking & Tea Company stores. He already had his own bakeries, which turned out Kroger bread and dinner rolls; he'd devised his own blend of coffee; once he added a meat counter (the first grocer in the country to do so), he would effectively be keeping his shoppers from having to go anywhere else. A shrewd plan, and so simple, except the butchers were used to working for themselves and not for grocers.

Trouble began almost immediately. Barney's butchers refused to use cash registers because they liked to short-weight meat and take sample cuts home, and also to make change for customers out of their own pockets, for obvious reasons. For those same obvious reasons, Barney insisted his butchers use cash registers. Within days, all the cash registers broke down. Barney repaired the cash registers and hired female cashiers to work them. It was wintertime. The butchers left the windows open, freezing the cashiers half to death. Barney built wooden enclosures around the cashiers and handed out lap rugs. The butchers retaliated by cursing so brutishly around the female cashiers that the cashiers wept and quit. Barney hired male cashiers. The butchers beat them up.

And so it went—for months. The last thing Barney needed was the Meat Inspection Act and government inspectors poking around his meat counters, inciting his butchers to further bad behavior, like wiping their bloody hands on the window sashes or spitting on the sausages.

Lucile, of course, sympathized. She was, first of all, a grocer's daughter. But from her school friends, daughters of some of the same politicians who voted to pass the Meat Inspection Act and the Pure Food and Drug Act in the House, Lucile heard horror stories of contaminated meat, maggoty meat, meat that poisoned little children and sent them to their graves, not to mention bad cheese that spread tuberculosis, and germ-filled unhomogenized milk that carried salmonella, and flour full of mealy worms that were just plain unwholesome. She read the papers. A world of bad food needed to be cleaned up.

The Federal Employers Liability Act for Labor was also being passed at around this same time. More bad news for Barney, who calculated every tenth of a cent as he tried to undercut his competitors with his "remarkably low prices." The only way to be able to offer those great deals, according to Barney, was to "run down the prices as far as you can go so the other fellow won't slice your throat." Which meant he had nothing to spare for any other kind of liability. Unless he sliced his own throat.

And yet, reasoned Lucile, shouldn't an employer look out for his employees? Shouldn't he have to take care of them if they got hurt on the job? How could she *not* agree with manly Teddy Roosevelt with his handsome children, his big chest and virile mustache, his mornings on horseback? Teddy Roosevelt, the compassionate Rough Rider, every American girl's ideal papa, who if more diplomatic than Lucile's own father when he spoke for publication, was equally pragmatic: "Let the watchwords of all our people be the old familiar watchwords of honesty, decency, fair-dealing and commonsense."

"Never sell anything except for just what it is," Barney said, in approximately the same language, "and don't sell it then if it isn't any good."

Admittedly, I don't know whether Lucile paid any attention whatsoever to Teddy Roosevelt and his Square Deal. How many high school girls spend much time thinking about politics? Nor do I know that she ever visited the White House—or even less likely, whether she had a math teacher who was related to Benjamin Harrison. However, it is true that President Benjamin Harrison's elderly widow was once invited to my grandfather's house on Indian Hill and sat through a theatrical staged by my ten-year-old father, and it's also true that I have a good friend who is a direct descendant of President William Henry Harrison, so there are some family connections to the Harrisons, even if they're not the right ones. I apologize for what may look like prevaricating here. Since all I have for facts about Lucile during this period are a couple of addresses on the flyleaf of an old schoolbook, I have to do a little historical tap dancing.

In her later years, when Alice Roosevelt Longworth was established as the grande dame of Washington, she kept on her sofa a needlepoint pillow on which were famously stitched the words: "If you can't say anything good about someone, sit right here by me." One day I would like to have such a pillow, but mine would read: "If you don't know what you're talking about, have a seat." In my opinion, writing about other people requires a certain stupid bravado—a willingness to chat up the unknowable. Especially since what you don't know about someone is always going to be more interesting than what you do, which is why telling the truth often means confessing that you don't have it.

"It is all very well to sell pink salmon provided it is sold as pink salmon," as Barney once observed, "not as red or top-grade salmon."

Guidelines for the fishy art of biography.

L ast summer I visited friends on an island in Lake Winnipe-
saukee. Their nearest neighbors own a border collie that
spent most of each day running back and forth to the end
of their wooden dock, where he stared frantically up at the sky and
turned in circles. None of us could figure out why the dog did this.
Finally, someone asked a child in the neighboring family why she
thought her dog stared at the sky and ran in silent circles.

The child said, "He's herding the clouds."

A few more clouds.

As much as I would like to insist that Lucile
was in Washington DC, just when she is supposed to be away at boarding school she has
inconveniently dated photographs of herself
at home with her brothers and sisters. In February and March of 1906, for example, she is
shown standing in the snow outside her house
in Cincinnati, wearing a long coat and carrying a muff (though one photograph shows her
standing with her back resolutely to the camera, as if denying that she is there).

These are photographs from that second al-
bum, a long black cloth-covered album with black pages, the size of
an accounting ledger, which begins in August 1905 and continues
into April 1906. Possibly Lucile was home on brief vacations when

the February and March pictures were taken in 1905 and 1906. Also possible that she twice tried boarding school and twice disliked it and came home to Cincinnati. Disliking boarding school could be a family failing. My father also disliked boarding school. I disliked boarding school so much that my second year I lived on apples and peanut butter rather than leave my room to go to the dining hall. Eventually I, too, came home. It is comforting to think your incapacities are foreordained, if only because then you aren't quite so alone with them.

THE FIRST PAGE of Lucile's second album is composed of scenic snapshots taken in 1905 of Eden Park and Spring Grove Cemetery, the sort of meditative pictures teenage girls find so irresistible and anyone else looking through their photo albums finds so dull. Leafy vistas, most featuring water. Pools, reservoirs, lakes. Snapshots of family and friends, everyone smiling a little vaguely, clustered in pairs or small groups. Subsequent pages display the Kroger family on vacation at Lake Charlevoix: rowing boats, walking in front of an enormous shingled hotel, standing by a Model A Ford. Lucile caught with her face screwed up, squinting unattractively into the sun. Children sitting on logs. A man plowing a field with a horse-drawn plow. Back at home: Shots of substantial prewar houses, a goat pulling a cart, children in the snow wearing dark hats and coats. Many pictures of dogs.

Then abruptly, like turning a corner and meeting a noisy troupe of schoolgirls, we come upon two pages devoted entirely to scores of little oval photographs of Lucile and her sisters and a few friends. Eighty-nine ovals in all. Twenty-two of the photographs feature Lucile in different poses. Wearing hats, holding a fan, reading a book, laughing, looking pensive, pretending to look pensive, some with another girl, most alone, never quite the same face twice. Ovals rise on those black pages like air bubbles from the past, within each one a trapped molecule of human time.

"Every photograph is a certificate of presence," notes Roland Barthes in *Camera Lucida,* his strange, wonderful, convoluted book on photography. But as Barthes goes on to point out, a presence can't be arrested, only registered. People change too quickly ever to be captured whole, and so a photograph of a person will always be "partially true, and therefore totally false."

Well, this is bad news. Of those twenty-two oval images, do none of them certifiably look like Lucile? Isn't at least one of those twenty-two expressions recognizable enough that, on being presented with it, her friends would have exclaimed, "Now *that's* our Lu! That's her to the life. That's just how she was." Then again, the different people who knew her knew her differently, and each might have chosen a different picture as the one that was really "her." And so on. I suppose the good news is that if a human being can't be caught by a photograph, then at least photographs suggest the multifariousness of being human.

A cloud-herder's definition of history: something that is always "partially true, and therefore totally false."

ONE LAST CLOUD.

His name, according to Lucile's photo album, is Ally Harris. The date of the photograph is August 20, 1905. Surrounded by a page full of summery snapshots of children in sandals and white dresses holding fanciful white parasols, Ally Harris is small and anxious looking. He is also black. He stands alone in the weeds and bracken by the side of a road in Eden Park, his weight on one bare foot. Baggy overalls, a white cotton shirt, a cloth cap. He looks like a Hollywood version of early twentieth-century black boys, so perfectly do those sharecropper overalls and that cap match our expectations of what young black boys at that time would be wearing. The sun is high overhead. It appears to be a very hot day.

Because the sun is overhead Ally Harris's face is partly in shadow and his expression is hard to read, even with a magnifying glass. Actually, given my poor eyesight, I have just invested in an Ultra Dome

Magnifier, a "light-gathering solid acrylic dome," two and a half inches in diameter, which offers "4x power" and "glides effortlessly across any surface." (Igneous rock? Tree bark? The Bronze Age?) But even with an Ultra Dome Magnifier there's no gliding across this encounter. For instance, I can't tell whether Ally Harris is smiling shyly at Lucile behind her Brownie camera or frowning impatiently. However, his posture—one foot forward, the other behind him not quite touching the ground—is one of hesitation and retreat. He looks ready to bolt.

Ally Harris is the only child identified by name in this album who has not been previously pictured. Could he have been invited along by Lucile on that summer outing to Eden Park? Did young upper-middle-class white girls in Cincinnati befriend black boys in 1905? Unlikely. And had such a friendship occurred, by some miracle of innocence and goodwill, it would not have not been conducted in public. Even in Eden Park. Cincinnati was about as southern as a northern city could be in 1905, and it had an unusually mixed history when it came to race relations, Ohio having been a border state during the Civil War, with Cincinnati right on the border of that border, both geographically and ideologically.

In the mid-1880s it was home to the influential Ladies' Anti-Slavery Sewing Circle as well as some of the mainstays of the Underground Railroad, including the abolitionists Mr. and Mrs. Levi Coffin, featured in Harriet Beecher Stowe's *Uncle Tom's Cabin,* who lived for a while next to Lyman Beecher's place in Walnut Hills. The Beechers were dedicated abolitionists as well; Stowe, in fact, collected most of the material for *Uncle Tom's Cabin* while she was in Cincinnati, where the book sold like mad when it first appeared in 1852.

Meanwhile runaway slaves were often kidnapped in broad daylight in Cincinnati, surrounded by passersby who did nothing to intervene. Even when the slaves wept and cried out to them before being hauled down to the river and sent back across to Kentucky. Even when some of those passersby had just finished reading *Uncle Tom's Cabin.*

Cincinnati largely supported the newly inaugurated Abraham Lincoln, who visited the Queen City on February 12, 1861. He rode from the train station to the Burnet House, the fanciest hotel in town, in a carriage drawn by six white horses—an occasion witnessed from a street corner by my grandfather's mother, a fat little cross-eyed girl of five. (My family has a history of marrying late, which is why I have school-age children and a great-grandmother who saw Abraham Lincoln.) Crowds cheered Lincoln and waved flags. Bunting decorated every building. A delegation of orphans sang "Hail Columbia" on the steps of the Burnet House. One of them presented Lincoln with a bouquet of flowers.

Six weeks later at the end of March, a week and a half before Fort Sumter was attacked in South Carolina and the Civil War ignited, three cannon arrived in Cincinnati from Baltimore plainly addressed "Southern Confederacy, Jackson, Mississippi." They were shipped on unchallenged.

How many of the four thousand cannonballs fired at Fort Sumter during those critical two days in April 1861 were shot from those three Baltimore cannon?

It's possible a Civil War historian could tell me; it's more probable that no one knows or considers this information important. And yet, unlike the future, answers to questions about the past *are* out there, somewhere, even if we'll never find them, or find them interesting. Once upon a time someone knew how many cannonballs were fired from those Baltimore cannon because someone had to load the cannonballs. Someone for whom every cannonball was significant, at least for the several seconds required for loading it. Someone with a forage cap and whiskers, and dirty fingernails and black blooms of gunpowder on his uniform—a person of history and not just the casualty of it he most likely became.

Once upon a time Lucile knew everything there was to know about what she did and why she did it. I don't believe it matters that I'll never know why she took a picture of little Ally Harris or what prompted her to cut up eighty-nine photographs of herself and friends into thumb-sized ovals and paste them in her photo album. Or even whether she ever went to school in Washington DC.

Certainly I'll never know if my father's political liberalism and his dedication to civil rights—his proudest achievement was helping to desegregate the town in Virginia where we lived until I was nine—had anything to do with his mother's politics and her childhood in racially conflicted Cincinnati. Or whether it all sprang instead from his deep affection for the family's black chauffeur, a kindly man called Wash who was nicer to him than anybody else. Frankly, it doesn't matter. What *does* matter, it seems to me, is wondering about it. Those odd concurrences between generations. The strange "differences" that turn out not to be so different. Every family needs a crazy border collie, or an unserious historian, whether or not anyone is reconstructing missing relatives. If we don't try to gather in the past, it's gone. If we don't wonder about who and what we came from, we're half in the clouds ourselves.

Clouds or no clouds, one thing from my grandmother's photo album does seem clear: at age fifteen, Lucile was just becoming capable of bifurcated vision. She saw Ally Harris and also something she thought he represented. Poverty, most likely. Or, less excusably, rustic simplicity. Whatever she thought, Ally Harris and his shabby-looking overalls appealed to her emerging social consciousness that sunny August day, just as the ramshackle farmhouse and those factory smokestacks had caught her attention a year earlier. She saw him distinctly enough as a person to want to know his name, and to want to record it in white ink in her album, where he never appears again. She saw him distinctly enough as an image that she wanted his photograph.

Unfortunately, moments of emerging social consciousness are almost always awkward and often prove injurious to bystanders. Unlike the other children in Lucile's photos from that day in Eden Park, Ally Harris knows he is a Subject. Not so different from those leafy vistas. Head cocked to the side, one foot placed carefully behind him, he looks not just uncomfortable but unwilling—he reminds me, in fact, of Raymond. That guarded expression, shy, maybe recalcitrant. Ally Harris is a boy, not a view. His overalls are his overalls, not a costume. His feet are bare because he has no shoes. How hard it is to remember that people exist outside of our ideas of them.

VI

College Girl

To Alma Mater, Wellesley's Daughters
    All together join and sing,
Thro' all her wealth of woods and waters
    Let your happy voices ring.
In every changing mood we love her—
    Love her towers and woods and lake
Oh changeful sky, bend blue above her,
    Wake ye birds, your chorus wake!

                —"Alma Mater"

One fall day several years ago, I stood on the lawn behind the library at Wellesley College gazing across the silvery expanse of Lake Waban, admiring the russet oaks and dark pine trees on the opposite shore. And I found myself thinking that simply by standing on the same ground where Lucile had stood during her college years, I might divine something essential about her. Perhaps *she* had once lingered on this exact grassy spot, looking across the lake at a tumult of red and gold leaves. Breathing in the scent of leaf mold and damp grass. Feeling the autumn sun warming the top of her head. Perhaps somehow, in this moment, she was there.

Or that's what I pretended to be thinking. Most biographers suffer from a necessary vanity regarding their subjects and I am no exception. What I was secretly hoping for that fall day was not communion with Lucile over the foliage but some sort of paranormal sighting—my feeling being that if she was going to appear to anyone, it would be to me, and that the likeliest place she might put in an appearance, spectral or otherwise, would be in a place where she had lived intensely. After all the summoning I was doing, was it so unlikely that Lucile might pay me a fleeting visit by the Hazard Quadrangle or up on Severance Hill? And so I spent several cool, sunny hours rambling around the Wellesley campus, trying to glimpse a shade of my grandmother against the bricks and shrubbery and within the lengthening shadows of the turning oak trees.

What is biography but another kind of ghost story?

Ambrose Bierce, that caustic necromancer, and one of my father's favorite writers, expresses more or less the same idea in one of his popular ghost stories being published at the time Lucile was in college, and which she very well may have read:

> I know, indeed, that one's environment may be so affected by one's personality as to yield, long afterward, an image of oneself to the eyes of another. Doubtless the impressing personality has to be the right kind of personality as the perceiving eyes have to be the right kind of eyes — mine, for instance.

Every biographer feels he has the "right kind of eyes" to perceive his subject. An irrational conviction, perhaps, unless one goes by Bierce's definition of "rational" in his famous *Devil's Dictionary*: "Devoid of all delusions save those of observation, experience and reflection."

My father has always said that his mother's happiest years were her years at Wellesley, although about that period of her life he knows next to nothing. But he loves colleges and was himself a brilliant college teacher, though his academic career, like his other careers, was haphazard, even slightly delusional. For instance, he has a PhD but no undergraduate degree — he was admitted to Yale in 1943 but left at the end of his freshman year to join the navy during World War II. After the war he attended Columbia for a semester and spent a semester at the University of Ohio; he was too impatient to get on with life to continue. Which I can understand — he'd just got out of the Navy, he was newly married, he was tired of being told what to do. Also, he wanted to write for newspapers, at a time when that profession did not demand a college degree, only a reasonable proficiency with spelling (my father has always been an excellent speller).

Still, leapfrogging the onerous stages of life has its consequences. Twenty years later, when we left Virginia and moved to Washington, my father realized he was fascinated by mythology and also that he wanted to teach, so he got his doctoral degree (Joseph Campbell sat on his thesis committee) through one of the unaccredited universities that blossomed like loosestrife in the 1970s, a degree that allowed him to teach mythology as an adjunct at Georgetown, where he had an influential friend in the psychology department, yet caused him grief later when he wanted to become an assistant professor. And still later, when other colleges would not hire him. Which he found enraging. The great mythology of my father's own life was that none of his failed pursuits failed because of his reluctance to do what was required, but only because of other people's lack of imagination.

I've always thought that his mother would have made him finish college.

WHEN I FINALLY realized that Lucile was not going to materialize for me, even as a flash of red hair by the rhododendrons, I changed tactics. I decided, very rationally, to contextualize her. A poor second to a mystical vision, but it was time to get on with things. So I stopped wandering around Lake Waban and looking at the leaves and went into the library instead, determined to describe Lucile's college years in such a way that I could address the history of women's suffrage in America, intellectualism before World War I, New England reformers, theories on higher education for women, and the settlement house movement from 1907 to 1911.

As it so happens, I don't know much about any of those subjects. Nor could I muster the energy to spend months reading up on them (I don't have much patience, either, for onerous stages). Also my own memories of college tell me it's a time that goes by very quickly—full of things one believes are important, but which turn out not to be, and things that actually *are* important, but which one hardly notices—and that to impose cultural coherence on college life means missing the experience altogether. So in the end I gave up and simply made my own devil's dictionary of things Lucile must have encountered from 1907 to 1911, while she was a student at Wellesley College.

In this enterprise I have been somewhat aided by fourteen mostly legible pages in Lucile's *Tagebuch,* preserved in that fruitcake tin, which describe a month in her life, from February 11 to March 13, during her senior year. Somewhat, because to call this diary sketchy would be generous (one entry reads simply: "Luncheon"), and it stops with no more explanation than why it was begun.

Her tone is usually wry. Her main interest is in recording events and participants. She views the world with a level gaze—not someone easily impressed or given to fulsome descriptions:

> Wednesday, 1st, 6:00 p.m. The Shakespeare Faculty Senior Dinner. Not an especially thrilling event. I took Laura Dwight and we sat at a table with Miss Kendrick and Miss Whiting. After dinner the faculty told us funny things said on examination papers.

Or:

> Sunday, March 6. Chestnut Hill. Our first riding lesson, Mary Rhodes and I each had half an hour. . . . Result of ride, practical inability to walk, especially upstairs.

Lucile was the first person in her family, male or female, to go to college, during an era when many people still considered higher education harmful for women, especially women who might want to get married one day. She was the first person in her family to look through a telescope at the stars and through a microscope at a cell, the first to study human psychology (at least without a view toward selling something) and to consider Transcendentalism. Nothing in the fourteen pages of her diary indicates that she thought any of this was extraordinary.

But then, why would she? Significance belongs to recollection. As Virginia Woolf observed, "The past is beautiful because one never realizes an emotion at the time." What Lucile realized at the time in her *Tagebuch* are horseback riding lessons, making snow angels with a friend, a sleigh ride, walking into Wellesley village. Supper, vespers, exams. Breakfast in South Natick, a weekend trip to Nahant. A visit to Boston to see a performance by Pavlova. She doesn't say much about any of these experiences, emotional or otherwise, only briskly reports they happened. But that Lucile Ida Kroger once took life so for granted that she barely bothered to comment on it is perhaps what is most extraordinary of all.

WHAT LUCILE
ENCOUNTERED AT WELLESLEY

Algebra. Taught by Professor Ellen Hayes, who stunned a Sunday crowd at Houghton Memorial Chapel by announcing that "God himself cannot change the laws of mathematics." Her freshman year, Lucile studied Ration and Proportion in Higher Algebra and the Theory of Exponents including Imaginaries, Radicals, and Equations involving Radicals. Also Inequalities. Useful at Wellesley, a place Calvin Coolidge called "a political hotbed of radicalism." A college founded on the revolutionary theory that women could be educated as well as men, and deserved to be. (Ambrose Bierce on education: "That which discloses to the wise, and disguises from the foolish, their lack of understanding.")

Also a place where people were fond of discussing inequalities.

The Barge, Barnswallows. In September of 1907, Lucile takes a train from Cincinnati to New York to Boston, where she has to change trains again at South Station for a rackety ride out to the town of Wellesley, twenty miles to the west. She is seventeen. I don't know whether she traveled to Wellesley alone, but it's quite possible that she did. At the station she is met by "the Barge," a dolorous-looking black carriage in which Wellesley College students and their baggage are conveyed down Washington Street. The Barge clatters through the stone pillars and past East Lodge, swaying alarmingly, and halts suddenly at the steps of College Hall. Lucile climbs carefully down from the Barge, aware than an intellectual waterway has just been crossed. Maple leaves are beginning to turn red; the breeze in the east feels cooler than it had in Cincinnati, and when she looks up at the five stories of College Hall the sky above seems bluer, higher. Somehow academic.

She is given a key and directed to a house half a mile down the Weston Road, where her baggage has already been deposited. No one greets her when she arrives, but she finds her room at the top of the stairs and enters with a feeling of trepidation and relief. For a few minutes she stands by the window looking out at a spreading oak tree, listening to other girls rustling about in nearby rooms, a door closing, someone laughing downstairs. Then visitors begin to arrive. Hats crowd her doorway. Are you a freshman? From Ohio? Do you want to join the Ohio Club? Do you play an instrument? Do you sing? Lucile is bombarded with invitations. Social groups, student government, the Consumers League, the College Settlement Association, the Christian Association, Bible Study. Framed by the window behind her, oak leaves toss in a sudden hectic breeze. The door to her room closes at last; shafts of sunlight advance across the carpet.

Sitting on the edge of her still unmade bed, twisting a white cotton handkerchief (Aunt Ida has provided her with ten, hemmed but not monogrammed, her prediction being that all ten will be lost before Christmas), Lucile considers the options. She is nervous about being at college; she is homesick. Bible Study would be a reassuring choice. The Consumers League would make her feel right at home. But finally it's the Barnswallows, Wellesley's theatrical group, which catches her interest.

The Barnswallows was a popular campus group, providing evening entertainment every third Saturday, ranging from plays and dances to children's parties. Wellesley's student newspaper, the *College News,* reviewed each of the Barnswallows' productions at length on the front page. Students lined up an hour ahead of time to get good seats in "the Barn" on performance nights. That December, Lucile participated in the Barnswallows' annual Christmas Carol variety show, appearing in a comic sketch called "The Ruggles Prepare to Dine Out"; she had a minor role as a little boy. A review in the *College News* praises the sketch and nearly every actor in it except Lucile. Her next appearance, as a playing card in an adaptation of *Alice in Wonderland,* again went unnoticed by the *College News.* This was apparently the end of Lucile's involvement with the Barnswallows, though she got elected to the Shakespeare Society, which also staged plays, also reviewed in the *College News.* Lucile appeared in a single production, *A Winter's Tale,* as a servant.

A paradox. Lucile is attracted to drama but plays only small parts in it.

Cast of Alice in Wonderland. *Lucile stands in back row, second from right*

College Hall, College Women, Crushes. College Hall was where most classes met at Wellesley during Lucile's years there, also where the library was located, mail was delivered, meals were served, and where half the students and faculty resided. It contained at the time administrative offices, laboratories, a gymnasium and an assembly hall, and was constructed in the shape of a double cross as a reminder that Wellesley was founded as a Christian college with Christian ideals (improving the world being the goal of improving one's mind). At the center of College Hall, a five-story atrium glowed with light, furnished with potted palms and marble sculpture. College Hall was nearly an eighth of a mile long, rising above three hundred acres of lawns, oaks, and Lake Waban. It took four years to build.

The first time Lucile enters College Hall she stands bewildered beside a potted palm, feeling she should have a map, or at least a compass. Suddenly an enormous bell tolls from above. It is the Japanese bell, rung to signal the beginning and end of classes, meals, and chapel. But the real purpose of the Japanese bell, according to its inscription, is "to awaken from earthly illusions and reveal the benighted ignorance of this world." Fully awakened to her benighted ignorance, Lucile remains motionless by the potted palm and wishes she could take the Barge back to Cincinnati.

College Hall burned to the ground in 1914. Sleeping students and faculty were alerted by the Japanese bell, rung when the fire was discovered, and all escaped safely, thanks to the vigilant and well-prepared student Fire Brigade, whose captains ran weekly fire drills that required even the most acrophobic girls to climb down rope ladders. The Japanese bell did not survive. But the spirit of wakefulness continues on to this day.

Being inducted into the mysteries and routines of Wellesley occupies most of Lucile's time during her first months as a freshman. Not only must she navigate the brick vastness of College Hall and master various rules of etiquette laid out in the freshman handbook ("precedence is given to upperclassmen on the boardwalks"), she also has to learn "all the College Songs immediately" and become conversant with obscure rites and customs ("Forensic Burning," for instance, an event conducted under extreme secrecy that involves the torching of English papers).

More dauntingly, she must find another girl to fall in love with. In November, a letter in the "Free Press" column of the *College News* notes that "it seems quite the proper thing for every Freshman to have a 'crush' on an upperclassman." The writer goes on to abjure this practice, ending sniffily: "I hope the Class of 1911 will have the moral courage to resist any such repugnant tendency." Signed by a member of the Class of 1911. Did Lucile gain "moral courage" from this letter and forego a crush? Or did she simply conclude that its writer was unable to find one?

Further confusions. Lucile believes that she is at Wellesley to become well educated. A college woman as opposed to a regular female. But in December, the *College News* carries a disturbing editorial that describes the "typical college woman" as a "stout-booted, stern-eyed person who talks Common Sense or Transcendentalism at afternoon teas."

What's this? Those boots are indispensable! It rains a lot in New England. It snows. Who wouldn't be stern eyed after braving a December afternoon that's ten degrees below zero, hoping for a cup of tea. And what's wrong with talking about Transcendentalism, a perfectly polite subject, at least compared to the French Revolution or Higher Algebra?

In consternation Lucile reads on, discovering that it is the duty of College Women "to look as well as we can, to have social charm as well as intellect. We do not want people to think we college girls are a race apart. . . . Remember that it is not always wise to be too sensible."

Tell that to Aunt Ida. And what happened to the hotbed of radicalism?

Nevertheless Lucile takes extra care with her hat for several days and remembers to scrape the snow off her boots before sitting down to lunch. Until the next issue of the *College News* appears, with yet another editorial, this one chiding girls for being too emotional and "touchy." Be more rational, urges the editorial. "Girls, as well as men ought to be able to forget self in entering a discussion."

In the same issue, a letter in the "Free Press" warns against a "growing tendency on the part of college girls to be unnatural, insincere or hypocritical, for the purpose of gaining some hoped-for appreciation or recognition."

Only the transgendered would know just how to behave at Wellesley in 1907.

Dress. Hosiery; "Velvet-grip" hose supporters; jabots; stocks; Ladies' Ready-to-Wear shirtwaists, in madras or linen; walking skirts; dress skirts; walking suits; street gloves; hats; storm coats; English ulsters; and of course, boots. Rubber boots, button boots, riding boots, skating boots, heavy calf street boots. Also: kimonos and lounging wraps. To be worn without boots, one hopes.

Exams. On September 24, the day after Lucile arrives at Wellesley, she has to sit for an examination that takes four days. The exams begin at 8:30 a.m. and last until almost five that evening. Her first exam requires her to translate Cicero, after which she is tested on Latin prose composition. After lunch she tackles Caesar (sections from all four books of the *Gallic War*), then Vergil (anything from any of the six books of the *Aeneid*).

The next day is spent entirely on English Composition and Literature, where she is also obliged to demonstrate at least minimal knowledge of French and German. In 1907, the literature section of the English exam asked that Lucile display "a general knowledge" of Shakespeare's *Macbeth* and the *Merchant of Venice*; the Sir Roger de Coverly Papers; Irving's *Life of Oliver Goldsmith* (old friend!); Coleridge's *The Ancient Mariner*; Scott's *Ivanhoe* and *The Lady of the Lake*; Tennyson's *Gareth and Lynette, Launcelot and Elaine,* and *Passing of Arthur*; Lowell's *Vision of Sir Launfal*; and Eliot's *Silas Marner.*

The "study and practice" part of the English exam, meanwhile, demanded that she be intimately acquainted with Shakespeare's *Julius Caesar*; Milton's *L'Allego, Il Penseroso, Comus,* and *Lycidas*; Burke's Speech on Conciliation with America, or Washington's Farewell Address and Webster's First Bunker Hill Oration; Macaulay's *Life of Johnson* and Carlyle's *Essay on Burns.* A note appended to this list states that "it is taken for granted that candidates will have learned by heart illustrative passages from all poems read."

For the history exam, Lucile needed to know the history of Greece "to the death of Alexander," the history of Rome, both "the Republic and the Empire," and essentially all of English history "with due regard to social and political development." As for American history: everything about the colonial and revolutionary periods, plus "the elements of Civil Government." Not to mention "some practice in drawing maps to illustrate territorial changes." The rest of the exams—covering mathematics, a second language (German or French), chemistry, and physics—all insisted on a similar depth of "general knowledge."

And these were the entrance exams.

PLEASE, GO AWAY AND LET ME GRIND, read signs posted on doors toward the end of each term at Wellesley. Perhaps Lucile posted a similar sign on her door. She may have suffered from benighted ignorance but she was good at grinding. At the end of her first year she received an honorable mention for "a high degree of excellence in academic work."

Field Day. It came as a surprise to me to discover that Lucile was athletic. No one else in my family is particularly athletic, except my daughters, and I figure they got it from their father. But in perusing copies of the *College News* and the Wellesley Athletic Association Scrapbook, I see that Lucile joined the running team her freshman year and participated in Field Day, an all-day event at Wellesley full of tournaments, matches, races, and challenging outfits. That first year, for instance, Lucile and her classmates came onto the field wearing green dunce caps. As girls played golf and tennis and ran races, "trim maids waited to serve peanuts and hot buns" (and probably fell over laughing—they may have been maids serving hot buns to rich girls, but at least they didn't have to wear green dunce caps while they ran a hundred-yard dash).

In 1909 Lucile was elected captain of the 1911 running team and awarded her "W." That year, the same year Robert Peary raced Frederick Cook to reach the North Pole, the 1911 running team beat 1910s.

"The excitement was great," according to the *College News*. Lucile accepted her "W" and, one imagines, vowed to uphold the honor of the running team. The next year she was named head of running altogether, a coveted distinction. Thus she arrived at the center of her hemisphere.

Yet mysteriously, in the fall of her senior year she was "disqualified for health" from running altogether. Though 1911 was again victorious on Field Day, Lucile did not share in their triumph. Her disqualification was mentioned passingly in a letter written by a classmate but with no indication of what health issue disqualified her.

To inquire into this mystery I wrote to the chair of Wellesley's physical education department, without much hope of enlightenment but feeling that I should make at least an investigatory attempt. To my surprise, she sent me Lucile's medical records. These records did not explain Lucile's disqualification as head of running, but they did hint at why she may have left boarding school. "Has been well since fall '06" is noted on a sheet appended to a medical history taken her freshman year. On another sheet she is asked how much time she spends on exercise outside of school and her response jotted down: "a good deal until last year."

So she was sick in the spring of 1906, her junior year in high school, wherever that was, and perhaps during the spring and fall of 1905 as well.

On her medical form, Lucile Kroger is listed as having had the following diseases and conditions:

Measles
Scarlet fever
Whooping cough
Tonsillitis
Enlarged glands
Diphtheria

The last one, naturally, caught my attention. Did she contract diphtheria when her brother Raymond fell sick with it and died? Or did she come down with diphtheria later, when she was alone, away at school? Perhaps it was scarlet fever, measles, whooping cough. All of which could be fatal in 1906. In May of Lucile's senior year a "scarlet fever scare" swept the Wellesley campus, scary enough to make the newspapers, as one student noted when she wrote to reassure her mother that "two of the cases are almost out of the hospital."

Lucile also, at some point, broke her arm.

She was ten years old when she began menstruating, according to those medical records, but her periods were irregular and she had been treated for amenorrhea, having experienced gaps from five weeks to six months between her periods. She had occasional colds.

She wore a corset. At age twelve she began wearing a girdle. (I find this heartrending.) She slept eight hours at night. Her diet was "varied," her appetite "good." Whoever examined her did not record her height or weight; in fact, there is no printed listing for anthropometric measurements on the medical form. The form *does* inquire whether one wears "Union Undergarments." (Lucile did not.)

The final notation on her medical history is dated January 23, 1911. "No illness. Periods more reg: never goes more than 7 weeks now. . . . No discomfort from neck." Most likely she was disqualified as head of running because she hurt her neck. Fell out of bed. Fell off a bike, or a horse, or a fence. (There's a picture of her sitting on a fence, wearing her Wellesley letter sweater—possible evidence?) The easily injured neck. Turn too suddenly to look at a passing goldfinch and you can't look over your shoulder again for a month. Mystery solved.

Or is it? From her college medical history, it's clear that Lucile could have died any number of times during her first twenty years. "No illness" was the exception, not the rule. Maybe the grind was getting to her. Maybe she didn't feel like running anymore. Her heart was beating fast enough already. Life before vaccines was its own

Field Day and she figured she might as well take her time while she had it.

German, Grades. Lucile took French courses all four years at Wellesley, but her freshman year she also enrolled in Elementary German. Besides learning to read, write, and speak German (spoken at home, though evidently not by her), she was required to memorize German poetry. An educational investment that paid unexpected dividends. Fifteen years later, she attended a dinner party in Cincinnati to which my grandfather was invited as well. It had been prearranged with the hostess that he sing some lieder afterward. His repertoire that evening included songs Schumann had composed to the poems of Heine. Most of the guests listened politely, probably wondering when they could expect to get another glass of champagne, then clapped enthusiastically and went back to the party. But as my grandfather was putting away his music, a small red-haired woman came up to him. She said quietly: "I know those poems."

That was the beginning of my grandparents' courtship. Lucile never went past Elementary German, but fortunately she learned just enough German poetry while she was at it or I might not be writing this sentence.

As for grades, despite that commendation for academic excellence her freshman year, Lucile's marks were pretty average. She received a B in German that first semester and a C the second. To my disappointment, she got a C both semesters in English 1. In fact, the only class in which she managed an A was Hygiene. It's sobering to realize that before grade inflation, these grades were considered impressive. (What did she do in Hygiene to get that A?) It was also sobering to receive her college transcript from the Wellesley registrar, who had to order a basement vault to be opened, then unspool a dark coil of microfiche to find it. All four years of Lucile's college academic life are laid out on a third of a page, her grades recorded in a sloping hand by someone with a weakness for orthographic flourishes—the C's look like copyright symbols, while the A's, what few there are, resemble sugarloaf hats. Lucile did her best work in history, chemistry, and economics. She struggled with philosophy (who doesn't?) and astronomy. Too many courses her freshman year (eight) and not enough her senior year (four). Her ambitions narrowed, or her energy waned. Or she was distracted by something beyond Wellesley (love, illness, a new constellation she glimpsed in the stars). Sadly, for me, the granddaughter who has taught college writing courses for two decades, she dropped English Composition that final year.

Halley's Comet, Halloween, Hillary Clinton, Homesickness. As a Wellesley freshman, Lucile was "a diffident, inarticulate girl, struggling under almost unbearable fits of homesickness." That's how she was described by five of her friends in a memorial tribute written for *Wellesley Magazine,* twenty-six years after she first stepped onto the Wellesley campus. Since there were five of them who said she was homesick, it must have been true. As if to agree, Lucile herself twice underlined this observation in her *Life of Oliver Goldsmith:* "A nature like Goldsmith's, so affectionate, so confiding—so dependent on others for the sunshine of existence, does not flower if deprived of the atmosphere of home."

A diffident, inarticulate girl, struggling under almost unbearable fits of homesickness. A wilting flower. How could this be the same woman whom my father confused with a marble statue of Athena?

But then my family is full of shy people, most of whom try to disguise their shyness, some in ways that can look quite gregarious, but meanwhile a lot of quiet shrinking is going on behind the scenes. In my view, Lucile seemed diffident and inarticulate because she was awkward and knew it, and she was afraid, for good reason, of making mistakes. Here she was, the daughter of an uneducated foul-mouthed grocer, at Wellesley College, surrounded by New England intellectuals and bluebloods. Hunnewells, Sedgwicks, Wymans. Chatting about the fine points of Grandma Gertrude's sauerkraut recipe was not going to fly. So what to say? And how in God's name to say it? She wants to please but dreads even more the failure to do so. Later in her life, this will look like reserve. At the moment, it passes for tongue tied.

As for those fits of homesickness, shy people are often homesick because home is the one place where they have already disappointed everyone, at some point, and survived the consequences.

Then again, a lot of freshmen are homesick. I recall watching my mother drive away in a taxi after she dropped me at college and experiencing actual vertigo. A feeling that lasted until about April. I don't know how long it took Lucile to recover from homesickness at Wellesley, but at least by senior year she was recording a friend as saying "How you do talk, Lucile!" and including herself in various "ribald" outings that were full of gossip and roughhousing.

Not surprisingly, Lucile's confidence improved once she had her own home and family. Twenty-six years later, those same friends who described her as diffident wrote that she eventually "forgot herself and the timidity that had hampered her and, with gracious and easy manner became mistress of herself in all situations." Furthermore she displayed "sane, cool judgment," which allowed her to "avoid the fanaticisms and wild enthusiasms of our modern world." She was, they said, full of "high courage and simple poise."

> She rarely volunteered advice or criticism, but when asked, gave it frankly and wisely. Though it might be unpalatable or severe, it never bore a sting, because the recipients knew the infinite tenderness and regard for their welfare in the steadfast friend who offered it.

Even allowing for the solemn hyperbole demanded by memorial tributes, this is moving praise. Lucile grew up to become a reasonable person, calm and measured in a crisis, not hasty or judgmental. Someone who had been shy long enough to know how to keep quiet until called upon to be otherwise. I would like to have inherited these qualities, but mostly what came down to me is a tendency toward homesickness.

To distract freshmen from being homesick, Wellesley made a fuss every year over Halloween. In 1907, the freshmen were entertained at College Hall by the upperclassmen, who staged a "realistic circus," appearing as clowns, a magician, a tame cow, a tiger, an elephant trainer with his "two good-humored beasts," and an assortment of freaks including a bearded lady, a snake charmer, "the Tattooed Woman" and "the Human Pincushion." The girls ate apples and doughnuts and drank cider, had their fortunes told, carved a few pumpkins, and admired the freaks, briefly forgetting that to most of the world they were the freaks, "a race apart," those grinding, commonsensical College Women.

Three weeks later, on November 25, Professor W. R. Brooks of Hobart College, discoverer of twenty-five comets, gave his "Comets & Meteors" lecture at Wellesley, illustrated "with various stereopticon views." During his lecture, he predicted, correctly, the return of Halley's Comet in 1910.

Lucile did not encounter Hillary Rodham Clinton while she was at Wellesley, but as it is currently impossible to consider Wellesley College without considering Hillary Clinton, Wellesley's most famous graduate, she must be acknowledged. Though whether you see Hillary Clinton as a freak or a comet depends on your political leanings.

Ice Cream. Ice cream pops up frequently on luncheon menus recorded in student letters ("Waldorf salad, rolls, strawberry ice cream and crackers") and in advertisements in the *College News*. Every drugstore offered ice cream at the counter. The Wellesley Ice

Cream Company, on Central Street, also sold "Frappes, Fancy Ices, Frozen Puddings and Mousse of All Flavors." Girls walked into the village for ice cream whenever they felt like it. The corset maker, who had a shop up the street from the Wellesley Ice Cream Company, watched them saunter by with joy.

I'm sure walking into the village for ice cream is just as popular at Wellesley now as it was when Lucile was ordering chocolate frappes, though the ice cream has turned "gourmet" and corset makers have turned into physical trainers. Parents must sigh with relief the first time they drive into the town of Wellesley and spot those ice cream parlors. Also the old-fashioned iron lampposts lining the streets. Window boxes overflowing with pink petunias and purple lobelia. Upscale New England "village" shops selling silver butter knives topped with ceramic seashells, monogrammed dog beds, baby clothes made out of organic cotton, cakes of hand-milled French soap.

College is full of risk and experimentation. Parents know this. Their daughters may take drugs or drink too much; they may decide to be vegans; they may major in Africana studies, despite being white and from Scarsdale and having spent their formative years wearing Lanz of Salzburg flannel nightgowns; they may plot to blow up buildings or plan to run for president. But at least at Wellesley they will do so in a secure environment. At least, in the midst of whatever revolution overtakes them, those daughters will be surrounded by silver butter knives and hand-milled French soap every time they step off campus for an ice cream cone.

In Wellesley's residential neighborhoods, ample old colonials rise like schooners from billows of shrubbery, set back from the streets by trimmed lawns and mulched gardens brimming in summer with daylilies and roses. On early fall mornings a bluish mist hovers above the lawns, the houses, the sidewalks and the park benches, making it seem as if the town has sunk into a deep leafy dream of itself. And yet amid all this plush suburban calm, Wellesley College remains a radical hive. A stately hive, with sweeping manicured lawns, manorial brick buildings and Galen Stone Tower rising majestically above the trees around gleaming Lake Waban. But fierce. Combative. (DID YOU KNOW, read a recent hand-lettered sign in the campus center, COLORADO IS TRYING TO BAN BIRTH CONTROL & ABORTION WITH A NEW AMENDMENT? DEFEND YOUR RIGHTS!) Also earnest, industrious, persistent. Abuzz with determined learning. A college that in 133 years has never had a male president. A college that educated the first (and so far only) serious woman presidential candidate, the first woman secretary of state, and also Madame Chiang Kai-shek. A college that inspired a major motion picture, starring Julia Roberts, to promulgate the idea that there's more to life for women than getting married — an idea that, alas, still needs promulgation. A college that has always taught her students that the pen is mightier than the silver butter knife, and that the ability to afford gourmet ice cream should not define one's ambitions.

Jews. Not many Jews on Wellesley's campus when Lucile was walking under the oak trees reciting poems by Heine or getting lost in the double-cross of College Hall, but there were a few, or at least I'm guessing there were a few based on surnames from the Class of 1911: Alma Mosenfelder, Meta Schwab, Nina Weiss. Did Lucile befriend any of these young women? Antisemitism was casual in Cincinnati but endemic, as in the most of the country, and Lucile would have carried whatever prejudices she had at home with her to college, so probably not. Alma Mosenfelder went on to marry a physician and live in St. Louis. Meta Schwab and Nina Weiss also married but their addresses and husbands' professions are not listed in the *Thirtieth Reunion Record of the Class of 1911,* where I got this information. None of them have submitted personal entries. No names of children or descriptions of hobbies, club memberships, war relief efforts. No fond salutes to other members of 1911 or announced plans to attend the upcoming reunion.

It can't have been easy to be Jewish at Wellesley between 1907 and 1911, surrounded by Bible lectures, Bible Study, Mission Study, those constant Christian Association teas and receptions, and with attendance at chapel required at eleven o'clock every Sunday morning. For Jewish girls, like shy girls, keeping quiet might have seemed the only option. No Hadassah on campus, or Shabbat services. Probably no freshmen having crushes on you either. Not an unfriendly atmosphere, exactly, but also not entirely welcoming. Who can blame Alma Mosenfelder, Meta Schwab, and Nina Weiss for neglecting to reply to the *Reunion Record* questionnaire. They had other things on their minds in 1941.

Kinder, Küche, Kirche. I can't say whether Lucile or any of the girls listed above attended a lecture on March 25, 1908, delivered by Jane Addams, world-famous urban reformer, head of Hull House in Chicago, and frequent visitor to the Boston Settlement House, where many Wellesley girls volunteered to work with poor children. But if they weren't at that lecture they heard about it. Jane Addams's topic that evening was equal suffrage and she spoke to a "large and enthusiastic audience" in College Hall chapel. As might be expected, Wellesley was already deep into debates over the proper sphere for women. Even girls who planned to get married right out of college wanted *kinder, küche, kirche* translated into a different language than the one understood by their mothers and grandmothers.

By the fall of 1909, an Equal Suffrage League had been founded at Wellesley (dues: twenty-five cents). Lecturers arrived from England to report on the suffrage movement overseas and instruct Wellesley students on the difference between *suffragettes,* "who go out and fight for votes, and are perfectly willing to knock people down in the process," and *suffragists,* "who choose more peaceful means and confine their work to talking."

Wellesley professor Emily Greene Balch, who would go on to win the Nobel Peace Prize in 1946 for her work as an outspoken pacifist (though, lamentably, Wellesley fired her in 1919 for the same reason), testified that spring at the Massachusetts State House in support of a recent bill for Women's Suffrage. Her words are recorded in the *College News:* "I believe that after a few years' experience of equal suffrage most people will be puzzled to know why it once seemed so questionable a step, why it was so long delayed, and that, looking back, a restriction on suffrage on lines of sex will seem to them a curiously unreasonable one."

A century later, Lucile's half-Jewish great-granddaughter asks me: "Why don't people think gay people should get married? I mean, what's the big deal?"

Lectures, Luminaries. While Lucile was at Wellesley, George Santayana gave a series of guest lectures on the history of the aesthetic. Santayana was then a professor at Harvard and had just published *The Life of Reason,* in which he famously states: "Those who cannot remember the past are condemned to repeat it." A reflection often cited by historians and biographers who feel the need to justify their research; he cribbed it from Euripides, I believe. That same year Professor Munsterberg delivered a series of lectures on beauty; Professor Kuhnmann, on Schiller's dramas; Professor Everett, "Friedrich Nietzsche: A Study on the Ethics of Might." Every week, the *College News* offered cautious summaries of lectures by visiting professors and luminaries. (George Santayana's "History of the Aesthetic" lecture series is approached with a caution amounting to panic.) There were lectures on the condition of women prisoners,

Babylonian myths, the intelligence of raccoons, the peace movement. Bernard Berenson's wife was supposed to lecture on how to tell a good picture from a bad one, but she fell sick so her daughter had to speak instead. "The lecture, though lacking the charm which one deeply interested in the subject might have given it, was nevertheless good," reports the *College News* judiciously, "in that it did not soar over our heads."

May Day. (Largely discontinued.) A bacchanalian event at Wellesley that began at eight o'clock in the morning with seniors rolling hoops from College Hall, down the hill and back up again. Followed by girls dressing up in children's clothing to play games and

frolic around a beribboned May Pole. In a half-empty album of her Wellesley photos, also from my brother's canvas bag, Lucile is pictured on May Day standing with friends, arms around each other's necks, all wearing white dresses very like the one she wore when she was ten.

Wellesley once abounded with gala days like this one, conceived as an antidote to academic rigor and grinding, and also as a way to keep restive young women occupied. "We danced around the Maypole and we ate candy," reads a May Day description in the 1911 *Legenda*, "we had thrills when Betty was crowned Queen; we played tag . . . and pulled curls and stole hair ribbons." A day that ended tristfully, as do all festivities where grown people try to forget for a little while that they are no longer children. "And then gradually we straggled away down Washington Street, under shrouding raincoats, to a late dinner."

Non Ministrari Sed Ministrare. Wellesley's motto. Not to be ministered unto, but to minister. Central to Wellesley's ideals. Lucile will repeat this motto often during the year she spends in France with the Wellesley College Relief Unit, where as part of her job as manager of the unit's general store, she has to drive a one-ton GMC truck on country roads so pocked with shell craters as to be all but impassable. She will repeat this motto especially whenever the truck gets a flat tire.

Off Campus Housing. Like the rest of her freshman class, Lucile lived in the village (or "the vil" as she refers to it) her first year instead of on campus. No one seems to know why Wellesley used to segregate freshmen in this way. Perhaps parents felt freshmen were too innocent to be housed with upperclassmen. (See earlier section on crushes.) A popular pamphlet at the time, *Is College Bad for Girls?,* warned parents of the pitfalls facing their daughters at college, including "Evils of Dormitory Life — Midnight Hours of Who Knows What?" Also: "Reading Improper Novels, Magazines, & Other Suggestive Literature," not to mention the "Forming of Unladylike Habits that May Harm the Health & Morals of a delicate girl — Such as Smoking & Card Playing." Distributed to doctors' offices around the country, this helpful pamphlet also hinted that educated women often did not marry, which could eventually lead to "race suicide."

Miraculously Lucile avoided these dangers, except for smoking. Her first address was at the corner of Washington Street and the Weston Road; I drove by it the other day and it turned out to be a barnlike rooming house with mold-streaked beige clapboards, looming above a busy intersection. Ten or fifteen other freshman lived there, overseen by a house mother. The girls decorated their rooms with artwork borrowed from the college, were fond of chintz pillows and a clutter of books and cards and flowers. Like college students of any age, they kept food in their rooms; they made illegal banquets using spirit lamps, thereby endangering themselves

and others, and left their clothing strewn about. A photograph of the house in 1907 shows essentially the same building as stands there now. Drafty and barnlike. Though now several scraggy pine trees grow listlessly beside the front porch, where I tried

to imagine Lucile sitting on the steps, chewing on a pencil and re-reading Milton's *Il Penseroso* the morning before the entrance exams. On the other side of Weston Road lies a parking lot, where I noticed several cigarette butts scattered on the ground.

Pioneers, Professors. Almost the entire tenured faculty was female when Lucile attended Wellesley. According to one history of the college, *An Adamless Eden,* nearly 50 percent came from New England. None were married. If they got married, they were expected to leave. This was true even for one of Wellesley's presidents.

The faculty included the leading female biologists, chemists, astronomers, botanists, sociologists, psychologists, literary scholars, and historians in the country. Some were famous, like Katharine Lee Bates of the English Department, author of "America the Beautiful." Others were controversial, like Emily Greene Balch in the Economics Department, a socialist as well as a pacifist. Some were romantic, like Sophie Hart, also of the English Department, a tall redhead fond of capes, whose long neck "gave her a Botticelli-like appearance." Others had romances with each other. Especially true of the English Department. ("Students gossiped that Miss Shackford stole Miss Sherwood from Miss Jewett.")

Left out of these romances was Charles Lowell Young, Emersonian scholar and lone man in the English Department.

He was not handsome, Mr. Young—face a little lumpy, eyes small and close set, thinning hair parted in the middle. Old looking even before middle age, Spencer Tracy crossed with Robert Frost. Though an unassuming appearance was not why Mr. Young was left out of Wellesley romances. Nor was it because he was married (a puzzling double standard at Wellesley: male teachers could marry while females were encouraged to remain single). He shared an office with Vida Scudder, known as a severe literary critic; but in a memorial tribute to him in *Wellesley Magazine* she remarked sympathetically on Mr. Young's isolation among an intimidating group of "pioneer women." Laura Emma Lockwood, for instance, whose favorite pastime was to lead students up the hills of South Natick while making them recite *Paradise Lost* from memory. Mr. Young tried to fit in, but failed. He was, oddly, too dainty. Not one of the boys. "His natural attitude toward women was exquisitely chivalrous," noted Miss Scudder dryly, "but chivalry and equal comradeship do not always agree very well."

And yet by his very isolation, the mannerly Mr. Young shimmers into a romantic figure. A modest Transcendentalist. Reticent and self-reliant, doing his best to live deliberately at Wellesley, a quiet Adam among a hotbed of Eves, constructing his own intellectual cabin at the far end of its Edenic shores. According to Miss Scudder, if Mr. Young was met "on his solitary walks, on the Aqueducts or by the lake, eyes open to the invisible might well see Thoreau by his side."

As I was thinking about Professor Young the other day, and what Lucile learned from him (she got a B in his class), my father telephoned. By chance while we were talking he brought up Henry David Thoreau. He mentioned that after Henry Thoreau died, Louisa May Alcott insisted she could still hear his flute in the woods around Concord. My father said he liked the idea of Thoreau's flute continuing to play for Louisa May Alcott. Though how much of that melody belonged to the flute and how much to the listener, one can only guess. My father hears Thoreau's flute in the tulip poplars outside his apartment in North Carolina.

In Young's American Authors course, which she took her senior year, Lucile studied Emerson and Thoreau and the rest of the "Concord Group" and also Cooper, Poe, Lowell, Lincoln, and Walt Whitman. Young was one of the first academics in the country to teach courses on American writers. But Emerson was his hero, and Emerson's essays and poems were what Lucile would have studied most closely, parts of which she would have memorized, as my father has done (Emerson being his hero as well). Passages she might have repeated to herself later whenever she needed to transcend something. In a review of Young's posthumously published book, *Emerson's Montaigne,* the *New England Quarterly* called it "sane, perceptive, beautifully written." The reviewer went on to add, "It is perhaps a merit of Professor Young's work that he suggests more questions than he answered."

In a poem my father sent me a few months ago, there is this stanza:

> Emerson wrote that when you lose your way,
> Drop the reins on the horse's neck and let him
> Lead you home.

Having just suggested a question I cannot answer, I will drop the reins on the horse's neck.

Quiet. Hard to find at Wellesley, especially in the library. Even the new library, built during Lucile's junior year, and much more spacious and accommodating than the old library in College Hall, was noisy. To get away from the whispering and chair scraping and pen scratching, students often went on long walks. The Wellesley campus was, and continues to be, an academic pastoral, much of which was designed by Frederick Law Olmsted Jr. It is almost impossible at Wellesley to resist the narrative drama of outdoors: Sweeping lawns like vast green pages. Tall inspirational oaks full of stirring leaves. Reflective Lake Waban. One of the photographs in Lucile's album shows a young woman sprawled on a hillside under a spreading tree, surrounded by books.

A fresh breeze blows, smelling faintly of wood smoke. Towers of cumulus clouds sail overhead, fabulous white cities, while from a distance comes the honking of wild geese. Walk along the lake, into the woods, across the hills. Into the village, out of the village. College girls suffer fits of walking. A classmate of Lucile's, Helen

Slagle, walked all the way from Wellesley to her mother's house in Brookline, just because she felt like getting a little air. "I left at three and landed home at just six—having gone the eleven miles through Wellesley Hills, Newton Lower Falls, etc. . . . It was a glorious walk." Though when Helen reached home, she found her mother "writing letters and crying, poor dear." Probably best not to walk home, when you're looking for quiet.

Many of Lucile's entries during February and March of her senior year note walks to "the vil," for lunch or to visit someone. Twice she walked all the way to South Natick for breakfast. In February, she writes of visiting a friend for a weekend in Nahant, on the North Shore, along with six or seven others, including her closest friends Ridie Guion and Mary Rhodes Christie, her horseback riding partner, whose brother would one day officiate at Lucile's wedding. Also Cristine Myrick, vice president of the senior class, who eight years later would join Lucile in France. Out they went, ignoring the wintry weather, to "walk along the cliffs to raise an appetite." They sat by the fire and ate chocolates and played with a baby in the house. They took more walks on the cliffs and had a "ribald" time teasing one of the girls, who was "so staid in contrast to the rest of us." (At last someone else was diffident.) At the end of the weekend, Lucile was "sorry to leave, it's so blissfully quiet (except when the baby cries or we rough house)." Quiet is relative. Even being ribald can be a form of peace if it's conducted on one's own terms. In concluding this entry, Lucile notes that everyone in the group is "especially joyous at having missed Glee Club," a different kind of noise altogether.

Religion. Lucile attended chapel on Sundays along with everyone else at Wellesley, though her own religious affiliation was ambiguous. Interestingly, listed on the results of her entrance exam, along with her Cincinnati address, is a space marked CHURCH and after it is written: "Roman Catholic." Which suggests that even after

Barney marched his children out of the church, Lucile clung to the idea that she was a Catholic, if only because Catholic was what she had been while her mother was alive. (The Krogers tried for a while to become Episcopalian. But it didn't really take, which often happens when Catholics, who are used to a certain level of pageantry, become Episcopalians. The Krogers then tried on the Unitarians. At least with Unitarians pageantry isn't much attempted.)

Last year I happened to be on the Wellesley College campus on December 16, the seventy-fifth anniversary of my grandmother's death. Wellesley is only a twenty-minute drive from my house, so small pilgrimages of this sort are not difficult. I took a quiet stroll by Lake Waban before visiting Houghton Memorial Chapel, where Lucile sat through four years of Sunday services. I can't imagine Houghton Memorial Chapel is much different than it was a century ago. Still drafty and echoing, an impressive granite vault that smells ruminatively of mildew and furniture polish. I leaned back in a wooden chair, looking up at the stained-glass windows and the stone arches and pillars, and at the names of deceased alumnae donors chiseled into stone tablets, trying to summon up what Lucile's weekly religious experience might have been as she listened to winter winds tear around the chapel roof while a visiting clergyman intoned from the dais. I remember closing my eyes and making an earnest attempt at reverence. I remember hoping for some sort of visitation. Mostly I remember thinking it was cold in the chapel, that my chair was hard, and that I wanted a cup of coffee.

Societies. Wellesley had six of them when Lucile was a student, and the most desirable was Shakespeare. In 1909 another classmate of Lucile's, Mary Sawyer, writes home to say, "Every 1911 girl I know of, with one or two exceptions, applied for Shakespeare, and there are just nine vacancies." I confess a small flutter of pride that my grandmother was one of the chosen nine. Even at twelve I must have had some presentiment that the Shakespeare Society was a big deal, Lucile's society pin being one of my prized finds from my grandfather's attic. During my own brief theatrical career I used to wear that pin for good luck, which it did not supply. My youngest sister is an actress in Los Angeles and has performed in a number of Shakespeare's plays; I should probably give the pin to her, except she has been doing pretty well without it and why press one's luck?

Each Wellesley society had its own "house," where its members could prepare dinner for each other and retreat from the rest of college life, or pretend to retreat, since college life was the sine qua non of these societies. Shakespeare House is a copy of Shakespeare's timbered Elizabethan birthplace, and like Houghton Memorial Chapel remains largely unchanged from the days when Lucile used to walk in and out the front door, muttering phrases from *Hamlet* to herself ("The air bites shrewdly; it is very cold"). Last spring I wrote twice to the current Shakespeare Society president to ask for a tour but received no reply. Hoping to get in anyway, one afternoon I tried the front door, but it was locked and a small sign warned away trespassers. I was reduced to peering in through the leaded-glass windows. Not much to see: two rather dusty looking downstairs rooms and nondescript furniture. Ostensibly dedicated to intellectual pursuits (i.e., Shakespeare was supposed to be about Shakespeare), and overseen by faculty members, who had often belonged to the same societies as undergraduates, Wellesley's societies were, and I suppose still are, mostly social clubs, formed as much to keep people out as to let people in.

Lucile was apparently untroubled by the exclusiveness of these societies, or at least she never mentioned being perturbed in her *Tagebuch,* even though fierce arguments were being carried on by both sides of the matter. In her day, girls were secretly proposed for society membership and their qualifications dissected; though good grades were required, acceptance or rejection appears to have been otherwise largely arbitrary. This caused great distress among the nonsociety Wellesleyites, and much of the fall of 1909 and the spring of 1910 were devoted to arguing over whether societies should be abolished. A congress on societies was convened, headed by Dean Ellen Pendleton. According to the Shakespeare Society minutes from November 17, 1909, a Miss Kelly, swept up in the furor, announced nobly that she wanted to resign her membership. "Miss Kelly said that she did not believe in societies . . . and wished to withdraw her name for otherwise she felt she would be living a falsehood." Helen Slagle, who walked all the way to Brookline to find her mother weeping in the parlor, recounts in her diary that on Valentine's Day 1910 she went to a meeting of nonsociety members. "Snobbishness was laid much stress on," she notes. Also "the perverting of friendships." Society members were accused of being elitist, discriminatory, and not very nice. That the societies continued despite all the opprobrium, that they are still part of Wellesley a century later, shows how deeply people want to belong to societies, especially after being shut out of them.

The very last entry Lucile made in the *Tagebuch* her senior year was a record of a Shakespeare Society meeting (she was the recording secretary, but she must have recorded the rest of her recording elsewhere). Two girls are "formally received into membership" that evening. What follows may be a secret ritual. If so, I apologize to the society, but not being a member, I feel free to disregard the rules.

During an "initiation ceremony," the girls were "blindfolded with dishtowels and taken upstairs, having first thoughtfully fortified themselves in the rear to guard against expert assaults." The initiates were forced to jump over a basket of firewood, and then they "ran the gauntlet, and were assailed with rolling pins, spoons and wet mops." Roll call followed, during which each society member responded with a quotation from the *Merry Wives of Windsor*. Followed by dinner, prepared by themselves. After first noting that the table's centerpiece, a bunch of celery, has gone missing, Lucile provides the evening menu:

Tomato soup with whipped cream.
Toast.
Frankfurters—fried apples.
Ginger ale. Coffee.

"The dinner was enlivened by many good stories," she writes in her official capacity as recording secretary, "especially from Miss Mortenson, who was responsible for 'The Card Game in Heaven,' 'The Fruit Piece (I'm Looking at the Pair Your Mother Gave You),' and 'In the Family Way.'" The talented Miss Mortenson then concluded with "several corset stories," which were "much applauded." Another ribald evening with Shakespeare, who loved a good off-color story himself, even more than he loved sad stories. No wonder so many girls wanted to belong to the Shakespeare Society. It can't have been for the food.

Tree Day. Celebrated the first Friday in June. Called Tree Day because the freshman class plants a tree, which is then marked with a stone engraved with their class year and remains as their perpetual representative at Wellesley. If the tree dies, another of the same species is planted in the same place.

A century ago Tree Day involved speeches, performances, and processions, which according to one historian of Wellesley, "required elaborate costumes, and a Senior and a Freshman Tree Day Mistress, each supposedly the most beautiful girl in her class." (Lucile was never Tree Day Mistress, I am sorry to report.) The Tree Day Mistresses were dressed like brides and each attended by a court. After much ceremony, a sophomore, designated as Giver of the Spade, presented a freshman, the Receiver of the Spade, with a shovel (presumably the

Spade) to plant the class tree. This was for many years the crowning event of the Wellesley year, not excepting commencement.

As soon as I found out about Tree Day quite naturally I wanted to find the 1911 tree. It was, I learned, an ailanthus, a tree of heaven, also known as stinking sumac because it smells like cat urine. The head archivist at Wellesley found a map for me that showed where each class tree was planted, from 1877 to 2010. One hundred thirty-three trees. I believe I found one hundred thirty-two of them.

Guess which one I couldn't locate.

Which, now that I think of it, seems apt.

Underwear. Large in the early 1900s, often white, made of heavy cotton or flannel. Petticoats, chemises, calf-length drawers. Knick-ers. Sometimes woolen, as in the case of the aforementioned union undergarments. Useful in New England, where it is often very cold. In her Wellesley photo album, Lucile included a photograph of underwear drying outside on a wooden rack. Probably a frequent sight in the days when one's monthlies required a good deal of hand-washed laundry.

The inclusion of this photograph highlights not just underwear, and its importance, but also what is missing from Lucile's Wellesley album. Photographs of the library, for instance. But then, all photograph albums are full of missing pictures. The pictures that are missing, in fact, vastly outnumber the ones in the album.

Vivisection. A major scandal at Wellesley Lucile's senior year. "Wellesley is living in an atmosphere of vivisection these days," writes her classmate Mary Sawyer in a letter to her parents back home in Lowell. "All these disgusting newspaper stories are the limit."

Here is what happened: The Wellesley Zoology Department contracted with a local man "who buys cats people want to get rid of and takes stray cats which are public nuisances." These cats were then purchased by the Zoology Department with the understanding that they were nobody's kitties and did nothing but make the neighborhood smell like an ailanthus tree. An understanding that worked well for everyone but the cats, until their procurer "happened to get a pet cat which had strayed." The owners complained. It was the end of February. Scandals were in low supply. The newspapers went wild. "The Post had a vivid two column account slandering Wellesley and everyone here," reports Miss Sawyer unhappily. (Imagine the headlines: WELLESLEY COLLEGE, DEN OF PUSSY KILLERS.) President Charles Eliot of Harvard had to come to the defense of Wellesley and vivisectionists everywhere.

Lucile herself refers to the scandal in her *Tagebuch* while describing tea with a friend and a former instructor: "much talk about the 'cat' excitement and the unpleasant zoology department. Dotty and Miss L. earnestly discussed vivisection and their crowded social schedules. I don't mean to imply that they were connected," she adds, archly.

But soon enough the Wellesley vivisection scandal was yesterday's news, fit only for wrapping fish and tearing up for kitty litter. Three weeks later the Triangle Shirtwaist Factory in New York City caught fire. One hundred forty-six women and girls were burned alive. Some of the factory doors, it was discovered, had been chained shut.

The word *scandal* was never quite the same.

Wellesley College Scholars. A select group of seniors, which in the spring of 1911 included Lucile. Honored for high academic achievement at Wellesley, apparently bestowed on those who had, like Lucile, a B average, which therefore must have been difficult to achieve. She may have stopped running her last year of college, but she was still grinding. I have to wonder for what, though, since she had no plans following graduation except to go home. That spring the *College News* lists a talk to be given on careers other than school teaching. But the list doesn't go much beyond nursing or library work. Lucile's transcript shows she took mostly history and English courses her junior and senior years, which hints that she herself may have harbored thoughts of teaching (at the very least, it tells me that she was interested in history and liked reading novels). Her *Tagebuch* does not reveal any postgraduate plans. Like most of her friends, she imagined she would become a wife sooner or later, the requirements for which were generally not academic.

Xanadu. First encountered in English 1, a survey course required of freshman. A long slog through Spenser to Hardy. By the time English 1 got around to the British Romantic poets — Byron, Shelley, Keats, and Coleridge — the apple trees and the lilacs at Wellesley were in bloom, the dogwoods, and the tupelos by the lake. Leaning her head on her hand in a classroom inside College Hall, Lucile stares at the first stanza of Coleridge's "Kubla Khan," listening to a fly bump against the window panes, and wondering — as everyone wonders — what would have happened if a "person from Porlock" hadn't interrupted Coleridge "on business" while he was writing down the dream from which he'd just awakened. A soft breeze blows in from the lake, smelling of grass and mud. Lucile breathes deeply and tries to imagine Xanadu, that marvelous pleasure-dome, with its "caverns measureless to man," its miles of "fertile ground." A separate, mysterious world "girdled round" by walls and towers.

> And there were gardens bright with sinuous rills
> Where blossomed many an incense-bearing tree;
> And here were forests ancient as the hills,
> Enfolding spots of sunny greenery.

By the end of the first stanza she knows exactly where Xanadu is. But it will take her the next three years to realize just how much of it is a dream and how hard it will be to awaken back into a world of people from Porlock.

Yearbooks. In the 1911 *Legenda,* Wellesley's yearbook, Lucile appears in an oval photograph staring with amused gravity at the camera. Like all the other seniors in those photographs, she wears a high-necked white blouse—although she also wears a tie, which appears to be unusual—and her hair is upswept in a modified pompadour. She has large, wide-spaced eyes, which I know were pale greenish blue, like my father's. Her face is round—she was plump all her adult life—and her lips pleasantly full. She is not pretty like the gracefully lovely Ridie Guion, a few pages ahead, but her features are attractive, mostly because her face gives the impression, even in this small formal portrait, of a bright vivid frankness. On that particular day she was looking slightly past the camera and over the shoulder of the photographer; her expression is of someone about to make a sly (ribald?) joke at her own expense.

She shares her yearbook page with three other girls. Gertrude E. Kranz is just to the left of her, lowering at the camera under heavy black eyebrows. Beneath Gertrude, Florence M. Kunkel glances away from the camera altogether, a stolid young person with a big clumsy jaw, a small mouth, and a look of military stoicism. Clearly she would rather not be sitting for a photograph at all, and certainly not while wearing a white blouse that looks too tight around the neck; but she accepts that it is her duty, as a Wellesley senior, to be on record in the yearbook.

Below Lucile is Margaret W. Landes, the kindliest-looking young woman on the page, with serene brown eyes and a wide nose, who tilts her head gently to the left and gives the camera a calm, forgiving gaze. She looks to be apologizing for her three classmates, who variously seem to be deploring, ignoring, or laughing at the photographer. By the time he reaches the end of the *K*s, the poor man has been taking senior class photographs all day. He is both tired and harried, used to being treated with more deference by his subjects—local merchants, housewives, schoolchildren—people for whom being photographed is still an event, who view the occasion, properly, as a chance to join history and become fixed in the past. But these are Wellesley women, who have lost some of their deference to history because they have been taught to believe they might play more than a static role in it someday themselves. Even though most of them can't expect to go beyond being wives, schoolteachers, nurses. This is what Keats called negative capability, something they all learned in English 1.

I have no idea whether Lucile socialized with any of the three young women with whom she is pictured in the *Legenda,* but thanks to the *Thirtieth Reunion Record* I do know something of what happened to

GERTRUDE E. KRANZ   LUCILE I. KROGER

FLORENCE M. KUNKEL   MARGARET W. LANDES

them. Gertrude Kranz gave her address at the time as an apartment in Passaic, New Jersey. She was unmarried. In response to a detailed questionnaire asking about avocations and activities, mailed out beforehand by the editor of the *Reunion Record,* she answered that her "avocation" centered on her "black coon cat 'Crispin.'" Florence Kunkel had not married either but was now Dean of Women at the State Teacher's College in Shippenberg, Pennsylvania, and a much livelier and more forthcoming correspondent than her big shy stoical jaw would have suggested thirty years earlier. Florence claimed that her avocations included "books, bridge, buying antiques, Buick-driving, 'Bundles for Britain,' keeping pace with young moderns, feeding the multitudes, tripping the light fantastic."

Reading through the *Thirtieth Reunion Record* of Lucile's classmates, I noticed that it was characteristic of this group of women, all by then in their early fifties, to adopt a wry, jaunty tone when writing about themselves. Europe was in ruins for the second time in twenty years. Pearl Harbor was about to be bombed. And yet the important thing, those good-humored notes suggest, was to avoid self-pity and move through life as nonchalantly as possible, to "trip the light fantastic" instead of tripping over one's own clay feet, despite whatever difficulties or disappointments one may have encountered. Quite a few had recently lost husbands. Their parents had died or required constant care; they themselves had fallen ill. ("I am well, if I am careful"; "The last couple of years have been difficult because of a very serious operation which left my none too good heart in a state.") Yet the tone of these entries is uniformly plucky. Lots of gardeners ("I have had gorgeous Camellias blooming for three months now"). Lots of club members and volunteers (Wellesley clubs, British War Relief, Disaster Relief, prison reform, Girl Scouts, Ladies Guild). Everyone was busy, including the women who list themselves as having no job, no children, no husband. Their advice to the world: If you have to grow old with only a cat for company, do it bravely. Keep up with your friends, make bundles for Britain, and weed your garden.

Many 1911s, of course, did have children. The mothers seem especially proud of their daughters, all of whom appear to be college material and many of them also Wellesleyites. The ones with sons are quietly aware of the coming draft.

A third of Lucile's freshman class never married. World War I may have contributed to these statistics, but these were also the "new women" of the twentieth century, the first sizable group of women who could choose professions for themselves over marriage and motherhood. Though *choice* is deceptive. Lucile's classmates who didn't marry were disproportionately high school teachers. Ethel Anderton, for instance, a Yale PhD, was teaching math in the West Haven School System. Edna Fisse taught social studies in St. Louis; Mildred Gray, English in New Bedford; Ella Pennell, history in Portland, Maine. Ridie Guion was teaching at Milton Academy. Administrators crop up, too, and social workers, secretaries, librarians, one physician, a couple of deans at women's colleges, like Florence Kunkel, and a registrar.

Of the 1911s who married, almost none worked outside the home. Most of them listed their vocation as homemaker or housewife. Mary Rhodes Christie, who got married late to a widower, wrote in tentatively that her sole achievement was "possibly being an acceptable step-mother and stepmother-in-law." Only one correspondent publicly regretted her lack of profession, noting that her vocation was "Generally worthless — Unemployed."

Gentle-faced Margaret Landes is not in the *Thirtieth Reunion Record*. Not even on the "In Memoriam" page, where Lucile appears under 1932, accompanied by Margaret Ulbrich and Grace Lincoln. Although it turns out that Margaret Landes died that year, too.

I had to search back through a series of old *Wellesley Alumnae*

Bulletins to find out what became of Margaret Landes. After graduating from Wellesley she went to Yale to study philosophy; the subject of her doctoral dissertation was Henri Bergson's doctrine of intuition. She received a PhD in 1923, the same year Lucile got married. By 1925 Margaret Landes was professor of psychology and philosophy at Constantinople College for Women in Turkey. Why she alighted in Turkey rather than in a philosophy department in the United States is anybody's guess. Maybe she wanted to travel; more likely she couldn't find a teaching job at an American university. No clubs or gardens for her. No husband or children either. Instead the hot dusty streets of Turkey and veiled, dark-eyed women sitting in her classroom wanting to know about Henri Bergson and his theories of intuition.

What did those women intuit about Margaret Landes? Did they guess how she wound up among them instead of teaching high school biology in Bridgeport or planting azaleas outside a Westchester farmhouse? I find myself so intrigued by Margaret Landes in Constantinople that it's tempting to abandon my grandmother and focus on her instead. Then again, Gertrude Kranz and Florence Kunkel are both intriguing as well, their lives suggesting novelistic possibilities (*My Life with Crispin, The Jolly Dean*), which leads me to the rather obvious realization that everyone's life is a promising novel when reduced to a few lines in a reunion record. Also that every yearbook is full of promising-looking people who have no idea what will happen to them.

Zeal. It is required in college that you become zealous about something. Whether it's religious, political, academic, or social hardly matters. (Ambrose Bierce on zeal: "A certain nervous disorder afflicting the young and inexperienced.") At Wellesley in 1911, young women could be zealous about Equal Suffrage, Field Day, physics, settlement work, Latin declensions, Greek iambics, Shakespeare, social justice, astronomy, zoology, German poetry, Glee Club, the

Debate Club, the History of Aesthetics, table decorations for the Garden Party. They were certainly zealous about ministering to the world's problems, and in 1911 they believed those problems could be fixed. Unchain factory doors. Teach hygiene and gymnastics to the children of the poor. Design more comfortable underwear. Whatever you do, do something! Good-bye to the narrow Victorian world of their mothers, focused on dark kitchens and stuffy parlors. Corsets were loosening. A wider age had arrived.

For some of them it did.

But no matter what became of them later, never again would those women feel as zealous about the future as they felt during their four years at Wellesley, when their abilities and the world's willingness to consider them seemed, briefly, commensurate. Never again would they have such capacity for optimism. They were young. They were single. They were patriotic. Quite a few of them were brilliant. They could walk for miles, up hill, reciting *Paradise Lost* from memory, confident that paradise had not been lost to them, at least not yet. Scarlet fever had just swept by, taking no one with it. The Vote was coming. World War I was three years away. The 1918 flu epidemic was a distant rattle in the chest. World War II was unimaginable. The atom had not been split.

In fact, if there could be a measure for such things, it is entirely possible that zeal for the future reached its zenith at exactly eleven o'clock on the morning of June 20, 1911, as commencement exercises began at Wellesley College, lasting until the final notes of the Glee Club's rendition of "'Neath the Oaks, O Heart of Mine" drifted across the lake and into the trees.

VII

Lucy Birdcage

Love is a kind of warfare.

—OVID, *Ars Amatoria*

In the fall of 1911, a few months after graduation, Lucile traveled back to Wellesley to see Dean Ellen Pendleton inaugurated as the college's fifth president. Several of her friends did the same. In a letter I found in the Wellesley College Archives, Mary Rhodes Christie describes herself and another girl rushing to the Huntington Avenue station in Boston, where "we found Lucile and fell on her neck with shrieks of joy, greatly astonishing the natives thereby." Off they went to visit their old house at Wellesley, Wood Hall, "where tidings of our arrival had preceded us. . . . We were just beaming with joy." The next day they hurried to Houghton Memorial Chapel for Miss Pendleton's inauguration "and greeted so many people so enthusiastically that our coiffures all came down."

My father has insisted so often that he never saw his mother smile — "she was always severe" — that I can't resist pointing out here that Lucile was not only capable of smiling but also of beaming and shrieking with joy. What this says about the nature of memory I'm not sure, except that the minute you use the words *never* or *always* someone else will go hunting for an exception.

WHEN MY MOTHER handed me that fruitcake tin from my grandfather's attic several years ago and I opened the lid, the first thing I saw among Lucile's artifacts was the olive green Kodak packet of negatives she had brought back with her from France after the war. Unceremoniously, I unsnapped the packet and leafed through the yellowed cellophane sleeves that held each negative. As I lifted several of those negatives up to the light, I glimpsed a plump lively looking woman. Who was, in fact, smiling. Not beaming or shrieking with joy but definitely smiling.

Though it was almost a full year before I did anything with that packet of negatives. It was late spring and the classes I was teaching were ending; the usual restlessness was beginning to set in, part anticipation of the summer ahead, part worry that I would not make good use of it, and so one afternoon I decided to take the negatives into Cambridge, to a camera shop that specialized in archival photographs. When I found out how much it was going to cost to print them, I almost lost my curiosity and left the camera shop. But I had gone to some trouble to drive to Harvard Square and had paid for parking, and the pale young woman with orange spiked hair behind the counter was looking at me expectantly, so I handed her the packet and went home with a wan sense of being about to invest more than I had intended or could really afford.

After I got the negatives printed, I had one print enlarged and framed, and sent it to my father.

I was not there when he received this photograph, but knowing his habits, I can imagine the scene. A sunny, mild afternoon in early October. Wearing a gray wool cap and his blue windbreaker with the reluctant zipper—which has just cost him several minutes of irritated fumbling—my father takes his cane and ventures out to his mailbox, one of a bank of mailboxes set into the wall of a covered walkway by the parking lot. Visiting his mailbox is an event in his day, so it is with modest but real ceremony that he opens the little brass mailbox door with his key. To his surprise, instead of the usual assortment of bills that he will put off paying, then forget about, his mailbox holds a padded manila envelope, which he pulls out along with a few circulars. On the way back to his apartment he pauses to look up at the blue sky and admire, as he always does, the English larch that grows outside the entrance to his section of the apartment complex. A light breeze kicks up the slender leaves of the larch tree. Around him the pavement of the parking lot glitters. He wasn't expecting anything in the mail, aside from those bills and harassing letters from creditors and solicitations for magazine subscriptions, so he can't imagine what's in the envelope.

Back in his darkened living room he parks his cane against the sofa and struggles once more with the zipper on his windbreaker, then takes off his cap. Freed at last of every encumbrance, he opens the flap of the envelope cautiously and draws out a large framed photograph, which he brings close to the window to examine. The Levelor blinds on the window are dusty. Several minutes later he is still standing by the window, staring through slatted light at the face which stares back at him. A faint chord sounds in the distance, a doorbell ringing in another apartment.

Or a note from Thoreau's flute.

THE PHOTOGRAPH IS of Lucile standing alone by a rough knotty pine door, wearing a smart-looking high-belted black wool suit and a black official-looking felt hat that is not especially flattering. A bit of a breeze has caught in her skirt. On her feet are sturdy black oxfords. Her hands hang at her sides as if she's standing at attention, though there's a convivial slouch to her shoulders. Behind her,  leaning against the plank wall, is a rifle. She is smiling with good-humored impatience, the slightly challenging, evasive look of someone who knows she is not particularly photogenic, who knows that she will be misunderstood in some essential way by the camera and still cares enough to find this regrettable. Who knows, also, not to be disconcerted by the presence of a rifle.

But there's a complicity in that smile as well, hinted in the amusement playing about the corners of her mouth, a qualified assent to something that's just been said or to a question just asked.

All right go ahead, that smile seems to say. *Go ahead and take my picture.*

If you can.

She was, as I've said, a restless person, a quality she passed down to my father and, more mildly, to me, though unlike us she also had an adventurous streak that occasionally turned rash. My sister Lucy, her namesake, sent me a photograph last year of Lucile sitting in the cockpit of an early seaplane, circa 1913. A placard in the foreground identifies it as Curtiss flying boat, rides available to paying customers. She is wearing a flight helmet and looks, naturally, like Amelia Earhart. The plane looks like something a child would make from balsa wood and glue. That Lucile would entrust herself to such a flimsy contraption strikes me as more fatalistic than restless, but then I am not an adventurous person at high altitudes, unlike my sister Lucy, who has been enam-  ored of airplanes all her life.

That this particular airplane was called a flying boat strikes me as yet another metaphor for biography.

Restless in Cincinnati after col- lege, Lucile enrolled in courses in practical nursing and also "Home Economics," an impressive title for what appears to have been a cook- ing class. A grocer's daughter, even one with a college degree, had better know how to cook, especially if she was soon to be the only daughter at home. In 1913, the Ohio River again flooded downtown

Cincinnati, forcing its citizens into rowboats and for a week the New Vienna became the New Venice. Barney bought a bigger house, on a bigger hill. Not long after the floodwaters receded, he retired his red horse-drawn wagons and bought a fleet of Model T delivery trucks from Henry Ford. Lucile learned to drive. Maybe she took one of those trucks out for a spin, but probably she learned on the family Packard. She was in charge of much of the grocery shopping, from the evidence of those grocery lists at the back of her *Tagebuch*. Apparently she also experimented with raising chickens. (A small rebellion disguised as home economics? Raising squawky chickens behind her father's fancy new house on Crescent Avenue.)

Meanwhile Lucile's three sisters were getting married. Gretchen, the youngest, was first, eloping at seventeen with a much older man, "Captain Jack" Patterson. He carried her across the river to Newport, Kentucky, along with her sister Helen, invited as chaperone. Captain Jack's true intentions may be divined from the presence of Helen. Both girls were tracked down and dragged home by their father, the marriage annulled while Captain Jack was paid off and disappears from family annals, along with whatever B. H. had to say to his daughters about this adventure. Which, given his typical vocabulary, must have sizzled their eyelashes.

And then in 1914 war was declared in Europe and the whole world became restless. Given those courses in practical nursing, I can guess Lucile considered joining the Red Cross, like some of her Wellesley classmates—an adventurous handful of whom wound up in base hospitals in the Bordeaux. But in the beginning the war must have seemed too distant and confusing (Who was Lord Kitchener again? And where exactly was Ypres?), too European, to receive much attention from a young woman living four thousand miles away in Ohio, gathering eggs and watching her sisters get engaged. Besides, her father had asked her to work for him at the Kroger Company as his private secretary.

As Barney's secretary, Lucile learns shorthand and soon begins to forget everything she learned at Wellesley. Why did she ever bother studying the treaty of Westphalia? What is Emerson's Over-Soul to her now? Why *isn't* she getting married? The war continues on, incomprehensibly. It seems mostly to consist of either the Germans or the British trying to cross the Marne. Lucile scans the newspaper, never imagining how often, one day, she will cross the Marne herself. She takes dictation from Barney, learns how to roast chicken and bake brown bread—staples of the Kroger dinner table—and wonders about getting married.

Then, one soft spring morning in May, during a stretch of exceptionally fine days, a German U-boat torpedoed the *Lusitania*. Not a transport ship this time, or even a hospital ship, but a luxury ocean liner that was carrying among its passengers almost 200 Americans, of whom 114 drowned. The nation was horrified. Tens of thousands of soldiers would die in the mud during the Battle of the Somme that summer, but it was the sinking of the *Lusitania* that got Americans aroused. Six weeks later the Secret Service swiped a briefcase from a German doctor in New York City after he visited the publisher of the pro-German weekly *Fatherland*. The briefcase contained documentation on an array of nefarious plots against America: German agents were behind a string of "accidental" fires in American munitions factories; German agents were planning to take over the American supply of liquid chlorine; they were encouraging strikes at American steel plants, persuading labor leaders to promote embargoes of munitions shipments to the Allies, spreading propaganda at American universities and newspapers, even scheming to infiltrate the Chautauqua lecture circuit. These plots were well financed. According to accounts the Secret Service found in the doctor's briefcase, he had about twenty-seven million dollars at his disposal.

Suddenly the war was not so incomprehensible. And just as suddenly it was a bad time to be German in America, even in Cincinnati, though Cincinnati was slow to realize this. The Huns, Germans were being called just about everywhere; and yet despite the *Lusitania* and the discovery of German spy rings, numerous Cincinnatians were still raising funds for German relief and buying German bonds. Still singing *"Die Wacht am Rhein"* in Mecklenburg's beer garden and bidding each other *auf Wiedersehen* on street corners. A stubborn innocence clung to the city. By the middle of 1915 everyone in Cincinnati knew what the western front meant; schoolchildren could trace its line on a map of Belgium and France. But it wasn't until two years later, when President Woodrow Wilson, after epic hesitations, announced that America was at last entering the war that everyone in Cincinnati finally realizes which side of that line they had better be on.

Henry and Chester Kroger both enlisted in the army. Chester was bound for France with Company H of the Twenty-sixth Infantry, First Division, where he would be promoted to second lieutenant and lead a platoon in battles at Montdidier and Noyon in the Somme, then get sent to Soissons to fight in the second battle of the Marne. In *Testament of Youth*, Vera Brittain's famous memoir of her service as British nurse during World War I, she describes her first sight of American troops marching past her camp on the way to the front in April of 1918: "so godlike, so magnificent, so splendidly unimpaired in comparison with the tired, nerve-racked men of the British Army. So these were our deliverers at last, marching up the road to Camiers in the spring sunshine!" Heartening to think Chester might have been one of those "god-like" soldiers in the spring sunshine, especially given what was to become of him.

Back at home, Henry was bound for USA Baking Company 413 in Pike, Arkansas, where he became a quartermaster in charge of bags of flour. One suspects the hand of Barney here—Henry was Bernard Henry Jr., now the eldest boy, heir apparent. No trenches and front lines for him. Kill two birds with one stone: get Henry in the army and get him some good solid grocery experience. What Henry thought about this plan, no one knows. Probably not much,

but he was used to doing what his father told him to do. The army portrait I found of him recently, buried under stacks of old papers in my father's apartment, shows a delicate-faced boy with heart-breakingly soft-looking lips and a worried gaze. He has curly red hair and gingery eyebrows and he looks entirely unprepared for what life was going to present to him, and entirely aware of it. As for Barney's part in the war effort, he got ap-

pointed to the Ohio Defense Council by the governor to keep an eye on food supplies.

Downtown in Cincinnati, Erkenbrecher Avenue was changed to Albany Avenue. The conductor of the Cincinnati Symphony Orchestra, Dr. Ernst Kunwald, found himself arrested and thrown in federal prison as an "enemy alien" after tearfully confessing to an audience one night that his "heart" was with Germany, right after the orchestra finished playing the "Star-Spangled Banner." The concertmeister, Professor Emil Heerman, was arrested as well but later released; he promptly sank his savings into Liberty Bonds in a show of fiscal patriotism. Maybe he bought them from Barney Kroger, who was, as usual, ahead of the game and had been promoting Liberty Bonds since the first days of the war. German was no longer spoken at schools. People started Anglicizing their names, though Kroger, with two sons in the army and a fistful of Liberty Bonds, stayed Kroger.

ALL THROUGH THE war Lucile worked for Barney; she was a trustworthy employee in untrustworthy times. In 1916, she wrote in to the *Class of 1911 Reunion Record* that she had "a definite position as

Treasurer of the Kroger Grocery and Baking Company. I also act as my father's private secretary." A job she'd held for "nearly a year and a half," and which she liked very much, although, she added, "I am certainly looking forward to my vacation in June." She worked through the flu epidemic of 1918, during which a quarter of the country got sick, though as far I know she did not.

In France, the war was intensifying for American troops. The following is from an official war bulletin, issued on July 16, 1918, which I found in Mark Sullivan's popular series on U.S. history called *Our Times,* not especially known for objectivity, which is where I also found the information about German spies trying to infiltrate the Chautauqua lecture circuit.

> Fighting on the Western battlefront continues unabated from Chateau-Thierry to the Argonne, with the Allied lines holding firmly nearly everywhere. More complete details of yesterday's bitter fighting disclose that the American soldiers, who had never before played a part in this great struggle, withstood the savage rushes of the Germans like veterans and held them at the most vital point in the allied line. Chateau-Thierry was the pivot about which the Germans hoped to swing their lines, but the courage and tenacity of the Americans fooled them.

Thousands of miles away from the breakfast table in Cincinnati, where dispatches like this were undoubtedly read with great interest, was Chester, for whom "bitter fighting" and "savage rushes" meant something entirely different than for everyone reading the newspaper.

By the time the armistice was declared four months later, on November 11, Lucile was nearing thirty years old. She had helped direct a company with nearly five thousand stores for almost three years.

As treasurer, she would have been intimate with every aspect of the Kroger Baking and Grocery Company, from the number of delivery trucks out on the road at any given moment, to the exact cost of a shipment of Smyrna figs, to how much Barney spent on newspaper ads and precisely what time he liked his midmorning cup of Kroger coffee.

Five months later, Henry returned home knowing a lot about flour. Chester returned home a decorated hero. Severely wounded at Soissons, wounded four times in two days, finally shot in the head by a machine gun, he refused to be evacuated and stayed to urge on his platoon, "staggering from loss of blood" (quoted from his citation), until he fell, for which he was awarded the Distinguished Service Cross. He was written up in all the Cincinnati papers with his photograph included, to his father's immense pride, thereby relegating Lucile to the background, also costing her that treasurer's job with the Kroger Company.

Though Chester has no head for numbers. Maybe he once did, but not anymore. In his head now is a steel plate, inserted to replace lost occipital bone. In his head now is a sheet of pain, which rattles every time the weather changes. And behind that sheet is mud, the thick yellowish viscous mud of Picardy. And bombed cottages, blackened trees, shell holes, rubble, trench mortar emplacements. Barbed wire, sandbags, chalk cliffs. Men on stretchers, men without legs, men without most of their faces, men eating rations while sitting on the bodies of other men, the stench of men who have been dead for days under a hot July sun, their bodies bloated and buzzing with flies. He can't forget any of it. He never forgets any of it.

(My father cannot forget Uncle Chester galloping on horseback across my grandfather's front lawn in the 1930s, believing he was charging an enemy machine-gun nest. Chester was a huge man who sometimes liked to wear a service revolver strapped to his thigh. In the end my grandfather, who was not without a certain courage of his own, talked Chester down from his horse and invited him into the house where, wisely or unwisely, he offered him a drink.)

With his boys back in Cincinnati, Barney promises both Henry and Chester executive jobs at the Kroger Company. Any father would have done the same. The trouble is, there are only so many executive positions to go around. Plus how many Krogers do you need to screw in a lightbulb? Anyway, daughters belong at home.

Oh, THE WORLD is such a hard place! Here is Lucile, so intelligent, so capable, a college graduate who can drive a car and roast a chicken and keep track of millions of dollars in ledger books, unmarried, about to be unemployed. Unneeded by anyone. The terrible phrase *on the shelf* comes to mind. It is spring 1919. The forsythia is in bloom. Gertrude has just had a baby and is absorbed in baby rattles and bassinets. (She is having sex.) Helen and Gretchen are both engaged, Gretchen for the second time, and planning their weddings. (Planning to have sex.) Barney is, as usual, busy. Even Aunt Ida doesn't have time for her, being preoccupied at the moment with bleaching all the bedsheets and spring cleaning that mansion on Crescent Avenue. (Aunt Ida's version of sex.)

Yet how can Lucile be resentful of her brother Chester, who sacrificed so much in the war? Or of Henry, sacrificing himself to please his father? Yet how can she *not* be resentful, with her superior executive experience and that head for numbers, which is currently calculating her dwindling opportunities? Dull panic sets in. It is an awful feeling to have been necessary and then suddenly not to be. Maybe one of the worst feelings there is. No surprise that Lucile cannot tolerate it for long.

ONE MILD AFTERNOON as Lucile is shut up in her bedroom, rereading Emerson on self-reliance ("Trust thyself: every heart vibrates to that iron string") and trying to avoid Aunt Ida's mops and brooms, the latest *Wellesley Alumnae Bulletin* arrives in the mail. For the past year, she has been following reports of Wellesley relief units sent to France. Their brave exploits — searching for wounded American soldiers in French hospitals, driving ambulances and dodging shells, running a recreation hut, handing out chocolate and cigarettes just behind the front lines — have been well publicized.

In this issue, an article describes a new unit just being formed, a reconstruction unit to be posted in the Aisne region near Château-Thierry, where American troops massed to push back the Germans during their final drive toward Paris. Exactly where, in fact, Chester was wounded. Several girls Lucile knows from Wellesley have already been selected. Her friend Cristine Myrick and also two younger graduates, Frances Bogert and Berenice van Slyke. Cristine will be the unit secretary; she has, as well, a degree in dietetics. Berenice has a social work degree; Frances is a nurse.

Lucile reads the article twice. By coincidence, a few days later she gets a letter from Cristine, who wonders if Lucile might be interested in going to France? There's a new unit that needs someone to run a general store. She can drive, can't she? And speak French? Just a thought. Naturally, with her job, Lucile must be so busy . . .

Though she hesitates.

Maybe she wants to see if Barney is really serious about giving her job to Chester, who has been convalescing at home since the end of March. Newspapers are beginning to publish announcements about the new Wellesley Unit and their upcoming mission in France. Four weeks go by. At the end of April, Lucile is still not on the unit roster.

He must have been serious. Two months later Lucile was on a Dutch steamship crossing the Atlantic Ocean, headed for a tiny ruined French village called Lucy-le-Bocage. A village situated in the middle of what was being referred to at the time as "the plain of death." She had with her a trunk, a new uniform, a mink coat, and her No. 2 Brownie camera. Also an attitude which I can only guess at: a combination of audacity, idealism, pent-up sexual energy, and unexamined hurt feelings. Or maybe a different combination altogether. But whatever ushered her onto the deck of that Dutch steamship in 1919, like whatever persuaded her into the cockpit of that Curtiss flying boat, seems more than a product of simple restlessness.

The News for May 22nd gave the names of the members of the Reconstruction Unit. Passports have been obtained and they will sail on June 11th, following Miss Stimson who sailed May 14th.

It is now expected that that three additional members will sail July 2nd. These are:

Dr. Mary Marvell, 1894, of Fall River, where she is held in high esteem. She is a graduate of Johns Hopkins Medical School, 'oo, has served as interne in the N.E. Hospital for Women and Children in Roxbury. . . . Her specialties are bacteriology and pathology. . . .

Julia Larimer, 'o7, has taught in the schools of Topeka, Kansas, and New York City. For two years she has been head of the boarding department of Miss Barstow's School, Kansas City [and] has served with great success in executive capacity in Red Cross work in Kansas.

Lucile Kroger, 'II, has taken a year's course in Home Economics at the University of Cincinnati, her home city. She has been treasurer of the Kroger Grocery and Baking Company, and buyer for the Premium Department. She is a practical nurse and has had considerable experience in farming, gardening, and raising chickens.

—Wellesley College News, June 25, 1919

Ten Wellesley graduates, each over twenty-five years old and possessing "a useful skill," ranging from medical degrees to backgrounds in social work—and in Lucile's case, executive know-how combined with some knowledge of nursing and her "considerable experience" in farming and chicken raising—are selected for the Wellesley College Reconstruction Unit in the spring of 1919, and designated, by request of the French government, for the Aisne. This is the *région dévastée*, a swath of farmland and vineyards between Belgium and Paris that was systematically destroyed during the Germans' advance in the summer of 1918, where they were stopped at the Marne by American troops. Selections were made by the Wellesley War Committee, a group of alumnae that included Candace Stimson, sister of Henry Stimson, former secretary of war, and then approved by the State Department.

It made news across the country: "college girls" heading off to help repair battered France.

> *Wellesley College girls are to work where their brothers and sweethearts fought. At Château Thierry and at Belleau Wood the Wellesley unit will start their initial work of reconstruction.*
>
> *To Wellesley College the French have assigned 20 villages, 12 in the vicinity of Belleau Wood and eight on the Marne east of Château Thierry.*
>
> —*Evening Record,* Boston, March 22, 1919

Medieval hamlets. Stone cottages surrounded by fields, woodlands, apple orchards. Where women still wash clothing in cold outdoor washing pools and men still plow with oxen, and a town crier still beats a drum and shouts announcements. In the center of each village stands a church, unless it has been bombed to nothing. Also a well, unless it has been poisoned, or a body was thrown down it, in which case it is no longer a well but just a hole in the ground full of bad water. No shops, no cafes, not even a post office—only a *facteur,* who before the war cycled from village to village with his scuffed leather mail pouch, and will do so again, unless he was killed at Chemin des Dames, or the Argonne, or Verdun.

*About Belleau Wood—that section of France the marines
and doughboys wiped up at the start of the big American
push—hardly a home stands. The cottages and farms of the
villagers have been shattered by the fire.*

*And a unit from Wellesley, the great American college
for young women, has been assigned by the French Government to undertake the reconstruction of these villages.*

—*Chicago American,* May 28, 1919

Château-Thierry was the local market town, known before the
war for her eponymous castle and for her most famous son, Jean de
La Fontaine, who set *Aesop's Fables* in this same countryside, among
the sloping fields and old slow rivers—the Marne, the Ourcq, the
Aisne, the Oise. A countryside that looked about the same at the
beginning of the war as it did in the seventeenth century when La
Fontaine was sitting by his fire in Château-Thierry in a powdered
wig and ruffled collar, dreaming up those wise tales of careful ants
and careless grasshoppers, talking frogs and spiders and crows. Each
fable with a moral attached. "We believe no evil till the evil's done,"
he wrote one afternoon, scratching on a piece of parchment with
his quill pen. Never believing such fabulous evil could be done to
his own birthplace, all the cottages turned to rubble and rafters, the
forests bewitched into tree stumps.

And no particular moral for any of it.

TEN MILES AWAY, Lucy-le-Bocage, where the Wellesley
College Reconstruction Unit was to be headquartered, must have
looked like a village a child might have built out of blocks and then
kicked down in a temper; one cottage left standing while the one beside it is half sheared away, the interior open to the road, mattresses
and tables ruined by rain. Wind blows through the rooms of the half-
open cottage, lifting the edge of what's left of a cheap muslin curtain,

stirring a few straws of hay drifted in from the farmyard. A china cup has been left on a table, sitting there for weeks and months, filling with rain, as if waiting for someone to pick it up.

The Germans shot all the village dogs. They also cut down every apple tree in the orchard just outside the village. Even the birds were gone. When the snow fell and covered the village, it was a relief.

Just before Christmas, the villagers who left Lucy when the fighting began, or who were taken away by the Germans, start to come back in twos and threes, most on foot, wheeling their possessions along in handcarts. They did their best to live through the winter in their roof-less cottages, tacking oiled paper over the empty window frames and stretching canvas tarps over any room with three walls. Some people, whose cottages were entirely destroyed, lived in cellars.

THE FIELDS ARE still full of mines and unexploded shells and grenades, so when March comes and the snow melts the villagers wait for the Service de Desobusage to clear the fields before the men start plowing. In the meantime, they roll up barbed wire into bales and collect abandoned things that might be useful, especially anything wooden that can be chopped up for firewood. Sometimes boys wander into the fields, though this is forbidden, to scavenge for brass buttons and pocketknives and bullet casings, flares, dummy shells. One afternoon they find a skeletal human hand attached to part of an arm, said to be American by the wristwatch that goes with it. For a half hour the boys chase each other around the village with the hand, holding it out like a claw, until the old curé catches them with it and takes it away. No one asks what he does with the hand. Or the wristwatch.

In June, as red poppies bloom among the shell craters, five U.S. Army soldiers drive into the village in two trucks. It takes them a day to set up a white canvas hospital tent in the muddy beet field behind the mayor's house. They lay duckboards across the mud, fill the biggest shell holes, and build a little wooden outhouse about fifteen yards away. Into the tent they carry twelve iron bedsteads, twelve mattresses, and crates stamped Red Cross. Then they close the tent flaps and drive away.

That evening some of the village children meet behind the mayor's house to look at the tent. The children are skinny and somber, with big watchful eyes. They wear whatever clothing has been found for them — oversized black dresses or trousers, woolen tunics, wooden sabots, a blue soldier's cap. Some have been back in the village for five or six months, some for only a few weeks. The smallest children have not realized they are back at all since they don't remember the village they left, or if they do, this isn't it.

In the gray evening light the tent looks even bigger than it is, both ghostly and promising. The children pace around it slowly. Who will live there? They can't imagine, though they've been told. The outhouse is even more interesting. Especially the little square window set in the door, covered by a square of chintz fabric; inside, instead of two narrow planks laid above the pit, like most outhouses, there is an actual wooden toilet seat.

A few days later seven women arrive by truck, riding in the truck bed on top of their trunks and bags. Americans. All of them in fitted gray wool uniforms. Five of them young, at least they look young, in a way that even the youngest woman in Lucy no longer does.

The mayor greets the American ladies in his courtyard, bowing over each of their hands. It's his beet field they are renting, his

barn they are renting to house their "fleet" (that's what they call it), an old *camionette,* a truck, a touring car. He's pleased to act as their host. The women explain, in awkward French, that they are a reconstruction unit. They explain that they all went to Wellesley College in Massachusetts. The villagers do not know what Wellesley College is, or anything about Massachusetts, but they are glad that the women have come to their village. Americans are very popular. Inside what's left of the church, on a shattered lintel, someone has carved the words: GOD WITH GERMANY, AMERICA WITH FRANCE.

Standing in the hot dusty sunlight in their gray wool uniforms, the women declare they want to help the villagers rebuild their cottages and start a new school for the children. They want to teach gymnastics, and running games, and calisthenics. One of the women is a doctor and one is a nurse and they intend to start seeing patients the very next day. They promise the mayor that they will requisition building supplies and wooden barracks for the villagers whose cottages were too damaged to be rebuilt. They promise to set up a general store to sell pots and pans, sheeting, stovepipes, shoes, blankets, even glass for the broken and missing windows. They promise to speak to the *préfet* in Paris about the Service de Desobusage, which still has not come to clear the fields of unexploded shells, and to arrange for a detail of German prisoners, interned two miles south, to help with the reconstruction.

A lot of promises, think the villagers. But the next day six or seven German prisoners march down the Marigny Road, accompanied by two French officers on horseback. Children stare. A stack of wooden palettes across from the tent turn out to be a dismantled wooden barracks, on loan from the U.S. Army. This, the women tell the villagers, will soon be a community room and the doctor's dispensary. The community room will have tables and wicker chairs, chintz curtains, and even a piano. The villagers can come in and sit by the stove and knit or play checkers and read magazines, if they want, or learn English. The villagers look doubtful. Most of them have never heard of a community room. Or read a magazine.

The German prisoners put up the prefabricated walls and then add a roof. For several days the villagers stand around with their arms folded and watch the Germans hammer nails and saw boards. The Germans are being supervised by one of the American women as well as by the French officers. The villagers wonder blandly about shooting them. But after a while they get used to the sight of Germans working in their village and go back to trying to fix up their own cottages.

Two weeks later, three more American women arrive, one of them with bright red hair. The village children present them with bouquets of wildflowers. Their mothers bring baskets of eggs. The doctor and the nurse have already seen every child in the village, stuck a tongue depressor in each of their mouths, listened to their lungs with a stethoscope, and then handed them a lollipop. The children hadn't known what to do with the lollipops, until the nurse showed them. One child kept her lollipop to wear on a ribbon around her neck. Too pretty to eat.

Every day two of the women walk around the village, knocking on doors. The villagers always invite the women inside and offer them coffee, even if they don't have any coffee. The women ask questions and write down their answers in notebooks. Are you married? Was your husband killed or wounded in the war? Can your children read? Can you read? Do you have any furniture? Are you sick? Is anyone in your household sick? Do you have a garden? Do you keep rabbits? The villagers find these questions impertinent, but the women smile pleasantly and offer to hold the baby, so why not answer?

I HAVE DOCUMENTS from the Wellesley College Archives that give me an idea of what life in Lucy-le-Bocage was like for my grandmother and her fellow relief workers: scrapbooks, official reports, articles in the Wellesley newspaper, and photo albums left by unit members. I also have a fragment of a journal kept by Lucile herself (or maybe the fragment was all that was written), twelve small loose-leaf pages stuck inside her *Tagebuch*. War awakens what it doesn't destroy—my father once told me that his stint as an enlisted man in the navy was the first time he got to know men his age who hadn't gone to prep school—but there's not a lot of awakening in Lucile's journal. Written first in English, then in French, it follows her calmly, even phlegmatically, from the day she waves good-bye to the Hoboken Piers, to the afternoon of July 25, when she sits writing in that stuffy hospital tent at Lucy-le-Bocage, dust motes swirling around her bed, and then breaks off midsentence.

July 2, 1919

Started this morning at twelve o'clock after a blissful week in N.Y. I arrived Thursday and went at once to
the Vanderbilt. Had a fitting in the afternoon and dinner
with Ridie. Met my co-workers for the first time. Friday
afternoon Arau arrived and we had dinner together at
the Samovar on 36th street. It was pouring rain so we sat
in the Waldorf all evening & talked. Saturday morning
we went down to Battery Park, saw the Aquarium and
watched the ships, then went through the Woolworth
bldg. up Wall St. & wandered about Trinity churchyard
where we saw one of Arau's ancestor's graves—William
Bradford. In the afternoon we went riding up to the end
of Riverside with Connie & Ridie & saw the Atlantic &
Pacific fleets in the Hudson. Went out to dinner & to see
Somebody's Sweetheart at night. Sunday sat in Central
Park & watched the small boats on the lake. Monday
shopped, Tuesday evening had dinner on the Waldorf
Roof then rode until about twelve. Arau came to the boat
with me but left about eleven as he couldn't come on
to the dock. Met Miss Lathrop and Mrs. Shields at the
ticket gate. Strange coincidence. Hate to say good-bye but
it must be done.

A gay montage, not so much restless now as lightheartedly energetic, and so privileged, especially compared to what she's about to
encounter in France. But who *is* this romantically named Arau, who
came to see Lucile during that "blissful" week before she sailed?
Who took her to Trinity churchyard to visit his ancestor and America's first publisher, William Bradford (does this count as introducing
her to the family?), then swept her off to the Samovar on Thirty-sixth
Street and the next night to see *Somebody's Sweetheart*? With whom
she talked one entire rainy evening?

Lucile is awfully brisk about Arau, whoever he is; he scarcely gets more mention than the Waldorf roof. *Hate to say good-bye but it must be done.* He may have been somebody's sweetheart, but he wasn't going to be hers.

Briskness pervades her description of her transatlantic voyage as well. Lucile sailed from New York on the *Nieuw Amsterdam,* of the Holland America line, an aging seventeen-thousand-ton ocean liner pressed into service as a transport ship during the war; she arrives in France in mid-July, almost exactly a year to the day when Chester was wounded in Soissons. The rest of the unit, including one of the two doctors, had sailed two weeks earlier and were already setting up camp at Lucy-le-Bocage.

Lucile writes that the voyage is "very uneventful" (though she has never been at sea before). She and Julia Larimer, the unit director from Kansas, take French lessons every day from another passenger. Lucile observes the "queer mixture" of people on board, "nine or ten nationalities in the 1st cabin, Spanish-Portugese-French-Italian-Dutch-Chinese-German-Japanese-English & American." The weather is fine. On to Paris.

> July 16 — Lucy-le-Bocage — Wednesday
> Yesterday did most of my [Paris] shopping — had a fine shampoo and lunch at Columbines, went to the Red Cross to see Charlotte Baueron but she was busy, but ran into Irene Brewer who is stationed in Laon, driving an ambulance. In the afternoon, Dr. Marvell and I went to Mrs. Shields for tea. On the way I stopped to see Major Warren, Polly's brother-in-law who is just as attractive as ever. Mrs. Shields has a charming apartment in an old house, beautifully furnished with lovely old furniture, prints and books. I had dinner alone and wrote letters afterwards. Today I shopped and had luncheon with Miss

Larimer & played about afterward. We all came out [to
Lucy-le-Bocage] in our big camion sitting on our trunks.
It is a gorgeous night but we are all tired and must go to
bed in the big tent where all twelve of us sleep for the
present. Tomorrow will go into more detail about camp,
and Lucy, etc.

A rather casual account for a youngish woman from Ohio who
has never traveled outside the United States, who suddenly finds
herself plunged into and then out of the motley splendor of postwar
Paris. Paris! Where only two weeks earlier President Wilson and
Lloyd George had signed the peace treaty in the Hall of Mirrors in
Versailles; they'd left town so recently their bedrooms were still being aired. Edith Wharton was living in the Faubourg Saint-Germain;
Gertrude Stein and Alice B. Toklas were racketing about the Left
Bank in their Ford motor car, dropping in on Picasso and his Rus-
sian dancer wife. Soldiers, diplomats, peaceniks, journalists crowded
the cafes, drinking aperitifs and smoking cigarettes, arguing about a
new world order, still hung over from the wild celebrations along the
Grandes Boulevards.

But shampoo, shopping, attractive Major Warren, tea with Mrs.
Shields in her charming apartment—that's all Lucile has to say
about Paris. She runs into this and that acquaintance; she "plays"
about; she might have been in downtown Cincinnati, having lunch
at Pogue's department store. Is this offhandedness the sign of a confirmed provincial, a rube on the Continent? Or the token of a true
sophisticate, at home almost anywhere?

Even more curious is her initial impression of Lucy-le-Bocage.
First, that breezy account of her bumpy ride in the back of a truck
from Paris to Château-Thierry and from there to Lucy, sitting on her
trunk—no description of the destruction she saw along the way. Of
her arrival that afternoon in the decimated village that will be her

home for the next ten months, she notes nothing at all. Only that it is now a "gorgeous night."

What troubles me most, of course, is that little "etc.," scribbled at the end of the entry. How careless it looks. And what does it stand for? Not, God forbid, for the devastation itself. Is it simply shorthand for all that Lucile could not write down in her loose-leaf journal, because she was too tired, because she was overwhelmed (though she sounds so cool), because she was sharing a tent with eleven other people who wanted to go to sleep and did not have time for a fuller account?

I have to think so. That same "etc." resurfaced in her last letter to Ridie Guion thirteen years later, during another period when Lucile confronted devastation, this time her own. Clearly she was not someone who liked to dwell on suffering, which is not the same thing as ignoring it. But for the first time I get a glimmer of what my father means when he says she seemed "remote."

July 18—Lucy-le-Bocage

It's hard to know how to begin about Lucy. It is so different from anything I have done before. Our settlement is in a field on a hill at the edge of the village. At present a big hospital tent furnishes our sleeping quarters. There are twelve beds, real ones of iron, with mattresses & sheets. There is no floor, only a heavy canvas over the field. I had to prop up one leg of my bed as it was in a deep shell hole.

Our French barracks contains a dining room-kitchen-storeroom-office & dispensary for the doctors. We have a chauffeur, a queer duck from the West who was wounded at Chateau Thierry & later drove a Red Cross ambulance. Then we have two maids who come in for several hours each day to cook & clean. It is a real community life, everyone helps. Fortunately at the moment we have

Boches to do the hard work, carrying and emptying water, chopping wood, Etc. I don't know what we shall do
when they are gone.

Etcetera this time of course refers to the labors of the "Boches,"
German prisoners who had been brought in to do the "hard work"
for the unit, including constructing their barracks and dormitory.
A collection of men who, from the photographs I've seen, would
not have looked out of place walking down Erkenbrecher Avenue.
Lying in bed at night above that shell hole, did Lucile reflect on
her hereditary connection with these "Boches" who are carrying
water and chopping wood for her? Any of whom might be a distant
cousin? Any of whom might have fired the machine gun that all but
killed her younger brother? If those thoughts occurred to her — and
they must have — she didn't reveal them. She is not a confessional
diarist. Yet to this composed entry she adds a curiously revealing
endnote:

> I have not done very much today, and as a matter of fact
> I don't quite see where my place in the Unit is to be. I'm
> supposed to be purchasing agent & assistant chauffeur &
> perhaps help with the housekeeping.
>   Alors nous verrons.

Alors nous verrons. We shall see.
A great expectation, or a small one, depending on what kind of
revelation one is hoping for.

THE AMERICAN WOMEN work very hard. They are always
walking, driving, organizing things. Even in the rain. One of them,
however, the tall sharp-nosed skinny doctor with glasses, does not

stay very long. She goes back to America before the fall and no one seems sorry to see her go, least of all the nurse. But the other doctor stays. She knows a lot about children. That they need to be weighed, for instance, and measured, and given milk to drink instead of coffee, though everyone knows children prefer coffee to milk. Two days

L. Kroper   G. Crocker   C. Myrick   R. Lindsay
B. van Slyke   F. Roger   Dr. Marvell
J. Larimer   Dr. T.J.   J. Drew

a week, villagers are invited to visit the doctor in her *dispensaire,* at one end of the tent, and the doctor will give them whatever they need: bandages, ointments, pills, sometimes a shot, sometimes a peppermint.

As soon as the barracks are finished, the American women organize a fete, the fete of St. Rémy. In the beet field they hold sack races for the children—the children have to be taught what a sack race is—and on boards propped on sawhorses outside the new barracks they serve cake and apple cider. The fete is a great success. The next day the Service de Desobusage finally appears and villagers stand in the lanes, watching explosions in the fields as shells and mines are uncovered and detonated.

A chauffeur for the American women now lives in the mayor's barn with the unit's three vehicles. Irish, though he has an American accent. He is very good at repairing engines; sometimes he makes the parts himself out of machine gun cartridges and what he can salvage from ammunition dumps. Mostly he drives the doctor and the nurse to different villages. Sometimes he drives to Paris to pick up supplies. All the villagers expect him to fall in love with one of the American women, but instead he falls in love with one of the villagers. One of the Desabeau sisters. The prettier one.

July 24 [in French]

It is necessary now that I write my journal in French because the practice is very good for my French. We have been here one week tomorrow night. Friday I drove the Ford with the doctors Marvell and Taylor-Jones and the nurse Frances Bogert to Belleau and after that I went to Chateau Thierry. I was a little afraid, driving the Ford for almost the first time. But everything went well. I went to the market and bought vegetables. Everything costs a lot. Chickens cost 20 francs, eggs are one franc each.

Clearly Lucile was still taking chickens seriously. Her duties soon included weekly trips to Paris and Laon to visit Red Cross relief warehouses and anywhere else that she could buy goods cheaply. Shoes, aprons, pinafores, pots and pans, stovepipes, material for pants and blouses and dresses, needles, thread, forks, knives, hammers, nails. When she visited Paris, she drove sixty miles each way in a rusty GMC truck that often broke down on lonely half-exploded roads.

> We have established a large store in the tent where we sell everything from shoes to stoves at wholesale rates or less. . . . In addition to the stock on hand, we take orders for anything anyone wants, and Lucile Kroger spends a good part of every week scouring Paris for bargains in men's shoes, wash boilers, lamps and sheeting.
> —Cristine Myrick, *Wellesley College News*, October 30, 1919

Sometimes another unit member rides with her, but often she drives alone through miles of ruined countryside into that mazy, traffic-clogged, luminous city. Crossing the glittering Seine on one of its dreamlike stone bridges, she finds her way down rain-scented streets crowded with shops and wrought-iron balconies and pots of red geraniums. Paris seems almost untouched by the war. Prim little girls walk to school in navy blue uniforms and crisp hair ribbons. Old ladies in black dresses sweep doorsteps. Crates of brilliantly colored vegetables stand at outdoor markets, where one can buy fish, apricots, chocolate. At cafes with striped awnings people sit at outdoor tables drinking wine in the afternoon. Overhead the sun is caught in tracery of branches arching above the boulevards, gleaming along the wet sidewalks. Soldiers with their arms around women. Old men sitting over coffee and smoking cigarettes, looking at women walking by. Women everywhere, young lovely women, in severe and beautiful hats. So many more women than men.

In Paris, orange trees bloom in the Tuileries; one can order sole meunière and fresh asparagus at the Continental and attend a performance of *Thais* at the opera; then spend the night at the American Women's Club on rue de Caumartin, a faded old hotel covered in ivy, where the elevator doesn't work, but the plumbing does, and so before bed one can enjoy a decent bath. And gaze down at one's own glistening body in the porcelain tub, and wonder if anyone else will ever see it. And then drive back out to Lucy with a truckload of stovepipes.

> *Mondays and Tuesdays the community room turns into a store, and you find counters laden with great heaps of shoes of all the popular varieties, all kinds of underwear, big rolls of materials, and assorted "batteries de cuisines." Ruth Lindsay administers the shoes, Lucile Kroger presides over the cutting of materials. . . . Other members of the Unit improve their vocabularies by being salesladies in general.*
> —Cristine Myrick, *Wellesley College News*, February 5, 1920

Monday, September 8, 1919. The first morning the Wellesley store opens inside the hospital tent a line of villagers stretches down the road. Peasant women in kerchiefs and black shawls, baskets on their arms, children in wooden sabots, old ragged bearded men in rabbit skin hats who stepped straight out of an Aesop's fable, all preferring to shop for what they need (almost everything) rather than wait for haphazard allocations from the *préfet* in Paris. Lucile presides over bolts of cloth with a heavy pair of shears, snipping out lengths for pants and shirts. She is assisted by Frances Bogert, the unit nurse, and Ruth Lindsay, one of the social workers. Frances Bogert has dark smooth hair, parted on the side, and pale skin. She is a former archery champion—perhaps that explains her affronted Diana-like air.

Ruth is not pretty at all. She is tall and gawky with big brown eyes and wild springy brown hair that is always escaping whatever pins she's stuck into it; but her face is soft and she laughs a lot. The villagers love shopping for shoes, and complaining about shoes, and asking for different kinds of shoes, and it's Ruth who listens patiently to them in the dusty hospital tent, and tries to understand what they're asking for, and searches one more time among the pile of shoes and boots for a different size. She is from Chicago and a believer in temperance.

The store travels by truck as well, two days a week. Lucile and Ruth tote merchandise and baskets of woolen sweaters knitted for children by Wellesley alumnae, to far-flung villages over roads one can hardly call roads, and set up shop in the squares, or what serves as a square. Muddy, flattened little villages with palmy, exotic-sounding names: Epaux-Bézu, Gandelu, Veuilly-la-Poterie, Coupru, and my favorite, Ecoute s'il Pleut. Villages so small that in some cases hardly two dozen people live there. But never so small that the inhabitants can't appreciate a chance to try on shoes.

> July 24 [in French]
> Today I received the first letter of my family. Aunt Ida says Mary Emily [Gertrude's baby] is well and the whole family also. I went to Chateau Thierry with Julia and William to find the parcel post but I wasn't able to find it. It is almost impossible to do anything, either at the station or at the Postal Service. Everyone speaks very fast and one can't understand at all. This evening Miss Stimson arrived from Paris, and she said that the three new automobiles that we have bought are en route.
>
> It has rained a lot today, really it rains every day. The nights are very cold, but in the day it is good weather, the sunshine and the clouds are the most beautiful that I have ever seen.
>
> Tonight while Cristine and I wrote letters, Berenice sat herself at the typewriter to write. I think she writes poetry but I am not sure. Berenice is very funny when she speaks to the Boches and the Boche have a lot of admiration for her. She makes them work a lot but she is very agreeable and nice.
>
> I must go to bed because it is necessary that I get up early to make breakfast.

At the end of September a storm comes in and blows down the tent, but by then the dormitory barracks is almost finished and so the women move in. A tiny bedroom for each of them, partitioned by heavy canvas, with canvas for a door curtain. A narrow window, a wooden box, a shelf, a bed, a chair. Opulence to the villagers, who crowd in to have a look. Most of them sleep three to a bed in the kitchen.

> We have been very busy during the summer getting "dug in" for the winter. When we arrived on the scene of action the first of July the only building completed was a large hospital tent which we used for a dormitory until the middle of August. A wooden barracks loaned us by the French Government was in process of erection and was finished during July. In it we have our kitchen and storeroom, the dispensary, the office and a combination living and dining room. Late in the summer the big wooden hospital barracks bought from the Red Cross arrived and was put up for our permanent dormitory.
> —Cristine Myrick, Wellesley College News, November 20, 1919

Between writing poetry (she had been published in the *Atlantic Monthly* and *Poetry*) and supervising the German work crew with the help of a German phrase book, Berenice van Slyke, a nice girl from Detroit, somehow engineered an indoor plumbing system for the new dormitory barracks, with hot and cold water, and a sewer line. The other unit members were equally occupied. The two social workers, Julia Drew, a recreation specialist who had previously run a fresh-air farm for girls, and Ruth Lindsay, who spoke the best French in the unit, worked their way through the village, taking case histories and trying to teach games to the children, who had either forgotten or never learned how to play during four years of war. They visited outlying villages as well and held weekly "play hours." The children especially liked Julia, who gave them piggyback rides and taught them hopscotch and four-square and how to jump rope. Occasionally she and Ruth minded cows for a bedraggled pair of skinny blonde

twins, the celestially named Angèle and Angelina, whose earthbound parents wanted them to work in the fields all the time instead of learning how to play hopscotch.

Dr. Mary Marvell and Frances Bogert, the medical team, drove back and forth across the countryside in the unit's touring car, piloted by that "queer duck," William Henry, the chauffeur. They traveled by pony cart when the car broke down and the trucks weren't working, visiting patients in twenty-five bombed-out villages where there was no running water or electricity. Occasionally they delivered babies (including one who was christened "Wellesley"); more often they treated ailments that had gone untreated all during the war. Psoriasis, seborrhea, ulcers, conjunctivitis, emphysema, head lice, broken arms and legs that had been badly set and never healed properly, infections, childbirth complications, ailments that had no name and no clear symptoms except a general feeling of malaise and bad temper. And the flu. The Spanish Influenza which killed so many people in 1918 was still hanging around the French countryside in 1919, though by then people were too used to dying to be especially afraid of it. Frances herself caught the flu; thankfully, she recovered.

Frances also got lice from one of her patients. Dr. Marvell picked bugs out of her hair, then pressed larkspur against her scalp and made her sleep with larkspur inside a cap that night. In the morning she washed Frances's head with vinegar.

The unit director from Kansas, Julia Larimer, was the principle go-between the unit and the authorities in Paris who allocated building material for the villages or, more often, forgot to allocate anything and had to be visited, cajoled, bullied, and pleaded with. Cristine Myrick filed monthly reports with the Wellesley War Committee on the unit's activities, recorded expenses, and wrote long, newsy, cheerful letters to the *Wellesley College News.*

> *The big one-ton truck presented by the Cleveland Wellesley Club has done yeoman's service ever since it came into our possession in hauling plaster and lumber, roofing tiles, and nails. When not doing that, it is usually bringing supplies from Paris for our store. Every Friday morning it carries a jubilant load of village women to the market in Chateau-Thierry with their chickens, rabbits and cheeses, and brings them out again with baskets of supplies. All this is so popular we have been obliged to give out tickets.*
>
> —Cristine Myrick, *Wellesley College News,* November 20, 1919

In photographs Cristine is lean-faced, intelligent, with small close-set eyes. Humorous looking. She is a positive, attentive correspondent, and fortunately much more detailed in her observations than Lucile. She knew her Wellesley readers wanted a jaunty tone. Proof that an industrious spirit and a good attitude could overcome any adversity. *Non Ministrare sed Minstrare.* Though could it be possible that life in Lucy was actually as buoyant as she describes?

> *Our first [party] passed into the annals of the Unit as very nearly our most harrowing experience. We invited the entire village of Lucy upon that occasion, and they all came! . . . They filled the little room in an all too solid mass, waited solemnly to see what would happen, and never forgot their company manners for a moment. By use of much persuasion we got enough of them outdoors to eat our refreshments and*

so leave a little space within. We improved the opportunity
to start dance music, and after that our troubles were over.
Dancing they adore, and that night they danced for the first
time since 1914.
—Cristine Myrick, *Wellesley College Bulletin,* October
1920

Every Wednesday evening the American women hold a dance for
the village in the barracks' community room. Some of the older girls
and boys volunteer each week to help decorate; they hang paper lanterns from the rafters of the community room and wrap garlands of
paper flowers around the posts. American soldiers and officers from
the Graves Registration Camp at Belleau Wood come to the dances.
The two French officers from the German prison camp always come,
too—the younger one even got down on his hands and knees one
day and sanded the floor in the big room to make it smoother for
dancing. Often they bring along one of the prisoners, a tall quiet man
with a limp, who can play waltzes and fox trots on the piano. The
upright piano is very out of tune—too many cigarette butts tossed
inside its cabinet. Still, no one minds.

The American women are in great demand as dance partners, especially among the American soldiers and the French officers. If the
prisoner isn't there to play the piano, someone from the unit cranks
the Victrola for polka music. On those Wednesday nights the village
is full of music, people crowding into the Wellesley barracks, where
every window is lit, chintz curtains open to let in air. Out in the
grassy yard men from the village play cards by yellow lantern light,
using crates as tables and sitting on rocks and piles of roof slates or
lumber, while women gossip on the porch, a pale half-moon overhead, their kerchiefs pushed back to enjoy the evening breeze.

Sometimes before the dancing begins, an old man from the village will stand in the middle of the dance floor and sing a sad ballad,

and tears will trickle down the faces of the old women, who have lost their sons. Afterward everyone claps and feels suddenly freer and more like laughing. American soldiers lean against the barracks walls, smoking and talking about when they will be going home. It is still that time after the war where people who have been missing suddenly show up, as if out of nowhere, and almost every Wednesday there is some kind of reunion of cousins or neighbors or an uncle thought to be dead.

There begins to be an attitude in the village that life is starting back up again. An attitude not accompanied by gladness, exactly, or even something as simple as relief. More like a renewed interest in routine. Nothing is the same as before the war, but it's not as different as it had been, just a few months ago, though no one, not even the Americans, believes that what's been lost can be recovered. Only reconstructed. And of course reconstructions go on forever.

Wellesley College girls are still in France and they intend to stay as long as anything remains to be done for the stricken French peasants in the vicinity of Lucy-le-Bocage.
—*Evening Sun,* New York, February 2, 1920

In two of the pictures from Lucile's negatives from France, she is posing with a shepherd dog, her long hair loose around her shoulders, and she is not only smiling but making eyes at the camera, too.

When I examined the rest of the negatives from the fruitcake tin, I found more pictures of the shepherd dog and also quite a few of a handsome mustachioed man in uniform. In Lucile's handwritten index at the back of the packet, the man is identified alternately as "Alsace" and "the Brigadier." He walks with a thin flexible-looking cane; he has been decorated with the Croix de Guerre; he looks like Clark Gable. The dog is named Wolf and resembles one. Other negatives depict roofless cottages, destroyed churches, rubble-strewn villages, bales of barbed wire and unexploded shells—but the dog and the handsome man are featured more than anyone or anything else, including village children, another popular subject, and Lucile's fellow unit members.

After I sent my father the photograph of Lucile smiling quizzically in her sensible oxfords, he called to thank me. Then he asked me to describe some of the other photographs, which I did as best I could, not knowing much at the time about what I was looking at. When I mentioned the handsome officer, I added that I wondered if there had been a romance. My father said, "Imagine that!" His voice was raspy and a little hesitant over the phone, as it has been ever since his radiation treatments, but in it was a note of real curiosity, something

I had rarely heard from him regarding his mother, which I found encouraging, even though it made me worry a little as well, in case I could not deliver as much as I was starting to promise.

WITHIN A WEEK of that conversation I paid the first of many visits to the Wellesley College Archives. After making several misdirected requests of the two patient archivists—I had never been inside an archive before, as they soon realized—I was presented with five or six boxes of photo albums, scrapbooks, letters, and official reports donated by members of Lucile's unit.

And there she was again. Kneeling by a galvanized tub, washing clothes outside in a pasture full of shell craters. Sitting on the tailgate of a rusty old truck in an enormous mink coat. Accepting a letter from the *facteur* from his mailbag. Standing with her unit on the rickety porch of their barracks, a blasted tree in the foreground. Petting Wolf the dog. Posing in a village wedding photo, a demolished house in the background. Smiling, smiling, smiling. Day after day in the Archives, I sat at a long wooden library table wearing white gloves, reading old letters and looking through brittle photo albums with a loaned magnifying glass, peering at a woman who was not my father's mother.

Or rather, she was my father's mother—no need to be so melodramatic—but she was not the woman he recalled. Nothing austere about her, at least in those photographs. No marble Athena in sensible shoes or distracted matron smoking Chesterfields and staring at a crossword puzzle. She looked bright faced and bustling and rather ordinary, someone absorbed in the business of the moment, contemplating neither the wisdom of the ages nor the uncertainties of the future, but only who and what was right in front of her.

I became passionately interested in the mustachioed officer.

My father, too, became interested in the officer. If his mother hadn't smiled at *him,* at least she had smiled at someone. I sent him a photograph of the officer, who is leaning on his thin cane and smiling tenderly at the camera. Quickly we both began to envision a doomed love affair. A broken heart especially appealed to my

father as a possible explanation for Lucile's later abstraction; also my father is drawn to stories where people are separated forever by fate. I promoted a less tragic scenario, with the brigadier as a charming cad attracted to the Kroger millions, which Lucile cannily recognized (she was Barney's daughter, after all, and knew not to misrepresent the merchandise—even to herself), while enjoying his attentions nonetheless. In my father's version, the dog was an extra. In mine, the dog had served as go-between, chaperone and canine guardian angel, carrying love notes across the blasted wheat fields, accompanying the lovers on fall rambles through treeless woods, sniffing out

land mines, locating half-concealed abandoned German dugouts for illicit trysts (the German dugouts were said to be drier and more comfortable than British or French ones). Like Lucile, I have always liked dogs.

Again and again I stared at those photographs of the handsome officer and Lucile and Wolf, my white gloves gathering the dust of 1919. A ménage à trois? Which one had Lucile loved more? Because of course she had loved them, the wolfish hero and the wolfish dog, and been loved in return. I couldn't imagine otherwise, because I didn't want to.

ONE MORNING LAST spring I was sitting at a table in the Archives looking at newspaper clippings in the unit's publicity scrap-book, when the head archivist handed me a box I hadn't seen before. The contents, she said, were still uncatalogued. In the box were papers belonging to Frances Bogert, the unit nurse, including roughly two dozen letters she had written from Lucy-le-Bocage and sent home to her father at his cattle farm in Keswick, Virginia. Chatty, clear eyed, occasionally carping letters that range from the tragic to the absurd to the trivial and back again.

In one, the body of an American soldier is discovered down a village well. In another, she complains about the overpriced taxis in Paris. She describes a careening truck ride through the Left Bank, where she had to lie on top of a load of goods because there was no room for a passenger in the cab. Another letter describes how one of the unit's vehicles, the unreliable *camionette,* gets a flat tire on the way home from Château-Thierry; Frances and three village women are all obliged to pile out with their market baskets to walk four miles back to Lucy. Frances has just had her hair done in Château-Thierry; it gets ruined as they cut across the oat fields. The same letter also includes a description of a tour of battlefields in Verdun. At Fort Douaumont, Frances sees where a shell had burst, "burying 27 Boches and 8 Frenchmen alive."

She sees wild boar, foxes, pheasants, and one day a rare snow white ermine runs across the road right in front of her. In a single week she takes care of ninety-three flu victims in six different towns.

She is homesick. She is tired of eating tinned meat. December is cold (the villagers say *"Pas chaud,"* or "It's not hot," when it's very cold). February is "heavenly." Mud is everywhere. In March she goes to Nice for a short holiday and stays in a hotel. ("I wanted to sleep in the tub to reacquaint myself with such an article.") Then a pair of dentists join the unit for a few days; ninety-nine children have teeth extracted, baby teeth pulled "by the sixes and sevens and eights," until one couldn't walk across the floor without stepping on teeth. In May, she attends William Henry's wedding, to Paule Desabeau, whose sister, Pierrette, gets married during the same ceremony.

A lot of her letters mention men.

It was very soon after I began looking through Frances Bogert's letters, for instance, that I discovered the handsome officer in Lucile's photographs was named Georges Lambert, nicknamed "Alsace" ("One of the guards is an Alsatian, very good-looking and apparently thoroughly nice"), that he was from Strasbourg and was second-in-command at a German POW camp, a few miles from Lucy-le-Bocage. His horse was named "Très Fatigué." From Frances, I also learned that Alsace and his charming young French lieutenant, M. Aubert, were in constant attendance at Lucy-le-Bocage. Their excuse in the beginning was the detail of German prisoners on loan to the unit; soon both officers were visiting almost every evening on their own. They attended all the dances, sat in the community room playing chess, asked for English lessons. And it wasn't long before Frances Bogert confirmed what I'd already guessed. ("Both [officers] are quite devoted to two of the girls here," she writes, identifying them later as Lucile and Ruth Lindsay.) Each officer had presented the object of his devotion with a "quite stunning" lamp made out of a defused .75 shell, which when polished could serve as an attractive vase. The lieutenant gave Ruth the ribbon from his Croix de Guerre along with his Sam Brown belt. Romantic possibilities, perfumed by the smell of cordite from ammunition dumps being blown up down the road, suddenly lit the air.

A mile in the other direction of Lucy-le-Bocage was a camp full of U.S. Marines, a graves registration unit, in charge of the gruesome task of identifying and reburying dead American soldiers who had been hastily interred during the Battle of Belleau Wood, and establishing an American cemetery. According to Frances, four of those marines became known as "the Wellesley bunch" because of their attentiveness to the unit—one of them, an ex-butcher, fell madly in love with Julia Drew, the recreation worker. ("I am afraid he doesn't realize the utter impossibility of it.") Frances  herself was in love with the camp's commanding officer, twice gassed, twice wounded, with whom she went dancing at Ciro's in Paris and allowed herself to get carried away. ("I am not sure I acted à la mode.") She and two other unit members also went on an evening picnic with the four marines; they found a wooded spot and toasted potatoes on a coal fire and fried hot dogs and gazed up at a gibbous moon.

Love among the ruins. Most of the American soldiers could not pronounce Lucy-le-Bocage, which roughly translated means "Lucy of the hedged field." So they called it Lucy Birdcage instead. And perhaps that's how they thought of it: a strange gorgeous aviary in the midst of rubble. Aflutter with women in gray whipcord and mud-caked boots, who quoted Shakespeare, and declined Latin verbs, and debated equal suffrage, and played equally good chess and poker, and could waltz, and tell the difference between a salad fork and dessert fork, and could also set a broken arm and change a flat tire. Women in rough wool stockings who spoke with upper-crust accents and yet were willing to spend hours talking to "a fellow" about his problems. They were a mutinous bunch, those marines, miserable at still being in France, depressed by the dead all around them, sick of mud and tinned beef. But whenever they visited Lucy-le-Bocage, a seductive optimism crept over them. The war they had hated so much had, at the very last minute, handed them a defused .75 shell, polished and turned into a vase. ("No, it's true they are not the kind of men we would meet at home ordinarily, but they have done all kinds of things for us, and I for one am glad to have known them, known all they have gone through in the war.") They were from Brooklyn, Chicago, Philadelphia. Workingmen. Butchers, steelworkers, lithographers. And all of them had problems—estranged wives, sick children, subversive thoughts—that they brought with them to that crude muddy little camp, where inside a barracks there were little white wicker tables and magazines and vases of fresh flowers, where a millionaire's daughter snipped bolts of cloth and a poet rigged up a plumbing system, and if you wanted to talk, someone with a soft intelligent face would listen, sometimes for hours. A place those men later felt they must have dreamed up, once they got back home, to Chicago or Brooklyn, where listeners were less patient, and millionaires' daughters and poets operated along less democratic lines.

EVERYONE SEEMED TO fall in love with the Wellesley women, those capable birds, *les dames américaines.* Gifts were laid at their feet, like tributes to goddesses.

From the villagers: chickens, baskets of pears ("apples, salads, plums and beaucoup, beaucoup flowers . . . as well as a rabbit").

From the American soldiers: Dodge spark plugs, gasoline, trinkets from Paris, chocolate almonds, soap, perfume, cakes for their birthdays. ("One would think we had come out here to receive and not to give!")

From the French officers: Croix de Guerre
medals, Sam Brown belts, boxes of little pas-
tries called *gaufrettes*. The handsome brigadier
also gave Lucile a small bronze commemorative medal with ALSACE engraved in the upper
left-hand corner, with the profile of a medieval
young woman on one side and nesting storks on
the other. The same medal I had so thought-
lessly thought to save in the fruitcake tin, hav-
ing no idea what it really commemorated.

From the German prisoners: another defused shell, presented to
Berenice, on which was carved a w, whether for Weimar or Wellesley, no one could tell.

Everyone, it seems, loved them. Did those women also fall in love
with each other? I don't know, and Frances Bogert certainly doesn't
say in her letters to her father. Half of the Wellesley unit never married, not that marriage itself is necessarily an indication of a person's sexual orientation, especially ninety years ago. I could go on to
speculate—I've certainly speculated about plenty of other things—
but for once I will confine myself to what I do know, which is that
for seven or eight months the unit was the focus of an exceptional
amount of attention, from every quarter, which they all seemed to
have enjoyed. That attention, combined with the equally exceptional
freedom they experienced as relief workers, created a kind of general
frisson and also a tremendous aplomb. As long as they got their work
done, no one particularly cared where they went, or with whom they
kept company, and so, like goddesses, like birds, they did as they
pleased.

They visited battlefields. Traveled alone across Europe. Attended
the opera in Paris in their uniforms and felt reasonably well dressed.
They went dancing unchaperoned, drank champagne, lost their
heads, and didn't seem to regret it. Admiring men cleaned their

boots, whisked them away on picnics, operated the projector for the silent films the unit carted around to different villages and projected onto the sides of houses, to the amazement of all—most villagers had never even seen a flashlight. On Thanksgiving Day, the four American Marines left their sad camp of filthy tents and unmarked graves to show up at Lucy-le-Bocage for a turkey dinner. "We had turkey, (12lbs, 6oz), chestnut dressing, cider, in fact all the side-kicks we could," records Frances. On the table, covered with a white table-cloth for the occasion, instead of the usual "white and yellow oil-cloth," rested "a centerpiece of mistletoe." It was cold and late and snowy when dinner was over, so the men spent the night sleeping under the table. Where they were discovered the next morning by the unit's elderly cook, who was horrified, gratified, and immediately quit.

IN THE SAME November letter that tells of Thanksgiving with the marines, Frances writes to her father that Lucile and Ruth Lindsay had recently been invited by the French officers to an evening concert at the prison camp. A concert given by the prisoners, on "instruments made by the boches themselves."

Frances doesn't say as much about this concert as I'd like (she seems slightly miffed at not having been invited) and so I will have to imagine Lucile and Ruth setting forth on a night that's dark and cold and full of stars. William Henry, the chauffeur, drives them from Lucy in the touring car and parks on the hard snow just outside the coils of barbed wire and wooden pickets that constitute the prison's front gate. They pass two sentries, who salute them. Alsace and the lieutenant meet them at the door, smiling and rubbing their hands together against the cold. They lead their guests into a prison bar-racks, used as a mess hall, which is crowded with men. Maybe two hundred men. Some of them have not been this close to a woman in years.

As soon as Lucile and Ruth appear all the men stop talking. Unsteady wooden chairs are found for them. The lieutenant lights a match for Lucile's cigarette. Alsace hands the two women tin cups of strong hot tea and a tin plate of *gaufrettes*. Every man in the room stares at them. The windows steam up.

In her letter, Frances describes the scene with a tremor of finical awe:

> The French guards at the camp sitting on the rafters of the barracks, on broken-down benches, on the floor, their coats open, bedroom slippers on, the air blue with smoke and odorigorous, the two American girls, the chauffeur with typical Irish blue eyes and Irish mug, the Lieutenant and Alsace, the many prisoners, and outside barbed wire entanglements and sentries.

Wearing fur coats and cloche hats, Lucile and Ruth sip their tea and eat the *gaufrettes,* and try to seem at ease in that hot dark breathless barracks, surrounded by men and blue tobacco smoke. Meanwhile an orchestra of prisoners shuffles into place at one end of the room. The musicians carry a motley collection of instruments. Two flutes fashioned out of lengths of copper pipe, a French horn made from parts of a cook stove, violins and cellos made from packing crates and strung with telephone wire. After a few minutes of anxious tuning up, the musicians look expectantly at the concertmaster (a former pharmacist from Dusseldorf). He raises his arm. The crowd hushes and the concert begins. Sousa's "Stars and Stripes" is the initial offering, followed by "Madelon de la Victoire." The musicians' faces are flushed with excitement and effort. Everyone claps after each piece. Lucile and Ruth loosen their fur coats as Alsace and the lieutenant watch them solicitously. William Henry has been handed a glass of whiskey and is half asleep, his wet boots stuck out in front of him. And outside stretches the snow and the barbed wire and the long dark night itself.

So how did Lucile, our reserved Cincinnati grocery heiress, *feel* that night as she sat in a prison barracks, half-suffocated by smoky "odorigorous" air? Was she thrilled or unsettled by the bedroom slippers, the blur of unshaven male faces, the rough babble of French and German, the makeshift instruments? Perhaps she hesitated before she sipped from that tin cup (had it been washed?), then swallowed her tea, felt it burn her throat, and held out her cup for more. Perhaps she choked on a bite of *gaufrette,* aware that every man in the room was watching her swallow. And what did she make of that impossible music that was at once so terrible and beautiful, so poignant and coarse, so embarrassing and touching, so completely and utterly and profoundly distracting?

I have no idea.

Between our two experiences, hers real and mine imagined, stretches snow and barbed wire and the long dark night itself.

THAT SPRING LUCILE and Ruth Lindsay had another adventure together, one that included Alsace and his parents. Ruth left an album of photos from her year at Lucy-le-Bocage to the Wellesley College Archives; that album contains, at the very end, several pages labeled "A Day at Fontainebleau with Lucille Kroger" featuring faded yellowed snapshots, in some cases so faded and yellow it's hard to make them out. The first are of the legendary château itself, vast and overdecorated, a *gaufrette* for giants. Partly designed by the overwrought Caterina de' Medici, the château was the site of Napoleon's famous farewell speech to his loyalists on the eve of his first exile on Elba, before he eventually wound up in a vast and overdecorated tomb in Les Invalides, where he was visited many years later by my grandfather.

On the next page: Alsace posed atop an oddly shaped cleft boulder, legs spread wide, assuming the stance of the victorious hero, infused perhaps with the ghost of Napoleon. Below him on the ground, smiling broadly, hatless, but unsubdued, stands Lucile.

Two more cracked and discolored photos capture a group of people sitting at a table outside the château. The first is labeled "Lucille, the Brigadier, Mme. Lambert and R. L.," the self-effacing Ruth having reduced herself to initials while again generously awarding Lucile an extra *l.* The four of them, Alsace and his mother and the two American women, sit on a bench and chairs, a  table between them. Though the sun is shining and the trees behind them have leaves, it looks to be chilly. Everyone is wearing a coat. Perhaps it's late April.

Madame has gray hair tucked under a turbanlike hat and wears spectacles. An arresting face, not handsome exactly but strong-boned and clever—the face of one's high school civics teacher, known for being sardonic in class. Her coat has a frayed hem. Her smile is carefully amused, slightly hungry.

In the second photo, Madame Lambert is no longer part of the group; in her place is "Captain Lambert," who must have taken that first picture, then handed the camera to his wife. Alsace clearly got his looks from his father, who is dapper, assured, sporting a sleek dark mustache as handsome as his son's. The captain, too, is in uniform, which includes tall polished leather boots with shiny buckles. An attractive pair certainly, the Lamberts. And determined to put a

good face on today, as they meet their son's charming American friend, Mademoiselle Lucile, whose father, they've heard, is J. P. Morgan.

But all is not well on that outing. In that first "family" photo, Lucile regards the camera under the brim of her hat, ankles crossed, hands folded demurely in her lap, her expression deliberately noncommittal. Even the agreeable Ruth looks on edge. Possibly the captain has been issuing orders? Acting officious, already assuming the role of presumptive father-in-law.

In the next picture, the one with Captain Lambert, Lucile is turned toward him on the bench they share and seems to be considering something he's just said, smiling askance. Ruth's smile, too, has grown more dubious. The captain himself is at ease, one of those handsome men who can't imagine that being handsome would not be enough to recommend him; he rests one shiny boot casually on a curved table leg, the other on the ground. As for Alsace, he alone appears oblivious to the silent, complicated calculations consuming the rest of the group. Relaxed, happy, he leans toward Lucile and grins directly at the camera.

He should be looking at Lucile. There's something so knowing in her face as she gazes toward his father. Something even compassionate. She has seen Captain Lambert's type before. Good looking, confident, dictatorial. A man who believes he deserves the best life has to offer. Meanwhile, his wife has an old coat.

The jig is up for Alsace, though he doesn't know it yet. Lucile cannot picture him in Cincinnati at the Kroger dinner table, discussing with Barney whether to buy a railroad, or a villa in Palm Beach, or even a shipment of Smyrna figs. He is thoroughly nice, he is very good looking; but there in the shadow of Napoleon, he is not Napoleon. Plus his parents are pushy. Her heart remains unconquered. Still there's enough time, and forbearance (he *is* so good looking), for another "family" photo of Alsace, Lucile, the captain, and Madame, all sitting gamely together on a rock, Alsace and Lucile close together, his knee grazing her arm. And then a final shot of marvelous, excessive Fontainebleau, with its endless embellishments—scrolls, arabesques, gothic nymphs—a passionate dream of a building, where imagination trumped reason, again and again, and vanity was always satisfied, at whatever expense. Except this time.

For my father's sake, for Lucile's sake, I wish I could say there was more to this wartime romance, but I don't think so. Lucile was reasonable. She was particular and thrifty and restless. She was even romantic enough to save that commemorative medal with ALSACE embossed above the profile of a severe-looking maiden, but most of all she was her father's daughter and, once again, nobody's sweetheart.

SOON IT WAS time for everyone to go home. The war was, after all, over. First the marine camp left. Next the prison camp was shut down, though Alsace and the lieutenant continued to visit the Wellesley unit. And then it was April and then it was May, and William Henry was marrying his village bride, with Lucile and Julia

Larimer standing in as his parents (in a letter, Frances included the menu for their wedding dinner, ten courses, not counting the wedding cake), and then it was time to close up the camp at Lucy.

The unit held a lottery to give away all their furnishings and villagers drew numbers from a hat. Within an hour it was over. Frances watched "a procession of wheelbarrows laden with tables, chairs, rugs" vanish down the road ("many of the people wept"). Lucile was on her way to Cincinnati by then. Frances herself was heading to Paris, planning to sail in two weeks to be in time for Wellesley's commencement. "The wild boar is still in the woods," she remarked pensively in her final letter from Lucy. But the birdcage was empty; the birds had flown.

WOLF, I FOUND out, was a Belgian shepherd Lucile bought during one of her purchasing trips to Paris. Frances reports that he's a "stunning dog." What became of Wolf after Lucile went home to Cincinnati, I don't know. I hope she gave him to Alsace, the handsome brigadier, and that Wolf's descendants frisk about the suburbs of Strasbourg even now, nosing into the trash and chasing cats.

My father is right to find only impossible romances interesting, because only the impossible ones remain that way. Especially the romance of time, which is like any romance in that we always believe that ours in particular will never end.

In July 1919, when Lucile first stood under the blue sky of that little ruined French country village, she'd had no idea of the future at all. Did not know if she would ever get married. Did not suppose that she would build a big house with an attic. Did not guess that another war would come, twenty years later, and ruin everything all over again. Or that she'd have two sons who would fight in that war. Or that both of those sons would miss her the rest of their lives and that one of them would die from not wanting to talk about her and that as an old man the other would talk of her constantly. Or that those two sons would pass on some of that longing to eight grandchildren, including a granddaughter who one summer afternoon ninety years later would visit this same country village, the rows of cottages so neat now, their little yards leafy with chestnut trees and full of roses. How could she have known? She was just an American woman in France that bright hot day in July, with all the time in the world.

VIII

Mrs. Albert Berne
and Her Sons

I have written a hundred poems
About the you I never knew

—HENRY BERNE, "Letter to My Mother"

So many pieces now, the clues are adding up. And yet I find myself reluctant to begin writing this last chapter.

I suppose I don't want to let go of Lucile, now that I've discovered her. (But have I? Who is this woman with whom I've spent almost 250 pages? Half-imagined, and half what else?) She has become a familiar and empathic companion, gazing out at me from photographs scattered across my desk, enduring my speculations. And my father and I haven't had so much to talk about in a long time. For much of the past twenty years, our phone conversations tended to be hesitant and self-conscious, confined to movie reviews, whatever politician was currently under indictment, and whether or not it was raining. Yet now, when it's almost too late, we once again share a life in common, of great interest to us both.

"Did you know that Lucile was captain of the Wellesley Running Team?" I tell him one day, knowing that he did not. "Did you know that she went to a concert at a prison camp?" She broke her arm, read the biography of Oliver Goldsmith, tried to raise chickens. She visited battlefields in France that were still full of bones and carried home two packets of postcards as proof of where she'd been. Whenever I visit my father in Charlotte, I bring along photographs or a letter I've found in the Wellesley College Archives, or lately, something I have written. We talk about Cincinnati, his aunts and uncles, the family trip to Bermuda when he was four. His lung cancer has returned, and there is no further treatment for it; but we don't talk about that. We talk about his mother. Also his father, and his brother, Albert, who died decades ago. He tells me that he would like to visit Cincinnati again.

One afternoon, on two big sheets of sketchpad paper, my father draws a blueprint of the house on Indian Hill and his mother's garden. We walk through the house together. We sit in the living room; take in the view of the lily pond, the rose bushes. Climb the nineteen steps of the curving staircase to the upper hallway, where we peer into Lucile's bedroom, which my father has drawn so large that it occupies three-quarters of the second floor. There is the dresser where she stood and did crossword puzzles. There is her fireplace. There is the gothic clock on the mantle. Our conversations grow longer, more loquacious and wide ranging.

Also I know how this part will end.

Perhaps it would be better not to write this last period of her life at all, but simply catalog what I know about Lucile's experience as a wife and mother. While the rest of the country was absorbed by flappers and F. Scott Fitzgerald and Prohibition, and then the Depression, she was getting married and settling down. I could write pages about F. Scott Fitzgerald and the Depression. But for Lucile's marriage a catalog might be more appropriate, since marriage is a subject about which one can gather and present all sorts of facts and yet conclude almost nothing.

For instance:

My grandfather never alluded to Lucile's year in France except to remark once that she'd found waltzing with French officers a trial because they smelled of garlic.

A curious detail to retain from the many anecdotes she must have told him, unless she decided not to tell them. She met my grandfather in 1922, two and a half years after she returned to Cincinnati from France; they were married eight months later. Was she being deliberately offhand with that garlic remark? (To disguise a lingering affection?) Or was my grandfather jealously dismissing those waltzes, even long after she was dead, not wanting to imagine Lucile pressed against the decorated chests of French officers, her eyes closed, heart pounding, imbibing the fragrance of Gallic love?

In any case, why didn't she simply eat some garlic herself?

ANOTHER FOR INSTANCE: my grandfather himself. I have already mentioned that he met Lucile at an evening reception in Cincinnati given by a mutual friend, who had arranged beforehand for him to sing.

It's Christmastime. He appears on the friend's doorstep with snowflakes on the collar of his black wool coat, a streetlight gilding the pink curves of his ears. Carrying a music stand, smiling deferentially, is Albert Berne, age forty-five, a widower and a voice teacher at the Cincinnati Conservatory of Music. Handsome, in an intelligent, gentlemanly way. A small man with deep blue eyes, gold-rimmed spectacles, and thick, wavy gray hair. Distinguished looking. He was distinguished looking even when he was a young and had dark brown hair. Even in a bathing suit, he was distinguished looking. An achievement when one considers men's bathing suits in the 1920s.

Come in, cries his hostess, extending a hand. Mr. Berne! I'm so glad you could come. Isn't it cold? Everyone is *dying* to hear you sing. I have a friend whom I'd especially like you to meet. She's very keen on music. You'll have heard of her father, of course . . . ? He smiles, nods, looks politely baffled.

In all my memories of him, my grandfather looks politely baffled, an apologetic, absent-minded expression that made him seem above ordinary human concerns. It was not that he didn't know what was going on, more that he didn't see his part in the program. That other-worldly expression must have been helpful once he married into the Krogerian empire, where ordinary human concerns were big business and music was for marching bands.

Further for instances concerning Albert Berne:

He spoke beautiful German.

He had excellent manners.

He could not ride a bicycle or drive a car.

He knew every note of Mozart's Concerto No. 22 in E-flat Major and Mozart's Piano Concerto No. 11 in F Major, but he did not know the difference between a frying pan and a stockpot.

He was gentle and anxious and dreamy, daunted by any kind of financial transaction, and he never, as far as I know, uttered a single profanity in his very long life.

So did Lucile set out to find the one man in Cincinnati who was the precise opposite of her father?

SHE WAS THIRTY-THREE years old by the time they met. She had the right to vote—the Constitution had finally been amended in 1920—but was once again living in her father's house, making his grocery lists, roasting his chickens, and ringing his dinner bell at precisely six thirty. Prohibition was in ascendancy, and so were bootleggers and bathtub gin. Not that Lucile cared much for drinking, unlike most of the rest of her family. Barney didn't drink at all. Not morally opposed, just too busy. (Asked once by a reporter to list his aversions, he answered, "Young man, I have no time for aversions.") All three of her sisters were now having babies; Gertrude already had two. Her brothers had her job with the Kroger Company. And so after Lucile complimented Albert Berne that night on his singing, and showed off a little by announcing that she knew those poems by Heine, she invited him to a dinner party the next week. On learning that he did not have a car, she promised to "send someone" for him, which she did on the appointed day.

Years later, my grandfather described that dinner party at the Kroger house to my mother, how Lucile had seated him next to her at the table, and then after dinner had asked him to dance. "Our cheeks touched," he said, "and that was it!"

Well, maybe. Having inherited some of my grandfather's German romanticism, I enjoy the idea of love sealed with the brush of a cheek, and it's true they got engaged just a month or two later. But having also inherited some of my grandmother's German pragmatism, I assume Lucile did a few computations and figured out that as a husband Albert was a fair bet. He had a good mind and a gentle disposition; he had traveled in Europe and could talk with her about poetry and art and music; and he would not be compared with her father (unlike her less fortunate brothers-in-law). Neither would he try to tell her what to do with her money. Or ask to spend much of it on himself. In fact, Albert was so worried about being considered a bounder that before he asked Lucile to marry him, he went to see Barney and offered him his entire savings: five hundred dollars.

How could Lucile not be touched? Who else had ever made such a gesture on her behalf? And yet, how much of her decision to marry Albert had to do with being over thirty and still living in her father's house, while her sisters were having babies?

THE FRUITCAKE TIN holds one final article I haven't examined: that charm bracelet, given to Lucile right before she got married, most likely by her sisters since it's a little too lighthearted and suggestive for Albert, who tended toward more sentimental gestures, and her sisters were a clubby bunch, who would have enjoyed getting together on this bracelet. Fourteen charms, most of them clearly emblematic of Lucile's past and present, some of them jokey. A tiny pack of Chesterfield cigarettes, set in sterling silver; a book of matches stamped HOT TIP; a globe; an American flag; a college banner; a dog in a doghouse; an engagement ring; a wishbone; a tiny silver marriage license that slides opens to display the words *State of Bliss*.

But then there are a few charms I don't get: an insignia with the Greek letters Phi Delta Lambda; the state of Texas in blue enamel; a tambourine, a sailboat; a wee gold jack-in-the-box that actually opens and actually pops up on a wee gold spring.

What did Lucile have to do with Texas? She never went there, as far as I know. Perhaps it's a reference to the Lone Star State, which was about to cease to be hers? The only current Phi Delta Lambdas I can locate are a sorority for Asian Americans and an honor society for graduates of Nazarene colleges. Was the sailboat an allusion to her overseas travel (they couldn't find an ocean-liner charm), or did she like to sail? The tambourine was probably to make fun of Lucile's support of women's suffrage, but I cannot for the life of me decode the jack-in-the-box. Unless it was a sly sisterly insinuation about her wedding night.

All day I have been wearing this charm bracelet, feeling the charms beat against the inside of my wrist, tiny reminders of a woman I can't quite divine, despite the hints, the tokens, the references I should be able to understand by now. But if I understand anything it's that the years I have spent thinking about Lucile are also years I have spent thinking about my father. Through the gaps of what was missing for him I have spied on her, tried to arrange her, define her, make her into a person who fills in the blank square, the central sadness of my father's life, so that he could stop being the central sadness of mine. And yet still Lucile leads a charmed life. No matter how I try, I cannot reduce her to a chain of facts, even for him, for whom, it seems, I would do almost anything. She remains always more, and less, than a reconstruction.

M y grandparents were married July 10, 1923, outside the house on Crescent Avenue. In the wedding portrait that hangs in my study, framed in a tarnished silver frame engraved with Barney's initials, Lucile wears a sleeveless white silk dress, a string of pearls, an Egyptian-looking lace head-dress trimmed with a flowing tulle veil, and carries a massive bouquet of white roses, lilies-of-the-valley and ferns. Peering out from beneath her phara-onic headdress, she looks lovely and diminutive and theatrically bridal. Finally she has the big-gest part in the play. Her clear steady light blue eyes are clearer and steadier than usual. Her ex-pression is muted but not unhopeful. If Lucile had reservations about getting married, it's not apparent in that photograph no matter how long I hang over it with my magnifying glass.

News of her engagement was not published in the *College News,* as was often the case, but in a 1924 *Wellesley Bulletin* I located this announcement:

> Lucile Kroger was married out of doors at her home in
> East Walnut Hills, Cincinnati, Ohio, July 10, to Mr. Al-
> bert Berne. Mabel Lee Wilson, Nell McCoy Shearer
> and Julia Larimer, 1907, were present. Mary Christie's
> brother officiated. Mr. Berne is a teacher in the Cincin-
> nati Conservatory of Music and himself the possessor of
> a very fine baritone voice.

Albert's "very fine baritone voice" must have been important to
Lucile, since it was she who provided this information to the *Wellesley Bulletin*. He wasn't a banker or a businessman, like the husbands
of some of her classmates. Still, he was an artist, a distinction that
conferred its own status.

Last winter I found a "family history" I had written in high school,
which focused mostly on my grandfather. I discovered this surprising
document in my own attic—surprising because I had completely
forgotten ever writing a previous family history. Yet there it was, the
title and name affixed to the front of a brown vinyl binder, the brown
vinyl designed to resemble wood grain, which I must have selected
for its lasting qualities. Inside, the handwritten text was on lined
notebook pages inserted between clear plastic sheets alternating
with black paper pages, on which I had glued a few old photographs.
I must have also carried those photographs away from my grandfather's attic, though I can't remember having done so. All along this
history has been up there, hovering like a holograph above the one
I am writing now.

This first history is notable both for its indestructible cover, and
for having survived my parents' divorce in the late 1970s and the
many house moves that followed, but most of all for the importance
I gave my father's family. Once again my family history is entirely
about the Bernes and the Krogers. It's as if my mother's family does
not exist. In fact, I conclude that earlier account by stating that my

father lives in Washington DC, "where he teaches at Georgetown University." Implying that he is a professor at Georgetown, which was not true—he was, as I've said, an adjunct, an auslander in the world of the academic department, without benefits or long-term prospects, akin to being a "consultant," or even a temp, as I well know, having long been an adjunct myself. A situation that bothered us both, since I wanted my father to have "a real job," with an office and secretaries and a door with his name on it, and so did he, though every time he got those things he got rid of them again. It seems even at age fifteen I was trying to give my father what he was missing. That first family history also implies that he lives in Washington alone. No mention of my mother or myself or my siblings. I don't know that I can explain this, except to say that my father's family always seemed more important to me than anyone else's family, including my own, because they were rich and had a recognizable name, which made them glamorous, and because he remained so troubled by them.

Inside that first family history was an old brochure of my grandfather's, Scotch-taped to a page. The brochure cover features a photograph of him at about thirty-five, looking sensitive yet commanding,

ALBERT BERNE, BARITONE
TEACHER OF SINGING

something like Christopher Plummer during the "Edelweiss" scene in *The Sound of Music*. Underneath reads: "Albert Berne, Baritone," then under that "Teacher of Singing." Inside the brochure is a short biography: Albert studied piano in Europe for three years under "the great Masters Godowsky and Barth," and composition with Hugo Kaun "the famous composer." Then he returned to America before the war and decided to study voice with Herbert Witherspoon, of the Metropolitan Opera in New York. This change of venue is not explained. Also left out of the biography are his beginnings as the son of a saloon keeper on Vine Street, and his brief marriage around 1905 to a young German woman he met in Berlin while he was a music student and brought home to Cincinnati.

A marriage my father knew nothing about until he was in his thirties. According to my mother, the night before she and my father got married (second time for both), my grandfather confessed to her that he had also been married twice. My grandfather loved my mother, who was pretty and sweet tempered and liked to listen to him; he told her all sorts of things he never told my father. That first bride, forever nameless, but newly pregnant, died in a streetcar accident.

A story that was later amended by my father: the German bride threw herself in front of a streetcar to escape her new mother-in-law, the fat little girl who saw Abraham Lincoln, with whom they were living. This conjecture seems unfair to both my grandfather and his bride, and even to his fussy complacent little mother, who in photographs always looks as if she's just finished consuming a large apple strudel. I've read a couple letters my great-grandmother wrote to my grandfather while she was visiting a friend in Brooklyn in 1925 and they are chattily boring, mostly about what time exactly the friend's husband gets up in the morning for his job at the New York grain elevator, when he gets home, and how much exactly he is paid by the hour. She has a great fondess for exactitude ("We had a very good lunch at 12 o' clock"), which I'm sure could be irritating, but even so.

Albert must have handed his brochures out to prospective voice students—it's not a bad piece of advertising. I'd always thought he specialized in lieder, but from the list of "Representative Programmes" included on the back, I see he sang everything from old English ballads ("Mary of Allendale" and "Twickenham Ferry") to Dvorak's gyspy songs to "Kentucky Mountain" folk tunes. The brochure includes blurbs from several reviews that ran in the *Cincinnati Enquirer*:

November 27, 1918: "Mr. Berne sings with a keen perception of the artistic content of his songs and an appreciation of the moods they command. His voice is refined and pure in quality and is commanded by genuine musical intelligence."

November 10, 1919: "Mr. Berne's beautiful, vibrant voice, poise and glowing interpretation of his group of songs was one of the great successes of the afternoon."

July 27, 1919: "Mr. Berne's program included old English, French, Russian and American songs. His colorful, sympathetic voice was particularly enjoyed in his Russian group, which he sang with great fervor."

He was not Caruso, but he could sing pretty much whatever he wanted to and sing it well. A serious artist, serious enough to give concerts that were reviewed in the newspaper anyway. I also notice that he was smart enough not to sing a lot of German songs in 1918 and 1919.

Perhaps being a widower also increased his value in Lucile's eyes, along with his very fine baritone voice. Maybe it aroused her compassion. Explained his sensitivity, his apologetic look. At least it explained why he was unmarried, at age forty-five, and therefore avoided any embarrassing questions.

AFTER MY GRANDFATHER died, my father's story of his parents' marriage, which had always been reported to us grandchildren as idyllic, began to change. He decided that his mother had been unhappy, that his father was "weak," a man who couldn't throw a baseball despite having climbed the horned Alps with only a bar of chocolate in his knapsack, while she was "tough," like her father and her sisters. In his mind, this imbalance was what Lucile brooded on, those evenings before dinner, when she smoked Chesterfields and did crossword puzzles standing at her bedroom dresser, pausing every so often to stare out the window.

Her unequal marriage was why she looked remote in all those later photographs. She would have been happier, my father thought, with someone more manly.

But it seems she'd had that opportunity in France, with the handsome brigadier, and as far as I can tell, she rejected it. And just how "womanly," given the terms of the day, was Lucile? She could drive. She smoked. She had a college degree. She had flown in an airplane when airplanes routinely broke up like matchsticks, had been entertained at a prison camp surrounded by sex-starved men, and slept in a bed that had one leg in a shell hole. She had helped run a multimillion-dollar company and plucked her own chickens. She was not so much a "new woman" as her own woman.

I have on my left hand this moment the slender gold wedding ring Albert gave Lucile, which is engraved with both their initials and with the date of their wedding. My mother found the ring in a box in my grandfather's bedroom after he died and gave it to me. An elegantly simple ring, patterned with orange blossoms. Lucile herself never wore it. Did she balk at being identified as someone's "wife," two years after women finally got the vote? Was her ringless hand a declaration of equal rights? My grandfather never wore a wedding ring either; few men did in those days.

It's 1923, I remind myself. Lucile is a modern woman in an old-fashioned city. She wants a modern marriage but one that will not shock anybody, including herself. She's been reading Emma Goldman ("if partial emancipation is to become a complete and true emancipation of women, it will have to do away with the ridiculous notion that to be loved, to be sweetheart and mother, is synonymous with being slave or subordinate"). By modern marriage, Lucile envisions something radical: a union of two people who intend to remain strangers. They will be friends, collaborators, partners. Lovers, too. But essentially separate. Because what she wants most is independence. She wants out of her father's kitchen. She wants her own house, which she's quite sure her father will not pay for if she remains single, and she can't think of a job in Cincinnati that suits her idea of herself. She does not want to be considered ridiculous: a "spinster," a maiden aunt tolerated at family events, another Aunt Ida. She wants what her sisters have. Only she wants more than what her sisters have.

And so she falls in love with a modest, intelligent, good-humored man who loves and admires her but will not dominate her. Plus he has a very fine baritone voice. Whatever inequality exists between Lucile and Albert because she is an heiress and he has five hundred dollars in savings, is righted, at least for the moment, whenever he sits down at the piano.

But she is still restless. Perhaps because she likes to be outside, where she feels freer, or because she wants to control her own perspective, she has become deeply interested in landscape architecture. In the next six years, she builds two houses, the first on East Grandin Road, where her children are born, and the second on Indian Hill. For each house she designs elaborate gardens, especially for the second. She is influenced heavily by Frederick Law Olmsted, first encountered through his son's work at Wellesley, who taught American gardeners that there was more to gardens than flower beds, and that designing a view was a spiritual exercise. No topiary. No paths of white crushed shells and clipped yew hedges. No regiments of rose bushes. Olmsted favored wide lawns and part of every garden left "wild." Grades should be gentle and sloping, not sharp and terraced. Water should be a feature — pools, small lakes — and borders should be as natural as possible. Some statuary here and there, nothing flashy. (No Greek gods with distracting fig leaves.) But perhaps an even more influential teacher was one whose work Lucile had been admiring, or at least noticing, since she was a child: Adolph Strauch, landscape architect of Spring Grove Cemetery, who thought of landscape in terms of grief and solace and wanted every vista as open as possible.

Lucile reads everything she can find on horticulture, and then on Indian Hill she begins to design her own world, a gift from her father, who could not bring himself to give her the company she should have been running instead. Twenty-five acres of hillside once hunted over by the Shawnee, where stone arrowheads could still be found when I was a child, land that Lucile turned into walks and slopes, flowers beds and pools, a green enclosure which affords a wide view from every window of her big cream-colored house, and which flows into the lawns of her sisters' houses.

She plants dogwood, oaks, maple, witch hazel. Trees and shrubs that grow wild around Ohio, that suggest a forest preserve. But an enclosure is an enclosure, as Lucile knows perfectly well. Her view can extend only so far. Like many educated women with money at that time, she has turned her ambitions inward and the landscape there can be rocky.

LUCILE IS IN her garden, planting bulbs. Albert is teaching at the conservatory and spending several hours every day singing and practicing the piano. A happy partnership. I will insist upon it. But my father has sown that seed of doubt and it's grown into a watermelon: were they in love?

"The sun always shone in your corner," Barney Kroger's second wife, Alice, wrote to my grandfather in 1966, after paying him a visit in Cincinnati when he was almost ninety and she seventy-eight, a letter that somehow made it into my brother's canvas bag. "You were a good husband to Lucile. No one could have shared her interests as you did. You were both intellectuals, enjoying music, books, and the garden. And she was the best gardener I ever knew."

Alice did not need to write such a complimentary letter to my grandfather (a simple thank-you note would have been sufficient), but she did, and what she said about my grandparents' marriage must have been sincere, at least in her opinion, or she wouldn't have bothered to say it, thirty-four years after Lucile was gone. Unless she was trying to reassure my grandfather of something he himself had always doubted.

They'd had music, books, and the garden.

They'd had music, books, and the garden.

They also had two little boys.

Albert Jr. was born in 1924, a year after his parents were married. A handsome infant in the small photograph I have of him with his mother, dark haired and wide eyed, with that mildly astonished look so common to babies. And for all her reputation for remoteness, Lucile looks quite maternal. One hand cupped gently around her baby's head, the other supporting him carefully under the arm, she gazes softly down at little Albert with what appears to be rapt approval. He rests a tiny fist on her breast. Both of them gleam with health and well-being. It's a studio portrait (she's had her hair done, is wearing pearls and a dark silk dress with a white collar and cuffs;

he's in a fancy white baby gown) and so there's more sense of consequence here, perhaps, than intimacy, and yet nothing in her face or her pose suggests Lucile was anything but a fond parent.

But then there was the matter of the oil painting. My father's impression that his mother never smiled at him was almost certainly reinforced by a portrait that hung in the dining room during his childhood, directly across from his place at the table. I remember sitting across from that portrait myself all through the December week following my grandfather's funeral. A nearly life-size formal portrait, in a heavy gilt frame, titled *Mrs. Albert Berne and Her Sons,* commissioned from the society painter Dixie Selden, protégée of Cincinnati's most famous artist, Frank Duveneck. The same portrait to which my grandfather daily bid good morning and good evening for forty years.

My father was not similarly attached to this portrait. After my grandfather died he sold it to an art dealer, who sold it to someone else, who eventually donated it to the University Club in Cincinnati, where it graced the ladies' lounge, the identity of its subjects unknown, until my cousin Carol encountered it by chance one afternoon and collared the manager, demanding to know why her grandmother was hanging in the bathroom. I've been told the painting has since been moved to a more dignified location on the second floor.

In the portrait Lucile wears a pale green velvet gown, to set off her red-gold hair, and sits on a lemon yellow sofa with my toddler father, holding his hand. He is in a white silk suit with short pants and a white ruffled silk shirt, his bare knees as ruddy as pomegranates. Behind them stands my uncle, also in a white silk suit. All three wear expressions of weary endurance. The boys have probably been ordered sharply and repeatedly not to fidget. My father's eyes look teary above his pudgy cheeks. His brother looks fed up. What child wants to sit for a portrait? Particularly one painted by a frumpy little woman in her sixties who, despite bribing the boys with pretzels to hold still, seems to have found children bothersome—at least, in the portraits I've seen her child subjects are often grimacing.

The painting must have been Lucile's idea: she would have paid for it, after all. Chosen the pale green velvet gown, the ruffled shirts. Conferred about who was to stand or sit where. Approved the final result, which was meant to be an enduring and public representation of who she was, at least at the time. Yet in it she does not look like the proud mother of two healthy little boys breathing and fidgeting right beside her, one of whom is hardly more than a baby, his sticky hand clasped in hers. She looks pensive, distracted, unreachable. Staring off into a middle distance, as if she's just glanced up from a sad passage in a book and can't quite relinquish the characters or what's become of them.

In yet another studio photograph sent to me by my sister Lucy, probably a study for this portrait—same white suits for the boys, though Lucile is in a sleeveless black dress and holding a picture book open to the tale of the Pied Piper—she looks even more detached, even stricken, like someone who's just received bad news she must keep to herself. Blank faced, she sits on a wooden chair with Albert Jr. standing beside her. My father leans into his mother, hands clasped over his belly. She should have her arm around him, but she doesn't; oddly, he's half sitting on the edge of a table, half suspended in midair, a precarious position for such a little boy.

Behind Lucile and Albert Jr., quite distinctly, are their shadows. There might as well be five people in that portrait.

"She never smiled at me," my father keeps repeating. If he is referring to the woman in these portraits, that's true.

So why, during years that should have been the happiest and most fulfilled of her life, when she has achieved a harmonious marriage (at least to the casual observer), borne two children, and is at work building a beautiful house on a hill with a vast, ambitious garden, wasn't Lucile smiling?

Why does anyone stop smiling? Uneasiness. Anxiety. Depression.

By 1929, when my father was three, the Great Depression had hit, and though Barney managed to protect his fortune by selling his company right before the stock market crashed in October, the rest of the country was in desperate shape. Banks began to fail. Thousands of them by 1931, though the bank Barney founded, the Provident Bank, was providentially spared. Stockbrokers were disgraced.

People were committing suicide. Businesses failed. Farms failed. Foreclosures in every neighborhood. (Eight decades later, history is repeating itself, as history seems bound to do, having nothing but itself to repeat, and I can feel it for myself, the dull gnaw of national worry.) Millions of people were out of work—by 1932, almost a third of the American workforce was unemployed. Lines of people waited on Cincinnati street corners, all the way down to the river, people hoping for work or waiting for soup kitchen doors to open. Past those lines of sad-faced men and women in thin coats and patched shoes glided Lucile in a chauffeured Studebaker. A profile, a fur collar, a cloche hat behind a glass window. Whoever bothered to notice her must have thought she was just one more uncaring rich person.

And she was, apparently. But this was also a woman who for four years had read the words *Non Minisitrare Sed Ministrare* every time she passed the Wellesley seal. Ruined lives were not an abstraction to her; she'd spent too much time in ruined France not to feel uneasy in that chauffeured car. Still, she didn't stop the car and get out of it, either. Barney was handing money to any charity that seemed reasonable (despite his revolt against Catholicism, he particularly favored the Little Sisters of the Poor); he was bailing out employees who were losing their houses, giving away overcoats, food, loans, and it wasn't making any difference. Herbert Hoover was president. His idea of economic stimulus was to figure the financial market would correct itself. Do nothing. Feel bad about it. Hope things change. Meanwhile, people were starving.

And Lucile herself may have been in a depression of her own, not as desperate as what was being experienced by the rest of the country, but try qualifying depression to a depressed person. Her father had just sold the Kroger Company—for forty-five years as inseparable from the family as their own name—partly because he sensed financial disaster was coming and partly because he was getting married to Aunt Alice, a woman thirty years younger than himself. After all those years of presiding over her father's table, Lucile had to give her seat to another woman. And there were other family displacements. Barney had put Lucile on the board of directors, in apology for not putting her in charge of the Kroger Company; when he resigned as CEO, the board voted unanimously, at Barney's instigation, against naming his son Henry as his replacement. A decision that was justified but to Lucile must have felt treacherous. Had she known what was to happen to Henry, she would have felt even worse.

Then late in 1928, not long before Dixie Selden began painting that portrait, Lucile miscarried what would have been a little girl.

No woman who has ever had a miscarriage can fail to be affected by it. One day she has a baby; the next day she doesn't. It's nature's way, her doctor says; the best thing is to forget about it, try again. But for years she does secret reckonings. The child would be three now. Six. Eighteen. But the child never existed. So why does it still seem to be missing? In the 1920s, women didn't talk about miscarriages. Especially to their husbands. So Lucile would have been alone with her reckonings, and one of those reckonings would have been that, at nearly forty, this had probably been her last chance at having a baby. My father believes that she'd always wanted a daughter.  One more reason he felt she never smiled at him.

If women did not talk about their miscarriages, they did, however, go on rest cures afterward—if they had the money. In May of 1929, four months before the stock market collapsed, Lucile went alone to the Summit Hotel in Uniontown, Pennsylvania, high up in the Allegheny Mountains, an enormous, rambling white hotel with red trim with wide breezy verandahs from which she could watch the sun set over three states. Henry Ford stayed there, and Thomas Edison, Henry Clay Frick, Cornelius Vanderbilt. The hotel was famous for its "elite table water," which was supposed to have medicinal properties — largely unspecified — its German cooking, and its homegrown vegetables.

I have a letter Albert sent to her while she was at the Summit Hotel — the only letter I can find that he wrote to her, another relic from my brother's canvas bag. Written on Cincinnati Conservatory of Music stationery, and dashed off between voice students, he addresses her as "My dear Honeylamb" and begins by describing a party he attended the night before at her sister Helen's house, complete with "strong" mint juleps mixed by Helen's husband. A party at which Albert sang, apparently with mixed success (he shouldn't have had a mint julep). "How I missed you," he writes, "especially when I am in a crowd. I feel lonelier than ever when you are not there."

Aside from this doleful confession, the letter is newsy and upbeat. The children, he reports, are "fine as ever and want to know when you are coming home — they miss their Mama, as I do." He goes on to describe high jinks among pupils at the conservatory (someone turned on the fire alarm in the middle of the night and one girl fainted, "most of the girls are incensed about it"). The house on Indian Hill is still under construction but almost finished ("the painters have done walls and woodwork and made fine progress"). He is looking forward to seeing her the following week but adds with a note of contrition, to atone for sounding needy in the previous paragraph, "I hope you are having a real rest and a good time, too."

A real rest. People who are sad, who are emotionally and physically worn out, need a real rest. This was a woman who had money, a doting husband, happy children, sisters close by, servants to do all the housework. Spring had arrived. She was not

sick yet. The stock market hadn't crashed yet. But she needed a real
rest at the Summit Hotel. What was going on, aside from the miscarriage (which after all was enough), to keep her from smiling?

Lucile's silence on this matter is instructive. It is as impossible to
understand the intricacies of other people's unhappiness as it is to understand their marriages. Who knows, for instance, what motherhood

may have stirred up for her, motherless herself at nine years old.
Maybe my father was right and
she never bonded with her little
boys, or at least with him. Maybe
it really is true that she never felt
much for her second son, though
he is so appealing in his baby pictures, so darling, a charming big-
eared little boy with a shy comical
look. But maybe she found him
exhausting, disappointing. Maybe
he just wasn't a girl.

I have written an entire book to convince my father that he once
had a mother who had loved him, that she was not as remote as she
looks in those photographs; but it seems I can't prove it after all.

I WRITE TO my father's cousin Nancy to inquire about some
home movies of the Kroger family in the 1920s that I hazily recollect
being shown at her house the week of my grandfather's funeral. A
month later a packet arrives in the mail. In it are three DVDs, which
Nancy has had made from the old silent reel-to-reel tapes she has kept
all these years. On my next visit to Charlotte my father and I watch
the DVDs together on his computer screen, and there—amid grainy
black-and-white footage of children jumping into waves in Florida,
children swimming in a swimming pool, men golfing, B. H. Kroger

doing a soft-shoe dance in front of a huge stone fireplace, aunts and uncles having a picnic on a Cape Cod beach, and a Scottish terrier leaping madly after a balloon at the edge of a field—there, and almost not there, because she is always turning away from the camera, flickers Lucile.

Moving, talking with her sisters, smoking a cigarette. She is at a party where all the adults are dressed as babies (some holding rattles) where she dances sedately with Albert, and it's clear that everyone but them is uproariously drunk. She is at a Christmas celebration, sitting alone by a fireplace holding a large doll. She is on the beach in a black bathing suit, clearly pregnant, walking in the sand with my father and my uncle, who are skinny little boys in oversized swim trunks, but not holding their hands. And finally there she is with my grandfather on that same beach, a beach on Cape Cod that must be Harwich Port. She leans toward him, smiling as he leans toward her, their hair blown by the wind, clouds scudding behind them, and for one instant, probably at the request of the person behind the camera, they share a kiss. Not a passionate kiss, but an affectionate, married one. The kiss of two people who move freely in and out of a private world that no one else will ever know about.

My father makes a small quiet ambiguous noise. Then he asks that the computer be turned off. We sit for a minute or two, neither of us speaking.

My father did say something eventually, but I can't remember what he said. All I recall was that he didn't want to watch the rest of the movies. Was it too much, seeing his mother in motion? Or was it not enough? There she was, right there, looking askance at the camera, looking askance at *us*—and yet once more she wasn't really there, at least not for him.

THE REST DOES not rest her, the cure isn't curative. Over the next year and a half it becomes clear to Lucile that something truly is wrong, something more than the blues and disappointments and feeling overwhelmed. She is always tired; she has persistent aches; unexplained bruises appear on her skin. Albert's newly widowed mother, the ever-exact "Mother Berne," comes to live with them, to help out with running the new house. Mother Berne now plans what they will have for dinner and oversees the grocery shopping, although curiously she refuses to shop at Kroger, but instead has Wash the chauffeur drive her to a more expensive grocery downtown, where she emerges from the Studebaker with impressive dignity, clutching a string bag.

A nursemaid for the boys has also been engaged, a troll-like character straight out of the Brothers Grimm with a hulking forehead and whiskery chin. Nanny Blum. Fond of enemas and castor oil. Nanny Blum comes highly recommended by someone Gretchen knows, and is supposed to be good with "high-spirited" children who may become unmanageable if not taken firmly in hand. Lucile is afraid that Henry is high spirited. He has fits, on occasion, and holds his breath long enough to turn blue. He cries loudly and furiously in his crib. He wants up, he wants down. When Mother Berne takes him outside to play, he has to be put on a leash; otherwise he runs away. He always seems to want what he doesn't have. The sign of a true romantic. Also the sign of a difficult child.

Children. House. Husband. Garden. In what order should Lucile put them? She does what she can, aware that it's not enough. That winter she agrees to take the whole family, including Mother Berne and Nanny Blum, with Helen's family to Bermuda for three weeks. They all need a rest. They all need to have a good time. And so in March of 1931, during the darkest stretch of the Depression, instead of boarding a train at a train station, they drive down Indian Hill to Fort Dennison, and stop the Pennsylvania Railroad's main-line afternoon train to New York. They climb onto a private Pullman car. A party of eleven people, five of them overdressed children, with trunks, suitcases, hatboxes, the women in furs, the men in handsome topcoats. Fort Dennison is populated mostly by poor black people. A small crowd of threadbare onlookers silently watches them depart.

In New York the two families stay for a night at the Savoy-Plaza Hotel and Lucile takes her boys to see their first movie, Charlie Chaplin's *City Lights*. The next morning they board the *Queen of Bermuda* and sail excitedly out of New York Harbor. But it's a rough March crossing. Almost everyone is sick. Mother Berne begs repeatedly to be allowed to die. Only Albert and Helen's five-year-old daughter are spared. The two of them stroll around the deck, taking deep breaths of sea air and congratulating each other on their good health.

My source of information for the Bermuda trip is my father, who about twelve years ago decided to write his memoirs, though he only got up to 1967. In brief single-spaced chapters, he describes his childhood and years at prep school, his service in the navy, his sojourn in New York and love of jazz clubs, his time working in newspapers in Cincinnati, and his civil rights work in Virginia as director of a conference center in the sixties. A life of event and diversity, though he has never seen it that way. He told me some years back that he felt he had done nothing. We had been visiting Sleepy Hollow Cemetery, in Concord, because he wanted to see Thoreau and Emerson's graves. As we were driving home along a country lane, the trees luminous with fall color, he lapsed into melancholy reflections on all he had not accomplished. "Dad," I said finally, exasperated. "You have six children. You have lived in beautiful houses, survived a war, and had all sorts of jobs, and met all sorts of people. You've had a wide life." He looked flattered but unconvinced. As soon as he had finished them, he entrusted these memoirs to me guessing, correctly, that among his six children I would be the most likely to read them.

He is a lively narrator of his own past, with a novelist's appreciation for fiasco. In an early section, for instance, he describes arriving at last in Bermuda and being taken by horse-drawn carriage to the stuffy Bermudiana Hotel in Hamilton. While the adults are disembarking, his older cousin David runs into the lobby and discovers a long brass ceremonial horn, mounted on a stand; seizing the horn, David blows "a mighty blast," creating a terrific noise — "The Angel Gabriel would have been hard put to blow any louder" — shocking then enraging everyone at the hotel, except my father, who is filled with admiration.

During the next week, the two families visit the Crystal Cave in glass-bottomed boats; they tour an "ancient tavern" called Tom Moore's, and sit on a pink beach surrounded by coral cliffs. A pleasant holiday. Then the weather turns stormy. One morning Aunt Helen steps into her bathroom and notices that the water in the toilet is swirling around in the bowl, even though the toilet had not been flushed. Aunt Helen becomes convinced that Bermuda is about to crack off its foundations and float off to sea. At her insistence, the family departs the next day, crowding onto the SS *Veendam* and steaming directly into what is now a howling storm. "The terrible weather of our return voyage," writes my father, "meted out more punishment to my stomach than I care to remember." In this Chaplinesque end to their vacation in Bermuda, which began with that shameful display by the train tracks at Fort Dennison, my father suggests the Krogers are really being punished for being rich and heedless. But of course, life doesn't work like that, only the narrative version of it.

My father's memoirs are, in their own way, as sketchy as Lucile's notations in her *Tagebuch*. He is a much more detailed and descriptive writer ("Soon we were out on the open sea, and the only visible thing other than sea and sky was another liner with a gray hull and tan stacks . . . which gradually pulled away to the left, probably bound for Europe. I remember watching it until it disappeared and feeling a shock of loneliness . . ."), and far more determined to capture the emotional atmosphere of his life at different times. But the theme of his unhappy lack of confidence, caused by the insensitivity of the adults around him, eventually obscures almost everything else. ("Even in early childhood I had no real feeling of security.")

Lucile features very little in these memoirs. He recalls her taking him downtown at around three years old to buy a navy blue sweater, which was scratchy. He recalls being scolded for spilling his milk. He recalls his mother slapping his hand. But the only time he wonders about her is when he briefly describes that painting in the dining room, and her "sad look into the distance."

A FINAL PORTRAIT, this one taken at the bottom of the stairs of the house on Indian Hill: Lucile is posed with one hand on the banister, wearing a silk wrap with an enormous mink collar and mink sleeves. October 1931. Does she know yet that she is sick? The steady somberness of her face suggests that she does but not that she realizes how little time is actually left. She is forty-two years old. She is not beautiful, but she has entered into a tenuous loveliness that graces some women her age, for whom beauty becomes a matter of chance, of the right light and the right angles, and is therefore more poignant, and sometimes more breathtaking, than the beauty of younger women. Her features are more distinct than when she was in her twenties and early thirties, her eyes are more expressive, and perhaps more deeply green now than blue. Though threaded with gray, her wavy red hair is more flatteringly arranged above her wide forehead, because of course at this age you make the most of what you have. Which explains the rich fur against her face, the elegant drape of silk. Half her face is in shadow, a dramatic effect planned by the photographer; but planned well, because the effect is indeed dramatic. The lighting is not deception but an enhancement.

She is still, for a little while yet, between the acts.

L ast year my brother sent me a tiny card he found by chance at the bottom of a drawer in his house. Inside a miniature en-velope, with a pretend stamp drawn in red crayon on the top left-hand corner, and addressed "to Mother," is a little folded piece of lined paper on which a note has been written laboriously in pencil.

It reads:

dear Mother.
Yesterday I got a new Book I am reading good in It I got A in French The garden is awfully pretty.
Can we go to the circus next week. We had David over for supper last night. We had ham and Beans — For desert we had Straw Berries.
Love From Henry

That this note was preserved when every other artifact of my fa-ther's early childhood (school reports, drawings, quizzes) was swept away, suggests to me that Lucile herself had treasured it and perhaps tucked it into the corner of her mirror or in a drawer of her bedside table, a place that indicated its value. A keepsake. A reminder of the little boy downstairs, dreaming of elephants and learning French verbs. The note is undated, but my father wrote it himself, in per-fectly legible handwriting. He is in school at Cincinnati Country Day, along with his brother and a pack of cousins. It's spring 1932, probably late May, when the garden is "pretty" and strawberries are in season. He can read "good." He turned six in January. He is finishing the first grade, and his mother has just come home from the hospital, where she had an operation. And so he writes her a note, because she is upstairs resting and he's been told to be quiet.

I took this card with me on a spring visit to Charlotte, just as the tulip poplars were coming into leaf, and with the flourish of a defense attorney producing a final exculpatory piece of evidence, handed it to my father after lunch while he sat in his red armchair. He had been telling me, again, that his mother never cared for him. As I cleared away his plate of egg salad, he took a sip of iced tea, adjusted his glasses and peered at the little card in his hand. He took another sip of iced tea. At last he said querulously, "So I wrote this?"

I came back in from the kitchen to assure him he had. Wiping my hands on a dishtowel and taking a seat on the sofa, I pointed out that this was a note written by a child who knew what mattered to his mother, namely that he was doing well in school and that her garden looked pretty. He also believed she cared about what mattered to him. Her good opinion, his cousin David, strawberries. She was a mother who would want to know what he ate for dinner, a full report down to "desert." A mother who could be applied to for favors—a trip to the circus, for instance—and who might well grant them. A mother who received notes and kept them. A mother who had to have smiled when she got this one. Smiling myself, I got up and pointed to the signature: Love From Henry.

Ergo: a mother who was not lost, even though she had died.

"Oh," said my father vaguely.

He was looking out the window over my head. I had the impression he had not been listening very hard. The afternoon must be later than I'd thought; light was draining out of the room, or perhaps it was a passing thundercloud. As I sat back down on the edge of the sofa, clutching the dishtowel and watching my father watch the budding trees outside the darkening window, it suddenly occurred to me that he might be having as much trouble giving up the idea of losing his mother as I was with giving up the idea that I could restore her.

For a time it seems she is better. Well enough that the family travels to Lake Charlevoix in August, where they stay in a picturesque cabin made of roughhewn logs. They journey by steamship across Lake Michigan to Mackinac Island to spend a few nights at a hotel, an adventure made memorable for my father when a carriage horse took a bite out of Nanny Blum's black straw hat.

An effort is being made to behave like a normal family, to take trips to lakes, to ride on steamships, to laugh at Nanny Blum's straw hat with a bite taken out of it.

The cool mineral air of northern Michigan is bracing. It smells of black basalt rocks, magnetic fields and iron. Maybe the air will be bracing for Lucile. Maybe those magnetic fields will reset her compass and point her in a different direction.

But soon enough they are back in Cincinnati. Lucile grows paler and paler. When she takes a deep breath it seems to whistle through her body. When she wears a white dress, it's like looking at a ghost.

One afternoon in early fall she leans for a few minutes on the sill of her bedroom window, gazing down at the lawn where Albert Jr. and Henry are playing. The two boys stand out vividly against the grass, sharply outlined in the late afternoon sunlight. Their slender arms and legs are golden. They appear to her like small beautiful gods as they run back and forth, dodging around the shrubbery and past a stand of birch trees. She would like to go out onto the lawn and call to them, hold out her arms in that apricot-colored light. She

would like to pull up grass and trickle it onto their hair, pull leaves from the birch trees and pretend they are cups and saucers. But it's not really true that she would like to do this. She is too tired. And even if she was not so tired, something has always prevented her from being free and playful with her children. A kind of discomfiture, an almost physical awkwardness. She is never quite sure how to act with them or what to say; when they were infants, she was afraid of dropping them. To be honest, they do not fully interest her, though she figures this will change when they are older; she is probably right. Mothers have different stages of competence and the one who is bored around babies may be insightful with teenagers. Illness, too, has hampered her. She is embarrassed to be so sick, which makes her seem abrupt. When the boys come to visit her in her room, they stand at the end of her bed, fidgeting and sneaking glances at each other, and look relieved when their father tells them to go downstairs. She is relieved, too. "I don't want them to see me this way," she has told Albert.

Down in the garden the boys' voices are high, serious, reaching her thinly through the glass of her window. Sunlight glows through their hair as they run in complicated patterns, zigzags and figure eights, trailed by long shadows. They run to the lily pond and stand on the stones surrounding it, then leap away. In the distance are those gentle lavender hills. She can't tell if the boys know she is watching or not; neither of them looks up to wave to her at the window. They do not seem to be enjoying their game, whatever it is, but they are determined to play it to the end.

Outside the bedroom windows the garden is full of snow. The lily pond is frozen, the dark branches of the apple tree, standing alone in its stone circle, are sharply defined against a winter sky. Snow caps the bronze statues at either end of the reflecting pool, each of a child offering water to birds. A thoughtful garden, with its matching statuary, its hedges and rows of flower beds flanking a grassy avenue, the garden of someone more than casually interested in symmetry and perspective.

Upstairs in the master bedroom, a red-haired woman lies in bed facing the southeast window, which has a long view of the Little Miami River and the low hills of Ohio's Clermont County. She spends her days mildly, does picture puzzles in bed, and reads. Every so often she looks at the old clock on her mantel, a clock set in a dark gothic wooden case above a glass panel painted with an idealized landscape in bright greens and blues. Then she looks away.

She is visited daily by her three sisters, Gertrude, Helen, and Gretchen; her father visits almost as often, and sends her flowers. Her two little boys like school and are doing well, though she has not yet seen their report cards. They are taking piano lessons.

Christmas is upon her. She is making plans, making lists, writing letters to old friends. Downstairs in the living room her husband is singing "Ave Maria," accompanying himself on the grand piano, as the children go cheerfully off to school on a Thursday morning.

But now the children have left. Her husband has stopped singing. The piano lid is closed, the house has gone quiet.

And inside that elegant room full of wintry light, the only sound is the distant crack of ice on the river.

AFTERWORD

"You sounded just like her," my father said one afternoon last fall. I had been talking to him by cell phone while walking in the woods near my house, when my dog had leapt into a muddy stream and I had to interrupt our conversation to shout at the dog. "I was listening to your voice," he said, "and for a moment I heard *her.*" His family had had a dog, a cocker spaniel, he reminded me; Lucile used to take the dog on walks around Indian Hill. "I *know* I heard her call to the dog," he said, sounding pleased at having come across an unbidden memory, "and she sounded just like that."

I wasn't sure whether to feel pleased myself or taken aback. It has never been my intention to be confused with Lucile, in my own mind or anyone else's, and yet when one spends a long time thinking hard about another person, isn't some confusion to be expected?

When I first began looking into my grandmother's life, I was only a year or so older than she was when she died. We were roughly the same ages when we had our children, and we both had two, spaced two years apart, though I have girls. Like Lucile, I am close to my sisters, one of whom lives nearby. She and I are raising our children together, cousins who go to the same schools, as those Kroger cousins did, and who run through each other's front doors without knocking, and spend vacations together, and sing Christmas carols together every December. One of my nephews looks a lot like my father as a little boy; one of my daughters has Lucile's steady gaze and wide-spaced eyes, though in hazel.

Naturally the similarities only go so far. I am not wealthy; my husband is not a professional baritone; we live in an ordinary suburban house. Lucile's garden involved avenues, lawns, pools, roses, raised flower beds, specimen trees, a lily pond edged in fieldstone. My garden is confined to a disreputable patch by the driveway where I have planted peonies that bloom upside down because I never bother to tie them up. I don't even have red hair, though I did as a little girl. Yet it seems inevitable that the more I discovered about Lucile the less she became my father's mother and the more she became someone not unlike myself.

"TODAY TOOK A long time," my father said to me one evening on the phone, his voice bemused. "It was light in the morning and then it was still light when the nurse was here, which was a long time ago. And now it's finally dark."

The nurse had come the day before; my father had lost the day in between. Since October he was supposed to be on oxygen most of the time, but he was always forgetting to put the tubes in his nose, or to turn on the machine, and the less oxygen he got, the more confused he became. He often spent all day looking out the window.

My sisters and brother and I wanted him to go into assisted living, but he remained adamantly against the idea. He loved his apartment, especially the trees outside, his "forest cathedral"; nothing could persuade him to give them up. He loved his friends. One came to see him every morning and evening to take his blood pressure, and occasionally took him out to a local bar. Another often drove him to doctors' appointments. His very best friend, a man of extraordinary thoughtfulness, for whom he had been another father and who now became a kind of father to him, sorted out all his pills and made sure he took them. He was fine. He would not move. And so we worried and hired caretakers, whom he did not like, and he lost a day here and there, and was not sure if he had seen the doctor yesterday or last week, or what he had eaten for lunch.

Though some of his confusion was deliberate, even invited. He didn't care, particularly, about his lunch. About Cincinnati and his childhood, his memory was crystalline, and as the importance of five minutes ago receded, the distant past became more and more immediate. Especially because for the last two years, since I began my research into Lucile's life, my father had begun having long conversations with a woman he hadn't seen for more than seven decades.

Photographs of Lucile were now displayed on his bookcase, including the first one I'd sent of her in France, wearing those sensible oxfords and posing in front of the barracks door. Also a photograph in her midthirties with a Spanish comb in her red hair. Whenever he wanted to talk with his mother, my father sat in his armchair facing the photographs and held out his hands, palms up. A psychic friend had instructed him to do this. The psychic has long curly red hair. Once when she and my father were having lunch at a restaurant, she suddenly exclaimed, "Henry, I see your mother over your right shoulder!" And though I pointed out that the psychic could have been seeing her own reflection in a window, my father was convinced it was a visitation.

Settled in his armchair, he would wait for a receptive moment, and then ask his mother to take his hand. Often he would hum a few bars from Sibelius's "Finlandia," music which he believed somehow linked them. "Energy" would seize his hand, a strong tingling sensation. He described it many times. And then — they would talk. Though so far their conversations were one sided.

In the beginning they talked about his childhood, mostly about his complaints: brutal Nanny Blum and his interfering grandmother; and his father, who did his best but was weak and anxious; and his brother, who gave up too early and drowned his sorrows; and why all of this was Lucile's fault, for leaving these fragile people at the mercy of each other. My father referred to these conversations openly, if sometimes ruefully. The very first time he spoke to her, I received a message on my answering machine that began, "Wanted you to know. I just spent an hour talking with Mother. I got a bit wordy, I'm afraid."

HANGING BESIDE HIS red armchair was the photograph of Lucile by the stairs. Just over his right shoulder, in fact, which was where two years ago his psychic friend saw his mother. I brought it to him last spring, along with that little card he had written as a boy. A few months ago he called me to say that something extraordinary was happening to the photograph.

"As I look at my mother's picture," he said, "it seems to be changing. More and more light is on her face and the shadow on the side is diminished."

I asked him what he thought this meant. He thought for a moment, then said cagily, "What do *you* think it means?"

We had fallen into the habit of talking on the phone almost every day, often about which of his caregivers was coming in to make dinner for him that afternoon and why whoever it was knew nothing about asparagus or how to roast a chicken. "She *says* she can cook," he told me more than once, with pained incredulity, having inherited his grandfather's particular nature, especially when it came to dinner, which my father also liked to have served at precisely six thirty, even if he was the one doing the serving. I would ask about his blood pressure reading that morning, and whether he had gone to the park, and if it was a Friday, about the poetry group meeting at his house the evening before.

But usually those conversations veered around to Lucile. In that same phone call about his mother's photograph, he said that lately he'd been telling her about the summer camp on Cape Cod he went to as a boy. About canoeing on Long Pond, and the smell of pine needles, and the time he made a speech standing on a picnic table. The next time we spoke, he'd been telling her about his freshman year at Yale and his roommate, the son of Alfred A. Knopf, and how they'd been invited out to dinner at a restaurant in New York with Dorothy Parker, who pointed to a blonde woman in a low-cut dress and asked, "Pray, who is the lady in the turtleneck sweater?" Then it was about his enlistment in the navy during World War II, and being stationed on Okinawa as a medical corpsman and trying to build an X-ray machine by himself in the jungle. And then about living in New York in the 1950s during his first marriage and studying journalism at Columbia and listening to Pee Wee Russell and Count Basie play in Harlem. And then about living in Virginia in the 1960s during his second marriage, and arguing with restaurant owners about desegregation and meeting Martin Luther King Jr. just before the March on Washington. He told her about the psychology department at Georgetown in the early 1970s, how freewheeling it was, and the student who came to class wearing a Freudian slip, and his Jesuit friends who wore leather vests and peace-sign necklaces, then eventually about leaving all of that with another wife, and losing for a while what seemed like everything, but then getting some things back, including his life now in Charlotte, with his friends and the poetry he was writing, and how he had taken up abstract painting, like his father, though his medium was watercolor not oil. And finally he told her about his children and grandchildren, who were visiting more often now, and about the ever-shifting green view of trees from his armchair.

"I guess what it is," he said just before Christmas, with one of his surprised-sounding laughs, "is that I'm telling her the story of my life."

MY FATHER CAME down with a bad cold at the beginning of last March, just as two of my sisters arrived for a long-scheduled visit. When it became clear that this was more than a cold, that he was very sick, my sisters took him to the hospital and sat up with him all night, watching a freak blizzard from the hospital window. A kind nurse had pushed my father's bed around so it faced the window and he lay there for hours, struggling to breathe, watching snow fall into the waving branches of an apple tree, lit from behind by a streetlight. "Magical!" he cried.

The next day I flew down to join them. His mind had begun to wander long before I got there and he was having more trouble breathing. Propped up in a hospital bed, looking like an El Greco saint with his gaunt white-bearded face and his long beautiful hands, he talked about his brother, Albert, and about a Weimaraner dog named Herman the German he and my mother had owned when they were first married that used to run away and wind up in chemistry class at the local high school, and about a poem he wanted us to read. He talked about a great many other things that made sense if you listened carefully and thought about the order in which he'd said them, and finally one afternoon he told us it was a privilege to have met us all. That same afternoon he announced that his mother had just died. A little while later he touched his green hospital johnny, which was patterned with leaves, and told me that he was wearing his mother's clothes.

I cannot remember very exactly now, but I think it was then that I put my arms around my father and said, "Your mother is holding you." I kissed him and said, "Your mother is kissing you." He looked at me for a moment with those clear light blue eyes, so much like hers, and then he said, "Thank you."

My father died on March 6, 2009. Though he did not get to see the completed manuscript for this book, he read significant portions of it, and I think for both of us the process of looking for Lucile was, in the end, something like finding her.

ACKNOWLEDGMENTS

I MUST BEGIN by thanking the two archivists at the Wellesley College Archive, Wilma Slaight and Ian Graham, who were so generous with their time as I struggled to understand what I was looking at in the boxes of photographs, scrapbooks, official reports, newspaper articles, alumnae bulletins, and letters they brought to me during the months I sat at their long tables. They were unfailingly patient in helping me navigate the Archives, suggesting resources, locating boxes I hadn't thought to ask for, and trying to answer my questions, which were not always entirely coherent. I am grateful to have had access to the diary of Helen Slagle ('11) and letters belonging to Ridie Guion ('11), Mary Sawyer ('11), Mary Rhodes Christie ('11), and especially the letters of Frances Bogert ('14), which were so critical in helping me understand the experiences of the Wellesley College Reconstruction Unit. I was also greatly aided by various Wellesley College publications, including back issues of the *College News,* the *Wellesley Alumnae Bulletin,* the *Wellesley Alumnae Quarterly,* the 1911 *Legenda,* and the *Fifth, Tenth and Thirtieth Reunion Records of the Class of 1911.* Many thanks to Ann Hamilton, the Wellesley registrar, and Bridget Belgiovine, head of Physical Education, Athletics and Recreation, who unearthed Lucile's medical records for me. I also benefited from reading *In Adamless Eden: The Community of Women Faculty at Wellesley,* by Patricia Ann Palmieri, and Arlene Cohen's *Wellesley College,* which had so many helpful photographs.

The rest my sources were chosen more haphazardly. Fortunately, most readers will not be turning to me as an authority on anything other than my grandmother. For information about American involvement in World War I, I relied quite a bit on *Our Times: Over Here, 1914–1918,* by Mark Sullivan. I found Paul Fussell's extraordinary history, *The Great War and Modern Memory,* very helpful, also Robert Asprey's *At Belleau Wood,* and especially Hugh Clout's *After the Ruins: Restoring the Countryside of Northern France after the Great War. The American Guide Book to France and Its Battlefields* by E. R. Garey, O. O. Ellis, and R. V. D. Magoffin was useful in trying to figure out the part Lucy-le-Bocage played in the war, as was Sommerville Story's *The Battlefields of France: III. The Marne Cities and Chateau-Thierry.* Ruth Gaines's *A Village in Picardy* and *Helping France,* accounts of her time as a relief worker in France, were also informative. Alison Cohn, my research assistant for a semester at Harvard, found most of these books for me, as well as ones I never managed to read, and was tireless in hunting down stray facts.

I don't know what I would have done without *The Kroger Story,* by George Laycock, as is evident from the sections about my great-grandfather B. H. Kroger. As I tried to figure out what Cincinnati was like during Lucile's lifetime, and also during her father's time, I returned again and again to Alvin F. Harlow's marvelously readable *The Serene Cincinnatians.* I am also indebted to *Cincinnati: Story of the Queen City* by Clara Longworth de Chambrun; *Cincinnati, a Chronological & Documentary History, 1676–1970,* compiled and edited by Robert I. Vexler; Paul Briol's beautiful book of photographs, *The City of Rivers and Hills;* two books of photographs from the Images of America series, *Cincinnati Revealed,* by Kevin Grace and Tom White, and *Cincinnati's Golden Age,* by Betty Ann Smiddy; and William H. Tishler's *Midwestern Landscape Architecture,* which introduced me to the work of Adolph Strauch. Rebecca West's *1900* gave me the idea for trying to capture Lucile's experience of Cincinnati at the turn of the century.

I benefited enormously from reading Susan Sontag's *On Photography* and Roland Barthes' *Camera Lucida. Telling Lives, the Biographer's Art,* edited by Marc Pachter, is where I found Geoffrey Wolff's essay, "Minor Lives." Judy Simons's *Diaries and Journals of Literary Women from Fanny Burney to Virginia Woolf* furnished me with the fragment from Edith Wharton's line-a-day diary as well as the quote from Katherine Mansfield's journal. Stacey A. Cordery's biography *Alice: Alice Roosevelt Longworth, from White House Princess to Washington Power Broker* was also very helpful.

A number of people also served as resources for me as I was writing this book. Maxine Rodburg read all my drafts and without her wise and humane literary counsel, as well as her encouragement, I would not be writing these acknowledgements. Marjorie Sandor accompanied me to France to visit the village of Lucy-le-Bocage, patiently listened as I tried to figure out where else to search, and finally suggested that I go back to the attic. Suzanne Matson read the final draft and gave invaluable last-minute advice. Sonya Mead spent days and days scanning photographs and helping me figure out which ones should go where. I can't thank any of them enough.

For so many reasons, I am grateful to my family: my brother, Henry Berne, gave me many of the family photographs and also several of the letters that became central to my understanding of Lucile. Lucy Sowell supplied me with photographs as well and spent hours researching our great-uncle Chester's service in the Great War. Nancy Ireland kindly sent me family home movies. Cathy Scott told me anecdotes I hadn't heard before, as did my mother, Patricia Berne; my cousins Carol and Chester Berne; and my youngest sister, Serena Berne. Eve Berne was, as always, my chief listener, sympathizer, and sounding board. It can't be easy to have someone hijack your family history for her own purposes, and so to all my siblings and cousins I offer my apologies as well as my gratitude. Thanks to Ken Kimmell for supporting what often seemed an unlikely enterprise and for helping me through the hardest part of it. Thanks, also, to my wonderful agent, Colleen Mohyde, on whom I rely for so much, and once again I deeply appreciate the guidance of Shannon Ravenel, a true writer's editor.

But most of all I thank my father, John Henry Berne, with whom I had so many conversations about his relatives and Cincinnati over the past few years, who sent me e-mails whenever he thought of something else, and called when an e-mail wouldn't do, gave me his memoirs, and always trusted that the story I would tell about his mother would be a story he would want to hear. This book is a gift I tried to give to him, and by accepting it, he gave it back to me.